LIVE BEAT 3

Teacher's Book

Liz Kilbey • Ingrid Freebairn • Jonathan Bygrave • Judy Copage

Pearson Education Limited
Edinburgh Gate
Harlow
Essex CM20 2JE
England
and Associated Companies throughout the world.

www.pearsonelt.com/livebeat

The right of Jonathan Bygrave, Judy Copage, Ingrid Freebairn, and Liz Kilbey to be identified as the authors of this work has been asserted by them in accordance with the Copyright, Designs and Patents Act, 1988.

First published 2015

ISBN: 9781447952954

Set in Helvetica Neue LT 55 Roman 9/12.5pt

Printed by L.E.G.O. S.p.A, Italy

Illustration Acknowledgements

(Key: b-bottom; c-centre; l-left; r-right; t-top; page numbers refer to embedded Students' Book pages)

David Banks page 107 (right); Adrian Barclay (Beehive Illustration) pages 26, 34, 73, 85; Kathy Baxendale pages 7, 116; Paco Cavero (Sylvie Poggio) page 102 (middle right); Stephen Elford page 109 (bottom left); Kevin Hopgood (Beehive Illustration) pages 23, 55, 74; Richard Jones (Beehive Illustration) page 88; Wes Lowe (Beehive Illustration) page 105; David Shenton page 104; Eric Smith (KJA Artists) page 13; Roger Wade Walker (Beehive Illustration) page 103; Ian West (Beehive Illustration) pages 108, 109 (right); Tony Wilkins pages 16, 56

Photo Acknowledgements

The publisher would like to thank the following for their kind permission to reproduce their photographs:

(Key: b – bottom; c – centre: l – left: r – right; t – top; page numbers refer to embedded Students' Book pages)

Alamy Images: AF archive 56br, Alex Segre 62l, Catchlight Visual Services 28b, Charles Bowman 96c (background), Chris Howes / Wild Places 106tl, Doug Houghton 62r, Doug Simpson 72cr, Greg Balfour Evans 44cl, i love images 51, INSADCO Photography 91br, Janine Wiedel Photolibrary 12bl, jeremy sutton-hibbert 72bl, Jim Forrest 12tr, Jon Arnold Images Ltd 58cr, Jorge Royan 54cr, JTB Media Creation, Inc 58br, Justin Kasez 12z 32cr, Marmaduke St. John 24cr, moodboard 6cr, National Geographic Image Collection 67bl, one-image photography 19bl, paul kennedy 78bl, Peter Phipp / Travelshots.com 32b, 39bl, Realimage 40cr, RMIreland 40tr, Robert Fried 58t, Roger Cracknell 01 / Classic 100tr, Steven Harrison 41br, Teddy 59t, The Photolibrary Wales 19tl, Washington Stock Photo 28tr, Westend61 Gmbtl 84tr; **Bananastock:** 24tr; **(c) Rough Guides:** Suzanne Porter 8b; **Corbis:** 106cr, Douglas Keister / Lived in Images 6br, Image Source 46t, Jack Jackson / Robert Harding World Imagery 80tr, Lothar Schulz / fstop 55b, Lowell Georgia 79c, Ocean 72br, Peter Stanley / Demotix 18br; **DK Images:** Chris Stowers 38br, Dave King 84t (inset)), James Tye 84cr, Peter Cook 60tr; **Fotolia.com:** Kwokfai 39tc, Peggy Stein 39br, photomic 39bc, Syda Productions 31tr; **Getty Images:** AFP 79b, James Hardy / Photo Alto 75, Jeff J Mitchell 48b, National Geographic 79t, Oliver Strewe 58b (inset); **Pearson Education Ltd:** Studio 8 59c, Gareth Boden 4, 6t, 8tr, 10, 11t, 11bl, 11br, 14, 22, 35tl, 42cl, 44tc, 44tr, 46, 52, 59b, 64, 76, 86, 93, 96tr, Handan Erek 78cl, Rob Judges 60bl, Naki Kouyioumtzis / Pearson Education Ltd 39tl, Tudor Photography /Pearson Education Ltd. 49, Jules Selmes 69tl, Sozaijiten 36tr, 36cr, 36b; **Press Association Images:** Brendan Donnelly / Demotix 98l, Clive Gee / PA Archive 78br, Geoff Robins / AP 99, Owen Humphreys / PA Archive 71t, Rick Rycroft / AP 98r; **Rex Features:** Mark Large / Daily Mail 67cr; **Shutterstock.com:** Alexander Yakoviev 110tr, auremar 69cl, Bikeworldtravel 33tr, Honza Hruby 45br, Jason Stitt 82, Neil Mitchell 32tr, Sebastien Burel 42b, Shae Cardenas 19cl, Stephen Clarke 62c; **SuperStock:** Sheltered Images 6bl; **The Kobal Collection:** Columbia / Marvel 16cr, New Line Cinema 16tr, 16br; **TopFoto:** 57cr, The Granger Collection, New York 106bl; **WENN:** 94tr, 94bl, 94br; **www.imagesource.com:** 108cr

All other images © Pearson Education

Cover photograph © Shutterstock.com / Rido

Every effort has been made to trace the copyright holders and we apologise in advance for any unintentional omissions. We would be pleased to insert the appropriate acknowledgement in any subsequent edition of this publication.

Contents

Students' Book Contents

Contents

2

3

Introduction

Principles behind *Live Beat*

We believe that three key principles need to be followed if language learning material is to be effective for teenagers.

1 Motivate and maintain interest

The visual presentation of the content, and the topics and issues it deals with, must motivate the students from the start. In addition the learning tasks in the course must involve and challenge students both linguistically and cognitively to maintain their interest and ensure that learning is effective. *Live Beat* achieves this by using:

- authentic location photography, magazine articles, website articles and emails, as well as material in puzzle formats.
- supplementary content in a variety of digital delivery formats such as authentic video blogs, video drama, grammar animations, interactive games, etc.
- a group of sympathetic teenage characters with whom students can easily identify.
- situations, topics and emotional issues (see in particular the **Real Life Issue** lessons) which students will recognise and respond to.
- authentic functional language and everyday expressions which young British and American people use in conversation with each other (see the **Phrases** boxes and the **Use your English** sections).
- topics which expand students' knowledge of the world (see the **Across Cultures** lessons).
- memory exercises and puzzles (see the **Solve it!** exercises in the Students' Book, the puzzle exercises in the **Motivator worksheets** and the **interactive games** on the eText) to provide cognitive stimulus.
- interesting and varied language exercises to encourage the practice of key language (e.g. quizzes and questionnaires).
- personalisation to allow the students to talk about themselves and their opinions as much as possible.

2 Enable *all* students to succeed

The course material should make it possible for every student to achieve success at his or her level of ability. *Live Beat* achieves this by providing:

- grammar in clear tables for easy processing of information, and **Grammar summaries** in the **Workbook**.
- clear signposting of the key language (highlighted in red) in the presentation texts and dialogue.

- memorable exemplification of grammar structures through **video animations** on the eText.
- **graded grammar practice** tasks with simple language manipulation exercises followed by more challenging tasks in the **Workbook** and on the **MyEnglishLab**.
- **Extra practice** activities in the back of the Students' Book for learners who need extra challenge (stretch activities) or support (remedial activities).
- additional **lead-in**, **revision** and **extension** activities in the **Teacher's Online Resource Materials** to help teachers tailor the material to individual class needs.
- multi-level exercises in the **Workbook**.

3 Set goals and monitor progress

The learning material should contain markers throughout the course to enable students to monitor their progress, gain a sense of achievement and develop independent learning strategies. *Live Beat* achieves this by providing:

- **Objectives boxes** at the beginning of each lesson, enabling students to focus on what their learning goals are.
- **Skills tip boxes** containing simple advice to help students develop their learning skills.
- a **Language Revision** every unit with a **Self-check score box** and **Audio answer key**.
- a **Skills Revision** every two units which concludes with a *Now I can* descriptors **checklist** to help students build awareness of their learning outcomes.
- **Language round-up** pages in each unit of the **Workbook** to help students monitor their own progress.
- an extensive **Assessment package** in the **Teacher's Online Resource Materials** and **Teacher's eText** and on the **MyEnglishLab**.

Course components

Students' Book

The **Students' Book** contains a Welcome unit for revision and 9 core units. The units are organised into lessons. **Video** and **animation** is an integral part of the course and can be accessed on the **eText** or **MyEnglishLab**.

Units 1, 3, 5, 7 and 9 follow this pattern:

- three language input lessons (a, b and c)
- an Across Cultures lesson (d)
- a Writing skills lesson (e)
- a Language Revision lesson

Units 2, 4, 6 and 8 follow this pattern:
• three language input lessons (a, b and c)
• a Real Life Issues lesson (d)
• a Language Revision
• a Skills Revision

The a, b and c **input lessons** present and practise grammar, vocabulary and functional language (Use your English).

Lesson d focuses on **skills development**. It consolidates and extends the language presented in the preceding three lessons and provides further reading, listening, speaking and writing practice. There are two types of skills development lessons – **Real Life Issues** and **Across Cultures** – and they both cover all four skills, reading, listening, speaking and writing.

The emphasis on particular skills is slightly different, however. In the **Across Cultures** lessons, the emphasis is on **reading**, with reading tips that offer strategies for reading different kinds of text more efficiently.

In the **Real Life Issue** lessons, the emphasis is on **listening** and **speaking**. Tips for listening and speaking are provided which train students to listen and speak more confidently.

The **Writing skills** pages focus on **writing** and provide tips and writing practice leading to the production of different kinds of text such as a description, a postcard, an email, etc. They contain a model text plus focus task, writing tips, one or two exercises based on the writing tips, and finally the main writing task. They are designed to build students' confidence and improve their performance by providing a lot of help and guidance.

There is a **Language Revision** page at the end of each unit. The pages contain accuracy exercises to revise grammar, vocabulary and communication, finishing with a simple self-assessment box to help students monitor their own progress. **Skills Revision** pages revise the skills taught in the preceding two units. The questions are designed to give students practice with the types of questions that come up in the Trinity, KET and PET exams.

At the end of the Students' Book, there are **Extra practice** exercises, **Pronunciation** exercises, a **Word bank** for revision of the main vocabulary from the previous level, a unit-by-unit **Word list** and an **Irregular verbs list**.

Workbook

The **Workbook** is divided into units and lessons which correspond to those in the **Students' Book**. The a, b and c input lessons provide practice of phrases, grammar, vocabulary and functions. It contains exercises

at two levels of difficulty, indicated by one or two stars, to cater for mixed ability classes. Most students will benefit from completing both levels of difficulty in the exercises, but students with a good basic knowledge may attempt just the higher levels of task. Additionally, each input lesson ends with a **Grammar summary** which contains example boxes and simple rules.

Language round-ups give extra practice of the unit. These exercises have a marking scheme and progress **Self-check score box** and **Audio answer key** so that students can check their knowledge.

Skills practice pages focus on reading, writing and listening. Odd numbered units concentrate on reading and writing whereas even numbered units focus on reading and listening with an additional short writing task.

Teacher's Book

The **Teacher's Book** contains the **Students' Books** pages, **Answer keys** for the **Students' Book** and **Workbook** exercises, **Audio scripts** for the **Class** and **Workbook audio** and informative **Background notes**. Optional Extra activities (**Look forward, Extension, Extra practice**) provide further practice which the teacher can draw on to tailor the course materials more closely to the needs of individual classes.

Class audio CDs

The **Class audio CDs** contain all the recorded material from the Students' Book.

Teacher's Online Resource Materials

The **Teacher's Online Resource Materials** can be accessed using the access code supplied on adoption of *Live Beat*. All material is provided in pdf format and can be printed, if preferred.

The **Teacher's Notes** contain **Answer keys** for the **Students' Book** and **Workbook** exercises, **Audio scripts** for the **Class** and **Workbook audio** and informative **Background notes**. Optional Extra activities (**Look forward, Extension, Extra practice**) provide further practice which the teacher can draw on to tailor the course materials more closely to the needs of individual classes. Hyperlinks take the teacher directly to the **Motivator worksheets**. These correspond to lessons a, b and c of the units in the **Students' Book** and, in addition, summative **Round-up worksheets** which revise the language from the three input lessons. The lively, stimulating activities are a mixture of puzzles, problem-solving exercises and information-gap tasks and include many authentic text types (e.g. maps, menus, notices and signs). Since some have been designed for the student to complete individually and some for pairwork, the worksheets can be used to vary the class dynamic, and as the activities are highly visual they are particularly suitable for use with students who have Specific Learning Differences. Specific teaching notes for the **Motivator worksheets** with integrated answer keys can be found in this section of the **Teacher's Online Resource Materials** as well.

The **Teacher's Online Resource Materials** also contain the complete **Assessment package** for *Live Beat*. This consists of:

- a **Diagnostic test** to be used at the start of the course to assess the level of students.
- individual **Unit tests** focusing on Grammar, Vocabulary and Functions.
- two **Skills tests** every two units, one focusing on Reading, Writing and Listening and the other specifically on Speaking.
- **Summative tests** every two units to assess students' progress at key points during the course.
- **End-of-year tests** to assess students' progress at the end of each academic year.
- **A** and **B versions** of all the tests above.

A version of all of the above test types is provided for students with Specific Learning Disabilities (SLD), such as dyslexia.

Teacher's eText

The **Teacher's eText** is a digital presentation tool designed for use with an Interactive whiteboard or a projector connected to a PC. It is a key component of the course permitting the teacher to vary the classroom dynamic, engage students' interest and so increase their motivation to learn. On the **Teacher's eText** the Students' Book pages can be shown on screen and the teacher can use the hotspots on them to navigate between the pages and connect directly to the key features of the tool:

- animated grammar presentations
- animated pronunciation presentations
- video clips with dialogues from the Use your English boxes
- additional video lessons based on teenagers' video blogs
- class audio-recordings
- enhanced interactivity built into the d lessons
- interactive games for revision
- Teaching notes
- Motivator worksheets
- Tests
- phonetics chart

In addition, the enhanced functionality of the Teacher's eText allows the teacher to:

- zoom in on any part of the page.
- play audio material and display the audio script while the audio is playing.
- view the course video material with the option to display or hide the video script.
- call up the answers to the activities on screen.
- highlight words or phrases on screen.
- write/delete notes.
- hide/reveal sections of the screen, etc.

Students' eText

The **Students' eText** is a simplified version of the Teacher's eText, designed for individual use on a tablet or PC. Essentially students have the same basic functionality as the teacher with the classroom version but without the Show answers facility, Teacher's materials or the write-on-screen tools. The Students' eText can be used instead of a print version of the Students' book.

MyEnglishLab

The **MyEnglishLab** is an online resource which allows teachers and students to interact beyond the classroom. It contains:

- the entire **Workbook** in an online, easy-to-manage, interactive and auto-graded environment.
- a wealth of extra **Skills practice** specifically written for the **MyEnglishLab** environment.
- student access to **Video blogs** with follow-up activities to consolidate learning from the classroom activities.
- additional *Five Days* drama video activities featuring yet more exposure to authentic use of English.
- **Pronunciation** activities with **Record and playback**.
- useful **tips** designed to help students complete activities and **feedback** on submission of an activity to help students understand why an answer is right or wrong.

MyEnglishLab gives teachers instant access to a range of diagnostic tools. The **Gradebook** enables teachers to see how students are progressing at a glance. The **Common Error Report** indicates which errors are the most common and which students are making these errors. The **Summative** and **Skills tests** are also available in interactive format. Teachers can assign tasks to the whole class, groups of students or individual students and communication tools enable teachers to send instant feedback on their students' work.

Features of *Live Beat*

Students' Book

a, b and c **input lessons** present and practise grammar, vocabulary and functional language (Use your English).

Objectives boxes make students aware of the language they are going to learn.

Key grammar is highlighted in red.

Photographs set the scene and present new language.

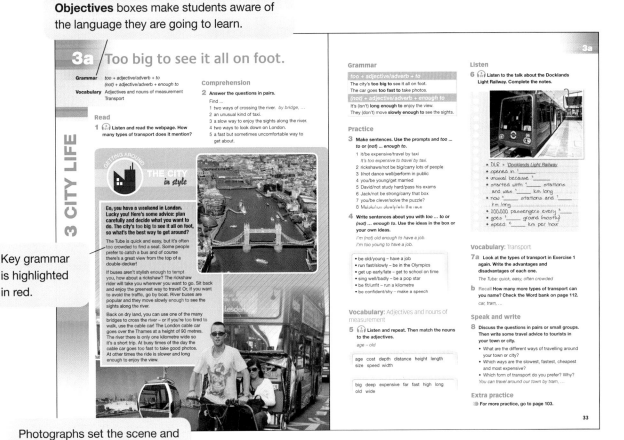

Photographs with teen characters engage students and set the scene.

Pronunciation exercises isolate and practise specific sounds, or stress and intonation patterns. Presentation animations with audio are included on the eText.

Communicative language is practised in functional contexts with video presentation on the eText.

Dialogues present new language in context.

Students learn useful everyday expressions.

9

Grammar boxes provide clear examples of grammar points. Animated cartoons on the eText present grammar in context.

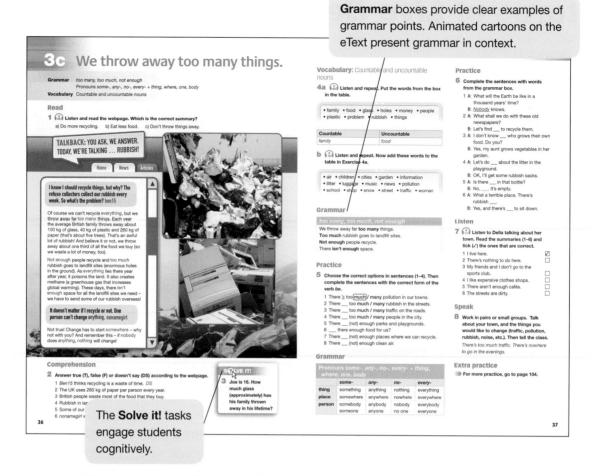

The **Solve it!** tasks engage students cognitively.

d lessons focus on **skills development**. They consolidate and extend the language presented in the input lessons and provide further reading, listening, speaking and writing practice.

Across Cultures lessons feature cultural aspects of the English-speaking world.

Get started activities make the topic relevant.

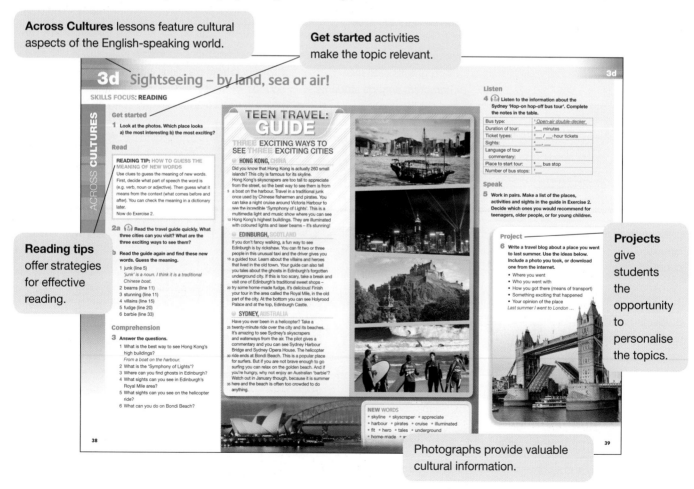

Reading tips offer strategies for effective reading.

Projects give students the opportunity to personalise the topics.

Photographs provide valuable cultural information.

Real Life Issues lessons highlight issues which are relevant to teenagers and contain moral dilemmas.

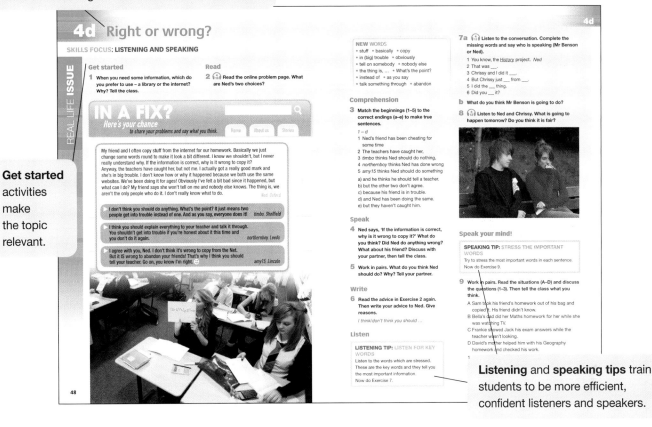

Get started activities make the topic relevant.

Listening and **speaking tips** train students to be more efficient, confident listeners and speakers.

Writing skills pages (e) focus on written communication and are designed to help build students' confidence.

Clear model texts provide guidance.

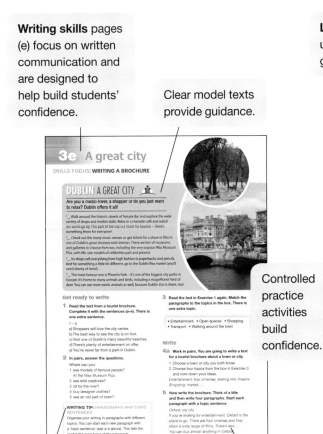

Controlled practice activities build confidence.

Writing tips focus on linguistic elements of writing, such as punctuation, connectors, etc.

Writing production task gives students the opportunity to demonstrate what they have learnt.

Language Revision pages for every unit contain accuracy exercises to revise grammar, vocabulary and communication.

Skills Revision pages revise skills taught in the preceding two units.

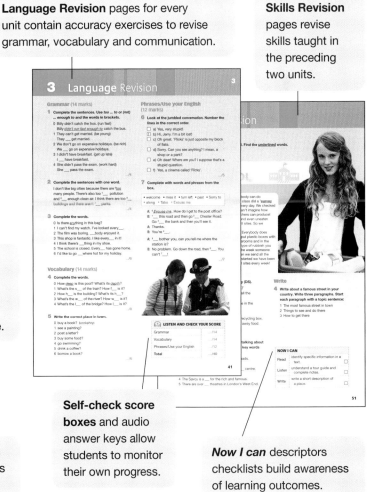

Self-check score boxes and audio answer keys allow students to monitor their own progress.

Now I can descriptors checklists build awareness of learning outcomes.

Extra practice activities provide stretch and remediation activities for every unit.

Pronunciation exercises for every unit isolate and practise specific sounds, or stress and intonation patterns.

The unit-by-unit **Word list** facilitates revision and memorisation of key vocabulary.

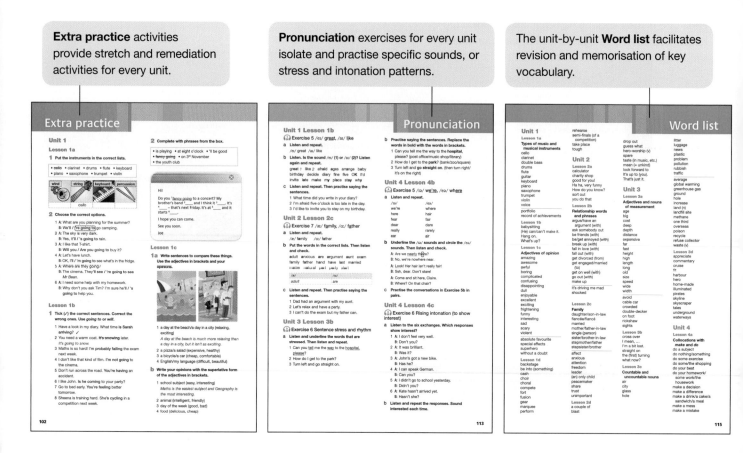

Workbook

a, b and c **input lessons** are multi-level and practise grammar, vocabulary, functional language (Use your English) and **Grammar reference** columns.

Grammar summaries contain example boxes and simple rules.

Multi-level exercises mean all students are able to succeed.

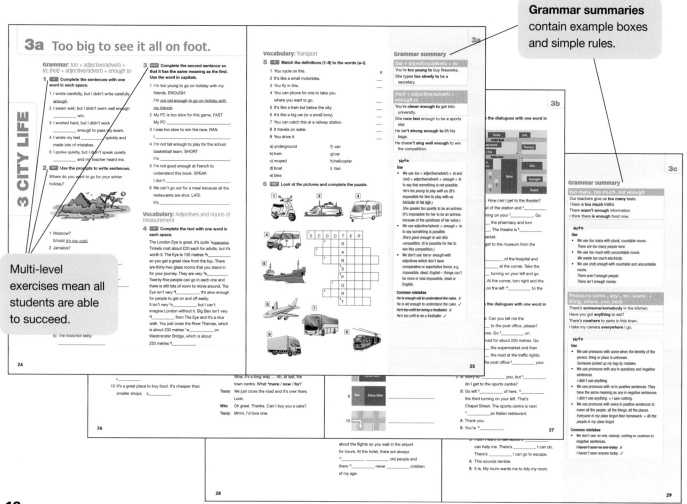

Language round-ups bring together all the language taught in the unit.

Skills practice pages focus on reading, writing and listening.

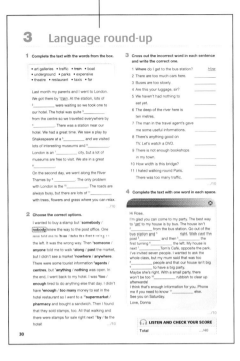
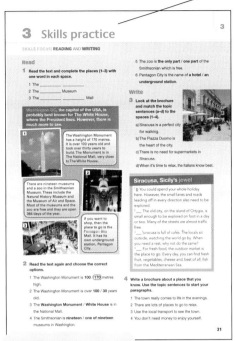

Odd units focus on reading and writing.

Even units focus on reading, listening and writing.

eText

eText brings *Live Beat* to life with integrated media to use on a variety of platforms.

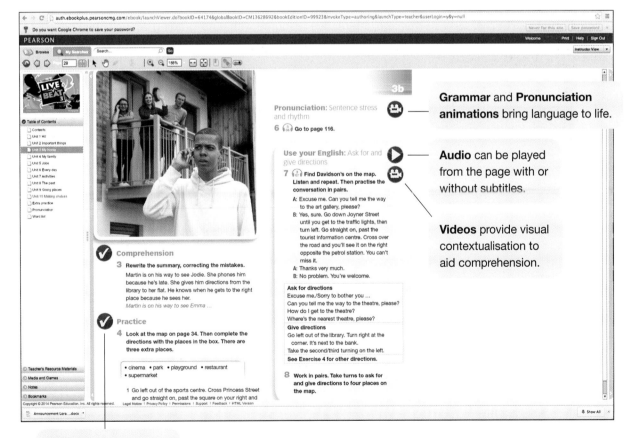

Grammar and **Pronunciation** animations bring language to life.

Audio can be played from the page with or without subtitles.

Videos provide visual contextualisation to aid comprehension.

Answer keys can be accessed via **Show answers** icons.

Interactive activities can be opened via the star icons.

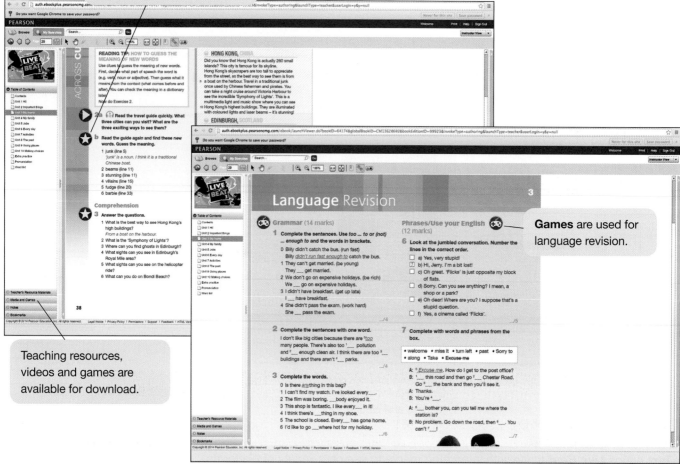

Games are used for language revision.

Teaching resources, videos and games are available for download.

MyEnglishLab

The **MyEnglishLab** is an online, easy-to-manage, interactive resource with auto-grading which allows teachers and students to interact in the classroom and beyond.

Interactive practice exercises and tests can be assigned to the whole class or to individual students.

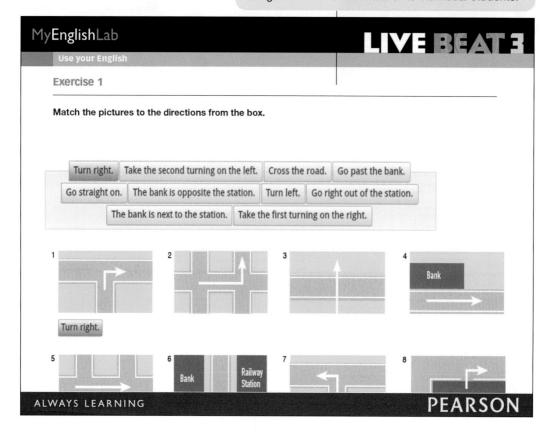

The **Gradebook** shows at a glance how students are progressing.

Teacher's Online Resource Material

The **Teacher's Online Resource Material** for *Live Beat* is available online or through your local Pearson representative.

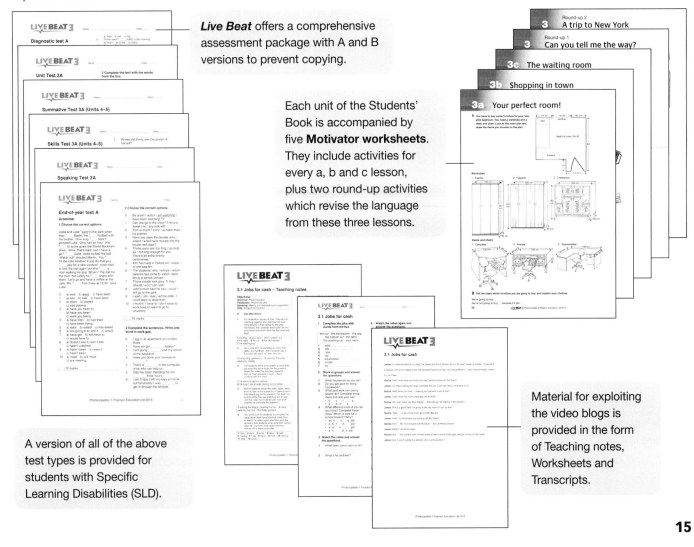

Live Beat offers a comprehensive assessment package with A and B versions to prevent copying.

Each unit of the Students' Book is accompanied by five **Motivator worksheets**. They include activities for every a, b and c lesson, plus two round-up activities which revise the language from these three lessons.

A version of all of the above test types is provided for students with Specific Learning Disabilities (SLD).

Material for exploiting the video blogs is provided in the form of Teaching notes, Worksheets and Transcripts.

Procedures

Photographs

The photographs which accompany the presentation material in each lesson in the Students' Book are an important teaching resource. They can be used for setting the scene, for presentation or revision of grammar and vocabulary, and for presenting additional language. In addition, the photographs frequently provide useful cultural information.

Learning objectives

The learning objectives box at the beginning of each input lesson of the Students' Book contains a list of the main areas of Grammar, Vocabulary and Functions in that lesson. The list is designed to make students aware of the language they are going to learn. It is often useful to discuss the learning objectives in the students' L1 (first language).

Suggested procedure

- Draw students' attention to the **Grammar** objective(s), and tell them that this language is highlighted in the presentation dialogue or text.
- Ask students to look at the **Vocabulary** objective(s), and elicit any words they may already know.
- Finally, ask students to look at the **Functional** objective and elicit any language they already know, or ask them what language they might expect to find in this part of the lesson.
- When the lesson has been completed, ask the students to go back to the learning objectives and give examples for each objective. Then get them to say which areas they found easy, and which ones they feel they need to practise more.

Get started

Some lessons contain a **Get started** task to introduce the topic of the lesson and generate some discussion. **Get started** tasks in the early units may be conducted in the L1. Later on, encourage students to use English as far as possible in these tasks. They can be conducted as a whole class activity or in pairs. It may be useful to write up any ideas or vocabulary deriving from the activity on the board.

Dialogue

The dialogues in *Live Beat* feature recurring teenage characters in different situations, and present the new language in context. All dialogues contain examples of the key grammar, vocabulary and functions of the relevant lesson. The key grammar is usually printed in red, and can be used later in the lesson to draw students' attention to the target language. The following guidelines may be useful for exploiting the dialogues in general.

Suggested procedure

- Check the teacher's notes for ideas to exploit the photo and introduce the situation. Present any language you think may cause problems, but don't focus explicitly on the grammar yet.
- All dialogues are preceded by a focus question in the instructions. Depending on students' confidence and ability, you could ask them to cover the dialogue in their books and look at the photo while they listen for the first time.
- Play the dialogue and ask for the answer to the focus question.
- Students look at the dialogue to check the answer.
- Students look at the comprehension questions. Check they understand all the questions. Play the dialogue again then check the answers to the questions. You may need to play the dialogue several times.
- If necessary, pause the audio recording to give students time to check and record their answers.

Suggested further work on the dialogue

- Play the dialogue again for the students to listen and repeat.
- Students read the dialogue aloud in pairs or groups.
- Some pairs or groups can act out the dialogue in front of the class.
- Write a skeleton version of the dialogue on the board. Students try to remember the missing parts. Slowly increase the number of gaps until students can recite the whole dialogue from memory.
- Students can then act out the dialogue without help from the book.

Read

Two types of reading texts are found in *Live Beat*. The first, shorter type is used to present new language in the a, b and c lessons. The key grammar is printed in red and can be used to focus on the target language later in the lesson. The second, longer type of reading text is used to develop reading skills in the d lessons. These texts are often adapted from authentic sources and cover a range of topics which are of interest to teenagers. They are presented in a variety of realistic formats such as website pages, magazine or newspaper articles, quizzes, etc. The following guidelines are for exploiting reading texts are used for language presentation in the a, b and c lessons. For guidelines on developing the skills practised in the d lessons, see the Skills focus section below.

Suggested procedure

- Use the photos or artwork to introduce the topic of the lesson. Present any language you think may cause problems, but don't focus explicitly on the grammar yet.
- Students look at the focus question in the instructions. This provides a purpose for reading.
- Students read the text silently. Encourage students to skim it quickly first to get a general idea, and then to scan for the answer to the focus question. Check the answer to the focus question.
- Students look at the comprehension questions. Check they understand all the questions. Students read the text silently again to find the answers. If desired, the audio of the text can be played so that students can read and listen.
- Students can compare their answers in pairs before you ask the class to give the answers.

Vocabulary

Vocabulary is presented in lexical sets. It is practised through exercises linked to the grammatical or functional goals of the lesson. Many of the new words are illustrated and their meaning will be clear. When there aren't illustrations, new words can be taught using a variety of techniques:

- mime the words; this is especially suitable for some verbs
- point to objects in the room to explain the words; this is especially suitable for common objects and personal possessions
- explain in simple English
- use L1 to translate certain words which are hard to explain or illustrate
- ask the students to use dictionaries

Suggested procedure

- Students look at the vocabulary in the box. Ask them to find some of the words in the text or dialogue.
- Play the audio recording and ask the students to mark the stress in longer words.
- Students complete the vocabulary exercise.
- Ask the students to use the words in sentences that are personal to them.
- Encourage students to keep a vocabulary notebook.
- After completing the vocabulary section in a lesson, students may record the vocabulary in their notebooks with an English explanation, an L1 translation if desired and an example sentence.
- Ask students to revise the vocabulary for each lesson as part of their homework. You can start the following lesson with a quick recall of the previous lesson's words. One way of checking what the students

remember is with the following game. Students work in pairs or small groups. Give them a time limit, for example, three minutes to write down as many words or phrases as they can from the last lesson. The pair or group that remembers the most items wins. To improve spelling, teams can also win an extra point for each correctly spelt item.

Solve it!

The Solve it! boxes contain tasks designed to engage students cognitively through problem-solving questions and activities as a way of maintaining motivation and providing a change of focus between the presentation materials and the language practice. They invite students to exercise their thinking skills and use English to solve problems. The short exercise is usually based on the presentation dialogue or text of that lesson. It often involves looking at a photo for clues as well as interpreting the written information.

Suggested procedure

- Students read the Solve it! question.
- Ask the students to work silently for one or two minutes. Do not allow anyone to shout out the answer in order to allow all the students time to find the answer.
- Students can compare their answers in pairs before you check with the whole class.

Grammar

The grammar boxes focus on the main grammar point in a lesson and are presented in tabular form for easy understanding by the student. The grammar boxes are followed by practice exercises. Although we recommend that the Grammar section is exploited after the presentation, since it's important to see the language in a natural context like a presentation dialogue or text before doing any analytical work, some teachers in certain teaching situations may wish to start a lesson with the main grammar point then continue with the dialogue or text. In this case the grammar animation provided on the Teacher's eText is a powerful aide-memoire to focus students' attention on the language form and usage.

Suggested procedure

- Students look at the grammar box and read the example sentences aloud.
- Draw students' attention to the highlighted words in the presentation text or dialogue.
- Students make more example sentences using the relevant grammar structure.
- If necessary, use the L1 to point out any significant differences between the grammar of the L1 and English.

Suggested procedure for eText

- The grammar animation can be used after the Dialogue section.
- Play the whole video animation for students and check if students understand the general context.
- Play the video again, pausing before key grammar points, and ask students to give you the next part of the dialogue.
- Resume the video for students to check if their answer was correct. Ask students to repeat the whole sentence.
- Refer students to the grammar box and pay attention to the highlighted words. If necessary point out any significant differences between the grammar of the L1 and English.
- Ask students to form groups and write their own dialogue using the appropriate grammatical structure. Encourage students to use the grammar box as reference while writing their dialogue.
- Ask groups to perform their dialogues in front of the class.

Practice

Practice exercises generally follow the Grammar box and are focused on accuracy. They can be done individually or in pairs where students can cooperate in finding the answers. Many of these exercises are personalised so that students can talk or write about their own lives and opinions, an important factor in maintaining motivation. **Revision** and **Extension** activities are given in the **Teacher's Book** notes.

Suggested procedure

- Make sure students understand the task.
- Read the example aloud while they follow.
- Ask the students to work silently on their own for five minutes while they do the exercise without writing. Do not allow anyone to shout out the answer. Allow all the students time to work out the answers.
- Ask individual students for the answers.
- If a student makes a mistake, ask another student to provide the answer.
- If there's time, get the students to write the answers in their notebooks.

Further practice exercises are to be found in the **Extra practice** section, in the **Workbook** or **MyEnglishLab** and the **Motivator** worksheets.

Listen, Speak, Write

Further practice of the main language goals is provided in the Speak, Listen and Write exercises of the input lessons (a, b and c). While grammar exercises are extremely valuable for initial accuracy practice, these skills-based exercises provide the opportunity to listen to and produce the key grammar and vocabulary in realistic and personalised contexts.

Suggested procedure for Listen exercises

- Make sure the students understand the task. Read the rubric aloud while they follow. If absolutely necessary, translate the instructions into L1. However, do not translate as a matter of course, since you want students to get used to reading instructions and to learn basic classroom language.
- Make sure they understand phrases like *True*, *False*, *Tick*, *Doesn't say*, *Choose the correct answer*, *Complete the table*.
- Where there are specific questions to answer about the recording, ask students to read through all the questions before you play the audio. They will then know what information they are listening for and it will help them to focus on this. Also, the questions often contain words that they are going to hear in the audio and it will help them to recognise these words on the audio if they have already read them.
- Play the audio once. Students write their answers.
- Ask students how they got on. Depending on time and the ability of the class, you may need to play the audio again.
- Check answers, asking individuals in the class. If a large number of students have made a mistake, replay the relevant bit of audio, stopping and explaining the issue/language which has caused misunderstanding.
- Depending on the amount of time available to you, you may want to follow the listening exercise with some speaking practice based on the answers.

Suggested procedure for Speak exercises

- Make sure the students understand the task. Read the rubric aloud while they follow. If necessary, translate the instructions into L1.
- Model the example with an able student, with you saying A's part and the student saying B's part.
- Students work in pairs while you go round the class checking on their work.
- Choose a couple of pairs to do the task while the rest of the class listens.
- Depending on the type of task, the amount of time you have and the ability of the class, you could ask students working in the same pairs to write the dialogues or questions and answers that they have just produced orally.

Suggested procedure for Write exercises

- Make sure the students understand the task. Read the rubric aloud while they follow. If necessary, translate the instructions into L1.

- Ask an able student to provide an example and write it on the board. Ask other students for examples and write them on the board. Elicit more examples from other students. Ask appropriate questions to elicit relevant answers.
- Ask students to do the writing task individually. Tell them they can use/adapt the examples on the board.
- While students are writing, go round the class checking their progress. Note the most common mistakes.
- Tell the class about five mistakes that you've seen in their work and write the correct version on the board. Ask students to check that they haven't made any of these mistakes.
- Tell the class that you will mark their written work individually when you next take in their exercise books.

Use your English

The **Use your English** sections provide communicative language practice in functional/situational contexts, e.g. ordering food, exchanging opinions, giving and accepting invitations, etc. This language is introduced in the presentation dialogues to provide a realistic context. Each Use your English section contains a short example dialogue followed by the key functional language in tabular form. Practice exercises follow. Videos of the dialogues are available on the *Live Beat* eText. These provide visual contextualisation to aid comprehension and offer students the opportunity to role play parts of the dialogue for additional speaking practice.

Suggested procedure

- Introduce the function/situation in the heading and translate it into L1, if necessary.
- Play the audio of the dialogue/conversation while students listen and read it.
- Play the audio again and, if you wish, pause it after each sentence so students can repeat.
- Correct any pronunciation problems.
- Ask the students to look at the box containing the functional phrases.
- If you wish, get the students to repeat the phrases in the box.
- Students practise the dialogue/conversation in pairs or groups, depending on the number of speakers.
- Demonstrate the practice exercise(s) with a volunteer.
- Students do the exercise(s) in pairs or groups.

Suggested procedure for eText

- Play the whole scene once and ask students who the people in the scene are and where they are (e.g. in Unit 1 **Use your English** video – a teacher and a student in a school). Students may read the dialogue in their books.

- Divide students into 2 groups: group A repeats A's part of the dialogue, group B repeat B's part. Play the recording again with students reading out loud their part of the dialogue together with the speakers in the video, keeping the same pace and intonation.
- Explain you are now going to play only A's part of the dialogue and students must reply with B's line. A timer on the screen will tell them how much time they have to reply.
- Follow the steps above for part B of the dialogue.
- Ask students to work in pairs and role play similar conversations using the prompts from Use your English box.

Pronunciation

Pronunciation exercises are found at the back of the Students' book and cross-referenced with the relevant lesson as well as on the MyEnglishLab. The exercises isolate and practise specific sounds, and stress or intonation patterns. The particular pronunciation point selected for the lesson occurs in the presentation dialogue. Each pronunciation section contains examples to repeat, and a further exercise to identify the point being practised. Short animations on the eText also provide a useful visual reference for students.

Suggested procedure

- Focus the students on the point to be practised.
- Play the recording of the Pronunciation exercise and ask the students to listen and repeat. Play the sounds several times if they are having difficulty producing them.
- Play the next part of the recording and ask the students to complete the task.

Suggested procedure for eText

Especially at lower levels it is very beneficial if students see the words they are learning and hear them pronounced at the same time. Apart from providing a clearly pronounced model the animations also show the phonetic transcription of the pronounced word. You can use this to teach your students phonetic transcription and show them how to check pronunciation of unknown words in a dictionary. For kinaesthetic learners especially it may be beneficial to ask them to stand up when they hear the stressed syllable in a word, to tap to the sentence stress or raise or lower their hands depending on the intonation pattern.

The presentation dialogues can also be used for additional pronunciation practice through straightforward repetition and chaining repetition techniques. The **MyEnglishLab** also contains practice exercises with **record and playback** so that students can assess their own performance.

Skills focus: Reading, Listening, Speaking and Writing

The Students' Book contains 9 skills focus lessons. These are the fourth lesson (lesson d) in each unit. They are divided into two categories: Across Cultures and Real Life Issues. Each lesson contains practice in all **four language skills**, and in addition, each concentrates on a specific skill or skills and includes a special 'tip' related to this skill, with an accompanying practice activity.

The **Across Cultures** lessons feature cultural aspects of the English-speaking world. They cover topics such as home, school, jobs, etc. and are written from a teen perspective. The texts in these lessons are often adapted from authentic sources and presented in a variety of realistic formats such as website pages, magazine or newspaper articles. The lessons also often present additional information in tables or charts.

Read

In the **Across Cultures** lessons, the skill of reading is given special emphasis. Reading tip boxes offer strategies for training students to be more efficient confident readers of different kinds of text. The following guidelines are for exploiting reading texts in general in all the d lessons, whether an Across Cultures, where reading tips are provided, or a Real Life Issue lesson, where the tips are for speaking and listening. It is important to treat the reading texts in the d lessons as opportunities for students to improve their reading comprehension and expand their vocabulary rather than treat them as opportunities for language analysis. (Lessons a, b and c serve this purpose.)

Suggested procedure for Reading

- Get students to look at the photographs/illustrations and ask them some questions to activate their background knowledge of the topic, and to establish the context of the text.
- Point out the New words box and ask students if they know any of the words. Tell the students they will meet these words when they read. Explain or translate any new words that are essential to the comprehension tasks or ask students to look them up in a dictionary before they read.
- Sometimes new words can be guessed from the context, so it is useful to encourage students to try and get the general idea of the text in the first reading and to guess the meaning of any new words they encounter. Students can be told the exact meaning of the words after the first reading. Guessing meaning is one of the most important skills when

reading in a foreign language, and it can help develop autonomous reading skills if the students are given the confidence to guess through class activities.

- Use the Get started activity (if provided), or ask some simple questions of your own to focus students on the topic of the text.
- Ask students to read the Reading tip, and check they understand it. Give more explanation or examples as needed.
- Ask the students to look at the focus question in the instructions and read the text silently. Check the answer to the focus question with the class.
- Students read the comprehension questions, and read the text again, focusing only on finding the information to answer the questions.
- Students can compare their answers in pairs before you check the answers with the class.
- Students read the text again to ensure they understand it. Ask for any comments which students might have about what they have read. Ask students if they found it easy or difficult, and, if there was a Reading tip, ask them if they managed to use it.

The texts are recorded, and the audio can be played for the students to follow. This is useful in the early stages of training reading skills. However, students should be encouraged to read silently as soon as they have built enough confidence.

The **Real Life Issue** lessons are designed to highlight issues which are of particular interest to students, and which contain moral dilemmas, such as bullying, honesty, family relationships, etc. They ae presented as, and based on, real incidents taken from life, and are fully illustrated.

Listen

In the Real Life Issue lessons, tips for listening and speaking are given special emphasis. These tips offer different strategies for training students to be more efficient, confident listeners and speakers. The following guidelines are for exploiting listening texts in general in all the d lessons, whether a Real Life Issue, where listening and speaking tips are provided, or an Across Cultures lesson, where listening and speaking tips are not provided. It is important to treat the listening texts in the d lessons as opportunities for students to improve their listening comprehension and to listen for important information, rather than to treat them as opportunities for language analysis. (Lessons a, b and c serve this purpose.) The listening texts are related to the theme of the lesson. They may provide a continuation of the story or topic, or another angle on it.

Suggested procedure for Listening

- Ask the students to predict what they think will happen in the text they are going to listen to. You can prompt students by writing some questions on the board for discussion. Make notes on the board of any predictions they make to provide focus for the first listening.
- Explain any new words which may discourage students from listening. There are usually very few new words in the listening texts.
- Ask the students to read the Listening tip, if there is one. Check that they understand the tip, and discuss it with the class, giving more explanation as needed.
- Play the recording for students to listen and grasp the gist. Discuss students' original predictions and what they actually heard.
- Students read the comprehension questions and listen again, keeping the Listening tip in mind, if there is one.
- Students can discuss their answers in pairs. Play the recording again, pausing if necessary for students to complete and check their answers.
- Ask for any comments students might have about what they have heard. Ask them if they found it easy or difficult, and if they managed to use the Listening tip strategy.

Speak/Speak your mind!

Students often find speaking at length difficult, and can be reticent because they are afraid of making mistakes. They need plenty of encouragement to 'have a go' and try to express themselves even if they make some accuracy errors. The **Speak** and **Speak your mind!** sections provide students with the opportunity to give their own opinions on the theme of the lesson. It is helpful to use pair and group work as much as possible so that all students have the chance to practise speaking at the same time. You can walk around the class to listen and note any errors and difficulties in order to give feedback after the task has been completed. The following guidelines are for exploiting speaking tasks in general in all d lessons, whether a Real Life Issue, where speaking tips are provided, or an Across Cultures lesson, where speaking tips are not provided.

Suggested procedure for Speaking

- If there's a Speaking tip, ask the students to read it. Check that students understand the tip, and discuss it with the class, giving more explanation as needed.
- Students read the task. Check that they understand what to do.
- Perform the first part of the task with the class, or use a confident student to demonstrate.
- If possible, put students into pairs or groups to carry out the task. Monitor and make notes for feedback later.
- Ask some students to report back what they said.
- Write any errors that you heard on the board and ask students if they can correct them. Praise students for their achievement of the task, and, if appropriate, ask if they managed to use the Speaking tip to help them speak.

Write

There are short writing tasks at the end of all the d lessons. The writing tasks follow the theme or topic of the texts, and give students the opportunity to produce a short text of the same type as one of the texts in the spread. So if, for example, there's a job advertisement somewhere on the spread, students may be asked to write a job advertisement. If there's information about a British festival, students may be asked to produce information about a festival in their country or town. The writing task that students do at the end of the Across Cultures lessons, is a project, and can be done cooperatively by groups of students. This project work can be displayed, if desired. All writing tasks in the d lessons can be set as homework if there isn't enough time to do them in class. However, it's always a good idea to allow preparation time in class before the students do them for homework, to increase confidence, improve performance, and reduce the time you will have to spend marking!

Suggested procedure for Writing

- Make sure the students understand the task. Read the rubric aloud while they follow. If necessary, translate the instructions into L1.
- Ask a confident student to provide an example and write it on the board. Elicit more examples from other students.
- Have students do the writing task individually, whether in class or as homework. Tell them they can use/adapt the examples on the board.
- If students do the task during the lesson, go round the class checking their progress and taking note of mistakes that occur most often.
- Tell the class about the five most common mistakes that you've noticed, and ask students to check that they haven't made any of these mistakes.
- Tell the class that you will mark their written work individually when you next take in their exercise books.
- If desired, display the students' Project work done for Across Cultures writing tasks in the classroom.

Skills focus: Writing

There are five **Writing** lessons in *Live Beat*. They recycle vocabulary and grammar from the unit in question and no new language is introduced.

Suggested procedure

- Check students understand the focus task before they read the model text. Check their answers to the focus task.
- Ask students to read the Writing tip. Check that they understand it, and discuss it with the class, giving more explanation or examples as needed.
- Students do the exercise(s) based on the writing tips. Check the answers.
- Ask students to look at the writing task, and if appropriate, get them to brainstorm a list of vocabulary that might be useful for the task. Write a list of these words on the board.
- Students look back at the text which serves as a model. Point out or elicit the sentences that can be used as a guide for students' own writing. Write the guide on the board.
- Students can then write in class or at home. Remind students that they must use the writing tips when they are writing. If students write in class, they can exchange their work and check for errors before giving it to the teacher.
- If the writing is done for homework, when you check it you can indicate errors using a series of symbols, and students can be encouraged to correct their own work. It can be a good idea to allow students to revisit their work in this way before giving the work a grade.

Extra practice

The **Extra practice** exercises are a bank of extra activities positioned at the back of the **Students' Book** and cross-referenced to the relevant lesson. There are one or two Extra practice exercises for each input lesson. They give further practice of the grammar, vocabulary or functional language in the lesson. At the end of each input lesson, students can be directed to these exercises. They are designed for use both by fast finishers and by those students who need more language consolidation.

Video Blogs

There are four additional **Video lessons** based on teenagers' video blogs available on the **Teacher's eText**. These lessons are after units 2, 4, 6 and 8. The video blogs (vlogs) feature teenagers discussing their own lives and a range of subjects such as recent trips, the pressures of school work or what they did at the weekend. They are casual, unscripted and very much in line with what students are used to seeing on

the Internet. They feature grammar and vocabulary from the previous lessons presented in a real context that students should instantly be able to identify with. The activities that follow ensure student understanding and are coupled with engaging productive activities. The videos, with further consolidation activities, are also available for students to watch again on the **MyEnglishLab**.

Teaching techniques

Most teachers find it useful to have a 'toolkit' of different teaching techniques that they can call on depending on whether they are presenting new language, getting students to practise a grammar point, encouraging discussion or teaching a skill. Choice of technique may also depend on the mood of the students. For example, if students are subdued and lacking energy, the teacher can change the pace by getting students to change places and work in groups. If students need quietening down, the teacher can set a writing task. The following is a selection of core teaching techniques that every teacher should have at their disposal, whichever combination of course components they have chosen for their class.

Repetition and choral practice

Repetition can help to reinforce pronunciation, grammatical patterns, vocabulary and functional phrases. It is essential for all students when meeting new language. Repeating chorally can help students increase their confidence before they are asked to perform individually. Choral work can be carried out with the whole class, with half the class at a time, in groups, in seating rows and with selected individuals.

Questioning patterns

Different question and answer patterns give the teacher the opportunity to demonstrate the language and give students the opportunity to practise it. A variety of patterns is possible:

- Teacher to self (to give a model).
- Teacher to one student (to give a model/to elicit and demonstrate before pairwork).
- Teacher to class (to elicit a choral response).
- Student to teacher (to allow students to ask as well as answer).
- Student to student (in pairwork).
- Student to student to student (in a chain).

Pairwork

Many of the language exercises in *Live Beat* can be done in pairs working simultaneously in the classroom. This means that students' talking time is increased dramatically and extensive practice can be done by all students in a relatively short space of time. Some frequently used pairwork patterns are:

- Closed pairs: Student A talks to Student B next to him/her, or turns round to talk to the student behind.
- Open pairs: Student A talks to Student B chosen from anywhere in the class.
- Pairwork chain: Student A talks to Student B next to him/her; Student B talks to Student C, and so on.

Cooperative pairwork can also be used. Students can be asked to work together on the answers to comprehension questions and practice exercises, and to prepare speaking tasks together. This helps to build confidence in weaker learners as well as allowing rehearsal before giving answers in front of the whole class.

Groupwork

For certain kinds of activities (e.g. roleplays, discussions and questionnaires), students can work together in groups. Groupwork can provide an opportunity for weak or shy students to practise without fear or embarrassment. Groups can also be used for cooperative work.

Groupwork needs to be set up and organised carefully. Give clear instructions, check that students understand what to do and train students to move into groups quickly and with as little fuss as possible.

Allocate roles in the group as necessary or appropriate to the task. One student might be the note-taker, another might be the spokesperson to report back to the class, another might be a time-keeper and tell the group how much time is left.

Always set a time limit and warn students when there is one minute left.

Monitor the students, spending a few minutes listening to each group before moving to the next. Take notes on any language errors to give feedback at the end of the activity. Don't interrupt unless the students ask for help.

Oral correction

Most students believe that their teachers should always correct them. However, oral correction should be carefully judged. When students are doing controlled practice, the teacher can correct immediately after the end of the utterance. When students are speaking to develop fluency (in discussions and roleplays, for example), they should not be interrupted. The teacher can listen and make notes of errors to give feedback later.

Written correction

If a written exercise is done for homework, when you check it you can indicate errors using a series of symbols, and students can be encouraged to correct their own work. It can be a good idea to allow the students to revisit their work in this way before giving the work a grade.

Suggested symbols

SP = spelling

GR = grammar

WO = word order

V = vocabulary

P = punctuation

Our aim when developing *Live Beat* was to create a course which would stimulate, educate and encourage teenage students of all abilities whilst at the same time providing extensive support and help for the teacher. We hope that we have achieved our aim, and that you and your students will enjoy using *Live Beat*!

WELCOME

Exercise 1
B – Luke,
C – Martin,
D – Emma

Exercise 2
2 Martin 3 Martin,
Luke 4 Luke, Jodie
5 Martin

Exercise 3
Positive: cute,
easy-going,
friendly, funny,
generous, hard-
working, helpful,
honest, kind, loyal,
polite, tidy

Negative:
annoying,
bad-tempered,
big-headed, bossy,
lazy, mean, rude,
unfriendly, untidy

Both: quiet, shy

1 🎧 **Listen and read. Name the people in the photo.**

A – Jodie

2 **Complete with *Luke, Jodie, Emma* or *Martin*.**

1 *Emma* is a member of the sports club.
2 ___ is American.
3 ___ and ___ are in the same class at school.
4 ___ is ___'s brother.
5 ___'s dad is a teacher.

Personality adjectives

3 **Look at the personality adjectives from the Word bank on page 111. Then write the words in the correct lists. Which words could go in both lists?**

😊	☹️
clever	

Emma:	Hi, Luke. Hi, Jodie. What are you doing here?
Luke:	Hi, Emma. We're applying for the free month. Are you a member?
Emma:	Yes, I play badminton here every week – but I'm not very good.
Jodie:	Don't listen to her. She's brilliant.
Luke:	Look, that's the new boy in my class. He's American.
Emma:	What's he like?
Luke:	He seems OK, quite friendly and easy-going. Oh cool, he's coming in ... Hi, Martin!
Martin:	Hi, er ... sorry, I don't remember ...
Luke:	Luke.
Jodie:	I'm his sister, Jodie, and this is Emma.
Martin:	Hi, nice to meet you. Do you live near here?
Luke:	Not far away. What about you?
Martin:	We're renting an apartment round the corner. My dad's a teacher. We're only here for a year.
Jodie:	Great. Welcome to London!

4

Present simple and present continuous

Name the tenses

1 What **are** you **doing** here?
2 I **play** badminton here every week.
3 He **seems** OK.
4 **I don't remember**.
5 We**'re renting** an apartment.

Stative verbs

We don't normally use these verbs in the continuous: *be, believe, forget, hate, hear, hope, know, like, love, mean, need, prefer, remember, see, seem, sound, understand, want*

Complete the rules.

We use the ¹___ tense for permanent situations and routines.
We use the ²___ tense for activities which are happening at or around the time of speaking.

5 **Choose the correct options.**

1 Sorry, I don't remember / 'm not remembering your name.
2 Hi! Where **do you go / are you going**?
3 Ssh! We **watch / 're watching** TV.
4 Jack **always sits / 's always sitting** at the back of the class.
5 We **study / 're studying** Shakespeare this term.
6 May **doesn't like / isn't liking** loud music.

6 **Complete the sentences with the present simple or present continuous form of the verbs.**

1 Luke, Jodie and Emma *live* (live) in London. Martin ___ (stay) in London for a year.
2 My sister ___ (love) adventure stories. At the moment she ___ (read) *The Hunger Games*.
3 I ___ (not want) to go out now – it ___ (rain).
4 What's funny? Why ___ (you laugh)? I ___ (not understand).
5 ___ (you enjoy) the party? I ___ (hope) so!
6 My mum ___ (call) me. She ___ (wait) for me downstairs.

7a **Take turns to talk about somebody in your family. Your partner takes notes.**

- What's he/she like?
- What does he/she do every day?
- What does he/she usually do at the weekend?
- What's he/she doing at the moment? (Guess!)

My brother's clever, but he's really lazy. He goes to this school. At the weekend he plays a lot of computer games. At the moment, he's having a Maths lesson.

b **Now write about the person your partner described.**

Anna's brother is clever, but …

4 **In pairs, describe the people using the adjectives in Exercise 3. Take turns to ask and answer.**

1 Ben gets good marks at school.
   A: What's Ben like?
   B: He's clever. He gets good marks at school.
2 Alex and Shaun like meeting people.
3 Amy doesn't like spending money.
4 Tom always makes people laugh.
5 Rosa likes helping people.
6 Jack always gets up late and doesn't work very hard.
7 Kate never says 'please' or 'thank you'.
8 Tim loves giving presents to his friends and family.

Extension ▰

Personality adjectives

Ask one S to go out of the room. The rest of the class chooses one personality adjective from the Word bank on page 111.

The S comes back and asks individual Ss to do certain actions. They have to act in the way suggested by the adjective, e.g. as though they are *bad-tempered* or *lazy*.

After two or three Ss have performed, the S tries to guess the adjective.

5

Exercise 4

2 They're friendly. 3 She's mean. 4 He's funny.
5 She's helpful. 6 He's lazy. 7 She's rude.
8 He's generous.

Grammar

1 present simple 2 present continuous

Exercise 5

2 are you going 3 're watching 4 always sits
5 're studying 6 doesn't like

Exercise 6

1 is/'s staying 2 loves, 's reading 3 don't want, 's raining 4 are you laughing, don't understand
5 Are you enjoying, hope 6 's calling, 's waiting

1 Listen and read. What does Martin like about his London home?

Martin: I've got some photos here – look, this is my house in California.

Jodie: Wow, it looks great! What about inside? Have you got any more photos?

Martin: Not on my phone. It's quite big inside, but there are only three bedrooms.

Jodie: Are all the rooms on one floor?

Martin: Yes, there aren't any stairs, but there is a small loft.

Jodie: Cool, I love lofts!

Martin: Not this one! It's dark and there's no window. There's just some old furniture up there.

Jodie: Well, now you're in a flat on the 5th floor. That's a big change.

Martin: Yes, it's different … but I like it. It's got a balcony! We haven't got one back home.

Jodie: But you've got a garden there. Have you got a swimming pool?

Martin: No, there isn't any space. But it doesn't matter, there's a pool next door!

2 Look at the photos (1–3). Which one is Martin's house?

6

House and furniture

3a Put the words from the box into the correct lists.

> • balcony • bathroom • bedroom • bookcase • carpet
> • ceiling • cooker • dishwasher • floor • fridge • hall
> • kitchen • lamp • mirror • sink • wall

Rooms: *bathroom, ...*   **Fittings:** *cooker, ...*
Parts of a house: *balcony, ...*   **Furniture:** *bookcase, ...*

b Work in pairs. Add more words to the lists, then check the Word bank on page 111.

4 Look at the picture for one minute, then cover it. How many things can you remember? Tell your partner.

a kitchen, a ...

Countable and uncountable nouns with *some, any, a/an* and *no*

Countable		Uncountable
Affirmative		
It's got **a** balcony. There is **a** loft.	I've got **some** photos. There are **some** photos.	There's **some** old furniture. It's got **some** old furniture.
Negative		
There isn't **a** window. There's **no** window.	There aren't **any** stairs. There are **no** stairs.	There isn't **any** space. There is **no** space.
Questions		
Have you got **a** swimming pool?	Have you got **any** photos?	Is there **any** furniture?

Note
Uncountable nouns do not have a plural form.

5 Complete the sentences with *some, any, a/an* or *no.*

1 There's <u>a</u> big fridge in the kitchen but there isn't ___ food in it!
2 There's ___ rubbish on the floor. Have you got ___ wastepaper bin?
3 Sorry, you can't sit here, there's ___ space – but there are ___ chairs over there.
4 I want to buy ___ chocolate. Have you got ___ money?
5 Yes, we've got ___ garden, but I'm afraid there aren't ___ flowers – only ___ grass.
6 There's ___ old bookcase in the hall with ___ mirror above it.

6 Match questions (1–6) to answers (a–f). Then complete them with *some, any, a/an* or *no.*

1 – b

1 Have you got *any* homework tonight?
2 Is there ___ food in the fridge?
3 Is there ___ furniture in the new classroom?
4 Has Joe got ___ new bike?
5 Have you got ___ good CDs?
6 Is there ___ computer in that classroom?

a) Not really, but I've got ___ cool music on my phone.
b) Yes, but I haven't got *any* time to do it!
c) Yes, there's ___ cheese and ___ box of eggs.
d) Yes, there are ___ chairs, but there are ___ desks.
e) Yes, but there's ___ printer.
f) No, he's got ___ old one.

7 Work in pairs. Take turns to describe your ideal bedroom or living room. Ask and answer questions about the room.

A: My ideal living room has got a big TV on one of the walls.
B: What about furniture? Is there a big sofa?

Extension

House and furniture

Play a simple 'Yes/No' question game. Demonstrate by thinking of a room, fitting, part of a house or an item of furniture and get the Ss to ask you *Yes/No* questions, e.g.:

A: *Is it a room?*
B: *No, it isn't.*
C: *Is it part of a house?*
B: *Yes, it is.*
A: *Is it outside?*
B: *Yes, it is.*
A: *Is it a garden?*
B: *Yes, it is.*

Put the Ss in small groups to continue with the game.

Exercise 3a
Rooms: bedroom, hall, kitchen
Parts of a house: ceiling, floor, wall
Fittings: dishwasher, fridge, sink
Furniture: carpet, lamp, mirror

Exercise 4
Rooms: kitchen, living room
Parts of a house: walls, floor
Fittings: cooker, fridge, sink, washing machine
Furniture: armchair, bookcase, carpet, chairs, clock, cupboards, curtains, lamp, sofa, table

Exercise 5
1 any 2 some, a 3 no, some 4 some, any
5 a, any, some 6 an, a

Exercise 6
2 c) any, some, a 3 d) any, some, no 4 f) a, an
5 a) any, some 6 e) a, no

Background note

Buckingham Palace: The official London home of the Queen. It was built at the beginning of the eighteenth century and became the official royal palace in 1837, when Victoria was crowned Queen. Buckingham Palace is used for important official occasions and for receptions. Parts of the Palace are also open to the public.

Exercise 1

Science

Exercise 2

2 F 3 T 4 T 5 DS

C

1 🎧 **Read Martin's blog. What does his father teach?**

My BLOG

Home   About   BLOG   Contact

Sept 5th

It was raining when we landed in London and after California it felt COLD. Our apartment isn't bad. The best thing is, Jamie and I have got our own rooms. When we arrived I wanted to go online straightaway, but there was no connection. This morning an engineer came … and here I am. Now what????

Sept 10th

I started school on Monday (it's a bit strange but OK) and I'm feeling more at home now. I went to the local sports centre on Saturday. A guy called Luke was there (he's in my new class), with his sister and her friend. While we were talking we discovered something embarrassing – the friend (her name's Emma) is in my dad's Science class, but luckily not at my school!

Sept 17th

Luke and I went sightseeing at the weekend and we saw Buckingham Palace. Lots of police officers and journalists were waiting outside while we were queuing – I think they were expecting someone important (they weren't waiting for us!).

2 Answer true (T), false (F) or doesn't say (DS).

1 Martin is from California. *T*
2 His apartment does not have an internet connection.
3 He's beginning to like his new home.
4 His father teaches Emma.
5 They visited several famous places in London.

8

Jobs

3a Find three jobs in the blog. Put them into the correct columns.

-er	-or	-ist	-ian	other
engineer				

b Now complete the jobs and add them to the table, then check the Word bank on page 111.

1 act<u>or</u> 6 direct__ 11 mod__
2 art__ 7 doct__ 12 music__
3 build__ 8 electric__ 13 reception__
4 dent__ 9 farm__ 14 shop assist__
5 detect__ 10 firefight__

4 Answer the questions. Sometimes there is more than one answer. Then check the Word bank on page 111.

Who …
1 fights fires? *a firefighter*
2 works with make-up?
3 cuts hair?
4 teaches skiing?
5 works with cars?
6 flies planes?
7 looks after the home?
8 cooks food?
9 serves food?
10 looks after animals?

Past simple and past continuous

Time markers: when, while

Name the tenses (1–9).

It ¹**was raining** when we ²**landed** in London.
When we ³**arrived** I ⁴**wanted** to go online.
While ⁵**we were talking**, we ⁶**discovered**
  something embarrassing.
Lots of police officers and journalists ⁷**were
  waiting** outside while we ⁸**were queuing**.
They ⁹**weren't waiting** for us!

Complete the rules.

We often use …
the ¹⁰___ tense to describe completed actions.
the ¹¹___ tense to describe actions that continued
  for some time in the past.
the word ¹²___ to introduce clauses in the past
  simple.
the word ¹³___ to introduce clauses in the past
  continuous.

5 Choose the correct options. Then complete the sentences with the correct form of the verbs.

1 Sam was cycling home [when] / while the police officer *stopped* (stop) him.
2 **When / While** the shop assistant opened the doors, a lot of customers ___ (wait) outside.
3 What was Jill doing **when / while** you ___ (see) her?
4 Dan ___ (play) football **when / while** he fell and hurt his leg.
5 I ___ (drop) my phone **when / while** I was walking home.
6 **When / While** the teacher ___ (talk), the students were taking notes.

6 Complete the next part of Martin's blog with the correct form of the verbs.

Sept 25th

Luke and I were at the sports centre yesterday. We ¹*didn't want* (not want) to do the same things. I ²___ (go) to the gym. While I ³___ (work) hard on the rowing machine, Luke ⁴___ (swim) lengths – he's a really good swimmer. After that we ⁵___ (decide) to go to the café. When we ⁶___ (walk) in, Jodie and Emma ⁷___ (sit) there, so we ⁸___ (join) them. While we ⁹___ (talk), I ¹⁰___ (ask) Emma about my dad. She ¹¹___ (say) he's quite a cool teacher! That's hard to believe.

7 Talk about your family. Use the prompts and *when* or *while*.

What were they doing when/while you …
• got home yesterday?
• went to bed last night?
• were having breakfast?
• left home this morning?
A: *What was your brother doing when you got home yesterday?*
B: *He was eating a sandwich.*

9

Grammar

1 past continuous
2 past simple
3 past simple
4 past simple
5 past continuous
6 past simple
7 past continuous
8 past continuous
9 past continuous
10 past simple
11 past continuous
12 when 13 while

Exercise 5
2 When, were waiting 3 when, saw 4 was playing, when 5 dropped, while 6 While, was talking

Exercise 6
2 went 3 was working 4 was swimming 5 decided 6 walked 7 were sitting 8 joined 9 were talking 10 asked 11 said

Extension ▰

Jobs
Play a game of 'What's my job?'

Write the names of different jobs on cards and turn them face down. Ask a S to pick up one card at random from the pile. The S then mimes the job for the rest of the class to guess. Ss may ask up to 10 questions. In response the S miming may only shake or nod their head. The S who guesses correctly takes the next card, and so on until all the jobs have been mimed and guessed.

Exercise 3a
-er: police officer
-ist: journalist

Exercise 3b
2 artist 3 builder 4 dentist 5 detective 6 director 7 doctor 8 electrician 9 farmer 10 firefighter 11 model 12 musician 13 receptionist 14 shop assistant
-er: builder, farmer, firefighter
-or: actor, director, doctor

-ist: artist, dentist, receptionist
-ian: electrician, musician
other: detective, model, shop assistant

Exercise 4
2 a beautician 3 a hairdresser 4 a ski instructor 5 a mechanic 6 a pilot 7 a housewife 8 a chef 9 a waiter/waitress 10 a vet

29

Exercise 1

He's phoning from the coffee shop.

Exercise 2

2 a) 3 b) 4 e) 5 c)

d

Jodie, Emma and Luke are shopping in a department store.

Emma: Let's look at the clothes.

Luke: No, thanks! I'm going to the coffee shop.

Emma: Where's that?

Luke: Upstairs. See you later.

...

Emma: I like this top!

Jodie: The plain red one?

Emma: No, this striped one. Oh, it's £50. Forget it.

Jodie: What do you think of the jeans?

Emma: Which ones do you mean?

Jodie: The ones next to the checked jackets.

Emma: Oh yes. How much are they?

Jodie: Let's have a look ... oh, £125!

Emma: Maybe not then.

[mobile phone rings]

Emma: Whose phone is that? Is it yours?

Jodie: Oh, yes ... Hello? Hang on, I can't hear ...

...

Emma: Who was it?

Jodie: Luke. He's bored.

Emma: I've got an idea.

Jodie: What is it?

Emma: Let's find a cheaper place!

10

1 🎧 0 04 **Listen and read. Where is Luke phoning from?**

2 **Match the beginnings (1–5) to the endings (a–e) to make true sentences.**

1 – d

1 The striped top is ...   a) £125.

2 The jeans are ...   b) checked.

3 The jackets are ...   c) in an expensive shop.

4 The phone call is ...   d) £50.

5 The friends are ...   e) from Luke.

30

Wh- questions

Which ones do you mean?
What do you think of the jeans?
Where's that?
How much are they?
Whose phone is that?
Who was it?
What is it?

Question words

• What • Who • Which • Where • When
• Why • How • What time • What sort/kind of
• Whose
• How much • How many • How long
• How old • How far • How often

3 Complete the questions with the words from the box.

• Whose • Where • How far • How much
• Why • Who (x2) • What • What sort of
• When • How • What time

1 A: _How_ did you get here?
   B: By bus.
2 A: ___ 's your name?
   B: Emma.
3 A: ___ bag is this?
   B: It's mine, thanks.
4 A: ___ was that?
   B: My brother.
5 A: ___ is this, please?
   B: It's £2.20.
6 A: ___ are you running?
   B: Because I'm late.
7 A: ___ do you sit next to?
   B: I sit next to Luke.
8 A: ___ films do you like?
   B: Comedies.
9 A: ___ did you go to bed last night?
   B: Ten o'clock.
10 A: ___ is your party?
   B: It's on Saturday.
11 A: ___ is your school from here?
   B: About a kilometre.
12 A: ___ are you going?
   B: Home.

4a 🎧 Listen to parts of six phone calls and respond with questions.

  1 Sorry, what's your name?

b 🎧 Now listen and check.

Clothes

5a Work in pairs. How many words can you add to the lists in two minutes?

Clothes:
top, dress, …

Styles:
casual, …

Accessories:
scarf, …

Patterns:
flowery, …

b Now check the Word bank on page 111.

6a Look at the photos and answer the questions below.

Emma
Jodie
Luke

1 Who's wearing a flowery shirt? *Luke*
2 Whose top is blue and white? *Emma's*
3 Who's in a plain, red top?
4 Who's wearing a belt?
5 Which two are wearing blue jeans?
6 Whose scarf is striped?

b Work in pairs. Take turns to ask similar questions about the people in your class. Use words from Exercise 5a.

  A: Whose sweater is green? **B:** *Mario's.*

7 Look at the photos on pages 10 and 11. What do you think of the clothes?

11

Exercise 3
2 What 3 Whose 4 Who 5 How much 6 Why 7 Who
8 What sort of 9 What time 10 When 11 How far
12 Where

Exercise 4a
2 Sorry, *who* do you want to speak to?
3 Sorry, *where* did you go yesterday?
4 Sorry, *why* can't you come?
5 Sorry, *how much* did it cost?
6 Sorry, *what's* your number?

Exercise 5a
Possible answers:
Clothes: baseball cap, boots, cardigan, coat, hat, hoodie, jacket, jeans, leggings, sandals, shirt, shoes, shorts, skirt, socks, sweater, sweatshirt, tights, trainers, trousers, T-shirt
Accessories: belt, gloves, pocket, tie, zip
Styles: baggy, sleeveless, smart, tight
Patterns: checked, patterned, plain, spotted, striped

Grammar Future with *going to* and *will*
Vocabulary Types of music and musical instruments

1 PERFORMANCE

Star Struck School of

Performing Arts

🏠 Home | Join in!

Interested? Come to our Open Day. You won't find a better way to make your dreams come true!

Auditions 1st and 2nd March

FAQs

What will the audition be like?
We'll ask you to perform two pieces. Then there'll be a short interview ... and that's it!

What qualifications will I get?
You'll take all the normal school exams (GCSE and A levels) as well as public examinations in Dance, Drama or Music. In addition, you'll leave school with your own portfolio – a record of all your achievements.

Will there be the chance to appear in West End shows?
Maybe! Every year, our students appear in all kinds of shows in and around London.

What musical instruments can I study at the school?
Our students study all kinds of instruments, from voice to double bass! We have an excellent orchestra as well as choirs and bands performing all kinds of music including classical, rock, jazz and pop.

Jess:	Hey Toby, have a look at this webpage for StarstruckSchool. It's their Open Day tomorrow.
Toby:	Are you going to have a look round?
Jess:	Yes, I'm going to apply for an audition.
Toby:	Wow! Do you think you'll get in?
Jess:	Who knows? But I'm going to try!
Toby:	What do your parents say?
Jess:	They're cool about it – but hey, it probably won't happen. It sounds like the audition is going to be quite hard. In fact, I think I'll go and practise now.
Toby:	Well, don't get a sore throat! Good luck, I'll keep my fingers crossed. 🙂

Read

1 🎧 Listen and read the webpage and the messages. How is Star Struck School different from yours?

Comprehension

2 Match the beginnings (1–6) to the endings (a–f) to make true sentences.

1 – e

1 Jess wants to study at
2 First of all, she has to do
3 Students at the school take
4 Some students get parts in
5 Students can study
6 They can join bands and

a) an audition.
b) London shows.
c) all kinds of music.
d) choirs.
e) the Star Struck School.
f) public exams.

12

16–18 year olds in England, Wales and Northern Ireland. Most students take between two and four A levels, prior to completing their secondary education and/or going to university.

West End show: Going to a West End show is a popular activity for Londoners and tourists to London and refers to plays or musicals in the many commercial theatres in the West End of London.

George Gershwin (1898–1937): A famous American composer and pianist. Gershwin composed the opera *Porgy and Bess*, songs such as *Rhapsody in Blue* and *Shall We Dance*, as well as many film scores.

Exercise 2

2 a) 3 f) 4 b) 5 c) 6 d)

S?LVE IT!

3 What is Jessica's instrument?

Vocabulary: Types of music and musical instruments

4a 🔊 **Recall** Listen and name the types of music (1–6). Then check the Word bank on page 111.

1 pop

b 🔊 **Extension** Listen and repeat. Then find these instruments in the picture below. Which one can't you see?

- cello • clarinet • double bass • drums
- flute • guitar • keyboard • piano
- saxophone • trumpet • violin • voice

Grammar

Future with *going to* and *will*

I'm **going to apply**.
The audition **is going to be** quite hard.
Do you think you**'ll get in**?
It probably **won't happen**.
I think I**'ll go** and practise now.
I**'ll keep** my fingers crossed

Complete the rules.

We use ¹___ for plans and intentions and when we use present evidence to make predictions.
We use ²___ for predictions, promises and decisions.

Practice

5 Complete the sentences with the correct form of *will* or *going to*.

1 This music is great. I think I/download/it
I think I'll download it.
2 This film is really sad. I/cry
3 We should call the police. They/help/us
4 Your exam probably/not be/difficult
5 It's Jo's birthday tomorrow. What/you give/her?
6 I'm busy now. I/do it tomorrow

6 Complete the conversation with the correct form of *will* or *going to*.

Toby: Good luck with your audition, Jess. What ¹*are you going to sing* (you/sing) for them?
Jess: I ²___ (sing) some Gershwin. Help, I'm so nervous, I feel terrible!
Toby: Don't worry, you ³___ (be) fine! What ⁴___ (you/wear)?
Jess: I don't know! I think I ⁵___ (probably buy) something new.
Toby: That ⁶___ (be) good. So, what kind of questions ⁷___ (they/ask) you?
Jess: I have no idea. Please stop the questions.
Toby: OK, OK. I ⁸___ (not ask) another thing!

Listen

7 🔊 Listen to Toby and Jess and choose the correct options.

1 Jess **is waiting for** / knows the result of the audition.
2 She's **happy** / upset.
3 She will probably **go out** / stay at home later.
4 She **will** / won't see Toby often.
5 Toby thinks she **is** / will be a star.

Speak and write

8a Talk about you. Ask and answer the questions in pairs.

- What types of music do you like?
- Who are your favourite performers?
- Do you ever go to live concerts?
- Do you play any instruments?
- Which instrument(s) would you like to play?

b Write your answers to the questions in sentences.

Extra practice

For more practice, go to page 102.

13

Exercise 7
2 happy 3 stay at home 4 will 5 will be

Extension ◼
going to/will
Ss mingle, asking each other about their plans for the weekend, e.g. *What are you going to do this weekend?*, followed by a question about their predictions for the weather, e.g. *Do you think it will rain/be sunny this weekend?*
Ss report back to the class on other Ss' plans and predictions, e.g. *Marco is going to the park this weekend to play baseball. He thinks it will be sunny.*

Extra practice
Page 122

eText
😀 **Video and Animation**

Grammar: Future with *going to* and *will*

MOTIVATOR 1a

Exercise 3
Her voice

Exercise 4a
2 classical 3 modern jazz 4 rock 5 rap 6 country

Exercise 4b
voice

Grammar
1 going to 2 will

Exercise 5
2 I'm going to cry.
3 They'll help us.
4 Your exam probably won't be difficult.
5 What are you going to give her?
6 I'll do it tomorrow.

Exercise 6
2 'm going to sing 3 'll be 4 are you going to wear
5 'll probably buy 6 'll be 7 will they ask 8 won't ask

Types of music and musical instruments

Divide the Ss into teams. With books closed, give Ss 30 seconds to try to remember as many types of music and musical instruments from Lesson 1a as they can.

A member of each team comes to the board and writes down a word or words in turn. Award two points for a correctly spelt answer, and one point for an answer with a spelling mistake.

Background notes

Finsbury Park:

A public park in North London, which holds outdoor music festivals from time to time.

Exercise 1

On Saturday: going out for her birthday
On Sunday: going to the cinema

Exercise 2

2 T 3 F 4 F 5 F 6 T

1b I'm going out.

Grammar	Present continuous for future arrangements
Function	Make arrangements: invite, accept, refuse (with excuses)

Dialogue

1 🎧 **Listen and read. What are Jodie's plans for next weekend?**

Jodie:	Hi, Martin.
Martin:	Hi. Can I stand under your umbrella?
Jodie:	Yes, sure. Listen, it's my birthday this Saturday, and …
Martin:	Oh, are you having a party?
Jodie:	No, I'm going out with Luke and some friends. Would you like to come?
Martin:	Sure, thanks. I'd love to.
Jodie:	Great! We're all meeting at our place at six.
Martin:	That's fine. … Oh no, hang on, I can't!
Jodie:	Why? What's the matter?
Martin:	I have to stay at home with Jamie on Saturday. My mom and dad are visiting friends.
Luke:	Hey guys. What's up?
Jodie:	Martin isn't coming on Saturday. He can't make it – he's babysitting.
Luke:	Well, what about going to the cinema on Sunday? *Batman*'s on.
Martin:	Cool. I'd love to!
Jodie:	Great. I'll have two birthdays!

Comprehension

2 Answer true (T) or false (F).

1 Jodie's birthday is on Saturday. *T*
2 Martin wants to go out with them.
3 He's going to change his plans for Saturday.
4 He has to go out with his parents.
5 Jodie decides to change Saturday's arrangements.
6 They decide to go to the cinema.

Phrases
- hang on
- What's up?
- (He) can/can't make it.

14

Grammar

1 fixed future plan

Exercise 3

3 On Tuesday, Luke isn't going to the dentist's at 4.00. He's going to football practice at 4.15 and Jodie's meeting Ann after school.
4 On Wednesday, (their) mum and dad are visiting Grandma.
5 On Thursday, Luke is going to the dentist's at 4.30. Jodie's studying for her English exam.

Grammar

Present continuous for future arrangements

Are you **having** a party?
I'm going out with Luke.
Martin **isn't coming** on Saturday.

Note
We often use a time phrase, like *this weekend*,
on Saturday, in May, at 2 p.m. with the present
continuous for future arrangements.

Choose the correct option.
We use the present continuous for a
fixed future plan / prediction.

Practice

3 Look at Luke and Jodie's family
calendar. Write sentences about their
arrangements.

Mon	Dad - start new job!
Tues	Luke - dentist's 4.00 go to football practice 4.15 Jodie - meet Ann after school
Wed	Mum and Dad - visit Grandma
Thurs	Luke - dentist's 4.30 Jodie - study for English exam
Fri	Jodie - hairdresser's 5.00
Sat	Jodie - hairdresser's 11.00 Evening: Luke and Jodie - have pizza with friends
Sun	Luke and Jodie - cinema

1 On Monday, their dad's starting a new job.
2 On Tuesday, Luke isn't going to the ...

Speak

4 Think of two arrangements for next
weekend, one true and one false. Ask and
answer about your arrangements. Guess
the true arrangement.

A: What are you doing next weekend?
B: I'm going shopping and I'm also playing
basketball.
A: You aren't playing basketball, you're going
shopping.

Pronunciation: /eɪ/ gr<u>ea</u>t, /aɪ/ l<u>i</u>ke

5 🎧 1/06 Go to page 116.

Use your English: Make arrangements:
invite, accept, refuse (with excuses)

6 🎧 1/07 Listen and repeat. Then practise the
conversation in pairs.

A: Would you like to go to a music festival?
B: That sounds good. When is it?
A: It's on Saturday 4th August. Is that OK?
B: Yes, fine. Where is it?
A: It's in Finsbury Park. Do you fancy going?
B: Yes, that would be great. Thanks.

Invite
Would you like to go to a music festival?
Do you want to go to the cinema?
Do you fancy going skateboarding?
What about going into town?

Accept
Yes, that sounds fun/great.
Thanks, that would be great.
Sure. I'd love to.

Refuse (with excuses)
I'm afraid I can't. I'm busy.
Sorry, I can't. I'm babysitting.
I'd like to, but my grandparents are visiting.
I don't really fancy it, but thanks.
Thanks for asking, but I don't think I can.

7a Practise similar conversations about the
events below.

What?	When?	Where?
an 80s disco!	on Sat 5th Oct	at the Youth Club
a fireworks display	on Sat 2nd Nov	in City Park
a fashion show	on Fri 8th Nov	in the Town Hall

b Now invite your partner to other events.

Extra practice

➡ For more practice, go to page 102.

15

Extension ■

**Present
continuous
for future
arrangements**
Ask Ss to imagine
that they are
rich and famous.
They write their
calendar with their
arrangements for
next week, then
ask and answer in
pairs, e.g.:
A: *What are
you doing on
Monday?*
B: *I'm flying to
New York to see
Katy Perry in
concert.*
More confident Ss
can act out their
conversation for the
rest of the class. Ss
can vote on whose
calendar is the
most interesting/
funniest.

**Extra
practice**
Page 122

eText
😊 **Video and
Animation**

Grammar:
Present continuous
for future
arrangements

Pronunciation:
/eɪ/, /aɪ/

Use your

English: Make
arrangements:
invite, accept,
refuse (with
excuses)

MOTIVATOR 1b

---

6 On Friday, Jodie isn't going to the hairdresser's
at 5.00.
7 On Saturday, Jodie's going to the hairdresser's
at 11.00. Jodie and Luke are having pizza with
friends (in the evening).
8 On Sunday, Luke and Jodie are going to the
cinema.

Exercise 5
1 afraid, ages, arrange, baby, birthday, OK,
late, make, place, stay
2 decide, diary, fine, five, I'd, invite, my, why

In a chain around the class, Ss invite, accept and refuse invitations, e.g.:

A: *Do you fancy going shopping?*

B: *I'm afraid I can't. I'm doing my homework. (Sam), would you like to go to the cinema on Friday?*

C: *Thanks, I'd love to.* etc.

Background notes

The Lord of the Rings: An epic fantasy novel by the British author JRR Tolkien, first published in the 1950s in three volumes. The film series, directed by Peter Jackson and based on the novel, includes *The Fellowship of the Ring* (2001), *The Two Towers* (2002) and *The Return of the King* (2003).

The Hobbit: A fantasy novel for children by the British author JRR Tolkien, first published in 1937. The film series, directed by Peter Jackson and based on the novel, includes *An Unexpected Journey* (2012), *The Desolation of Smaug* (2013) and *There and Back Again (2014).*

Andy Serkis: A British actor and

36

1c They're the best films ever!

Grammar	Comparison of adjectives: *much* + comparative adjective *(not) as … as* Superlatives
Vocabulary	Adjectives of opinion

Reviews

DVD > film > box sets > reviews

What's your favourite box set? Here's your chance to tell us what you think. Read other people's opinions and rate them, too.

I think the *Lord of the Rings* and *The Hobbit* are the best films ever! The three *LOTR* films are scarier and more exciting than *The Hobbit*, but *The Hobbit* films are less complicated. The plot gets much more confusing in *LOTR*! The actors in *The Hobbit* are as brilliant as the actors in *LOTR*. My absolute favourite is Andy Serkis (Gollum).   *GANDALFTHEGREY 55 minutes ago*

🔺 10 🔻 6

I'm a big *X-Men* fan, but the later ones are a bit disappointing – they aren't as good as the first three. I think the *Spider-Man* films are much better. I didn't like the third one much (it was a bit dull), but the last one is amazing.

FILMFREAK3 3 hours 35 minutes ago

🔺 12 🔻 0

The *X-Men* series are my favourite films, without a doubt. They're all fantastic, but in my opinion *X-Men First Class* is the most enjoyable of all. It has great action scenes and the special effects look amazing. The acting is excellent and the music is awesome.   *XMENROCK 4 hours ago*

🔺 6 🔻 2

Personally I don't like films about superheroes. I prefer funny ones, like *Men in Black*. The first two films are much older than the third, but they're still pretty good and very amusing. The third one is much funnier than the others, but it's also more violent. Don't watch it with your little brother or sister.   *OXFORDBOY 4 hours 10 minutes ago*

🔺 7 🔻 0

Get started

1 What was the last film you saw? What was it like?

Read

2 Listen and read the online film reviews. Who makes only positive comments?

16

Comprehension

3 What is the name of the film series and who is speaking?

1 'I really like them all except one.' *Spider-Man – filmfreak3*
2 'All the films are very good, but one of them is extra special.'
3 'They're great – but difficult!'
4 'They're good, but some of them aren't great.'
5 'They all make me laugh.'

director, born in 1964. Films include *The Lord of the Rings* film series (2001, 2002 and 2003) and *The Hobbit* film series (2012, 2013 and 2014).

X-Men: A team of mutant superheroes, who first appeared in comic book form in the 1960s. There have been seven *X-Men* films (2000–2014), starring Hugh Jackman as Wolverine.

Spider-Man: An American superhero, who first appeared in comic book form in the 1960s. There have been five *Spider-Man* films (2002, 2004, 2007, 2012 and 2014), starring Tobey Maguire as the superhero.

Men in Black: A comic science fiction film (1997), starring Will Smith and Tommy Lee Jones. There have been two sequels, *Men in Black II* (2002) and *Men in Black 3* (2012).

The Matrix: A science fiction film (1999), starring Keanu Reeves. There have been two sequels, *The Matrix Reloaded* (2003) and *The Matrix Revolutions* (2003).

Exercise 2

xmenrock

Vocabulary: Adjectives of opinion

4a 🎧 Listen and repeat. Which words are usually positive and which are usually negative?

Positive: *amazing, …*
Negative: *awful, …*

> • amazing • awesome • awful • boring
> • brilliant • complicated • confusing
> • disappointing • dull • enjoyable • exciting
> • frightening • funny • interesting • sad
> • scary • violent

b Which words have the same meaning? Which ones are opposites?

c Match words in Exercise 4a to the sentences.

1 I enjoyed it. It was *enjoyable*.
2 Hmmm, I didn't really understand it.
  It was ___ / ___.
3 There were lots of fights. It was ___.
4 I hid behind the sofa! It was ___ / ___ .
5 I really wanted to see it but then I didn't like it.
  It was ___.
6 It made me laugh. It was ___.
7 I cried! It was___.
8 The film was very, very good.
  It was ___ / ___ / ___.
9 Sorry, I fell asleep halfway through!
  It wasn't ___ / ___ – it was ___ / ___.
10 I hated it. It was very bad. It was ___.

Grammar

> **Comparison of adjectives**
>
> *much* + comparative adjective
>
> I think the *Spider-Man* films are **much better/worse**.
> The third one is **much funnier** than the others.
> They're **much more/less exciting**.
>
> *(not) as … as*
>
> They are(**n't**) **as good as** the first three.
>
> **Superlatives**
>
> *X-Men First Class* is **the most/least enjoyable** of all.
> They're **the best/worst** films ever!

Practice

5 Write sentences to compare the three films. Use superlatives, *(not) as … as* or *(much)* and comparative adjectives. Then compare sentences with your partner.

FILM	scary	exciting	good
The Midnight Man	***	*	***
No Time Like Now	****	*****	*****
Come Back Soon	*	**	*

1 *The Midnight Man* (scary)
  'The Midnight Man' isn't as scary as 'No Time Like Now' but it's much scarier than 'Come Back Soon'.
2 *Come Back Soon* (exciting)
3 *No Time Like Now* (good)
4 *Come Back Soon* (bad)
5 *No Time Like Now* (scary)
6 *The Midnight Man* (exciting)

Speak

6 Work in pairs. Choose three film series that you like. Give each one a score from one to five stars for the adjectives in the box. Then discuss your ideas with the class.

> • exciting • funny • good • interesting
> • sad • scary

We think the Matrix films are better than X-Men, but they aren't as good as Spider-Man. The first Spider-Man film is …

Write

7 Read the reviews in Exercise 2 again. Then write about the three film series you chose in Exercise 6, using adjectives of opinion.

… are great films, but in my opinion they aren't as good as … I think …

Extra practice

▶ For more practice, go to page 102.

Exercise 3

2 *X-Men – xmenrock*
3 *Lord of the Rings – gandalfthegrey*
4 *X-Men – filmfreak3*
5 *Men in Black – oxfordboy*

Exercise 4a

Positive: awesome, brilliant, enjoyable, exciting, funny, interesting

Negative: boring, complicated, confusing, disappointing, dull, frightening, sad, scary, violent

Exercise 4b

Suggested answers:

Same meaning: amazing/awesome/brilliant, complicated/confusing, frightening/scary, boring/dull

Opposites: amazing/disappointing, awesome/awful, boring/exciting, interesting/dull, funny/sad

Exercise 4c

2 complicated/confusing 3 violent 4 frightening/scary 5 disappointing 6 funny 7 sad 8 amazing/awesome/ brilliant 9 interesting/exciting, dull/boring 10 awful

Exercise 5

Suggested answers:

2 *Come Back Soon* isn't as exciting as *No Time Like Now*, but it's more exciting than *The Midnight Man*.
3 *No Time Like Now* is the best film.
4 *Come Back Soon* is the worst film.
5 *No Time Like Now* is scarier than *Come Back Soon*.
6 *The Midnight Man* is the least exciting film of all.

Extension ◼

Adjectives of opinion

Ask Ss to work in pairs to agree on a film which they like/ don't like. They share each other's opinions and make notes, if necessary. Then put two pairs together and get each pair to take it in turns to describe their chosen film. Their description should give clues about the film without actually naming it and should include adjectives of opinion, as appropriate. The other pair has to guess the name of the film.

Extra practice
Page 122

eText
🔲 **Video and Animation**

Grammar:
Comparison of adjectives: *much* + comparative adjective *not … as*

MOTIVATOR 1c

37

Background notes

Zanzibar City: The capital city of the island of Zanzibar, off the east coast of Africa.

Glastonbury: A three-day music festival, held most summers on a farm in Somerset in the west of England. It is the largest and best-known outdoor festival in the world. Recent headline acts have included Stevie Wonder, Beyoncé and the Rolling Stones.

The National Youth Orchestra of Great Britain: An orchestra of 165 teenage musicians, aged between 13 and 19 years.

The Royal Albert Hall: A world famous concert hall in Kensington, London. The Albert Hall holds the annual BBC Promenade concerts, the Proms, an eight-week summer programme of mostly classical music.

Exercise 2a

1 C 2 B 3 D 4 A

Exercise 2b

1 d) 2 c) 3 a) 4 b)

Exercise 3

2 c) 3 a) 4 b) 5 a) 6 b)

ACROSS CULTURES

1d Music festivals

SKILLS FOCUS: READING

Get started

1 Look at the photos. What's the most famous music festival in your country?

Read

> **READING TIP:** HOW TO PREPARE FOR READING
>
> When you prepare for reading, look at the title, pictures and the headings. This will help you to understand the text.
> Now do Exercise 2.

2a Read the text quickly, then match the photos (A–D) to the paragraphs (1–4).

b 🎧 Read the text again and match the headings (a–d) to the paragraphs (1–4). Then listen and check.

a) Rock band wants prize
b) All kinds of African music
c) A wide range of music and nationalities
d) Music and youth around the world

Comprehension

3 Read the text. Choose the correct options.

1 The text is ___.
   a) an interview b) a magazine article
   c) an encyclopedia entry
2 The International Festival in Wales is a ___ festival.
   a) jazz b) rock c) music and dance
3 Emma thinks it will be ___ to get to the semi-finals.
   a) difficult b) easy c) impossible
4 Sanjay is going to ___ the Mumbai Rock Festival.
   a) watch b) compete at c) rehearse at
5 The music festival in Zanzibar takes place ___.
   a) in the old city centre b) in a field
   c) in a football stadium
6 Farrokh is going to ___ at the music festival in Zanzibar City.
   a) perform b) work c) compete

18

Music festivals around the world

1 ___

All around the world young people are going to festivals to listen to music, to perform and to take part in competitions. We meet three teenagers from different countries and ask about their experiences.

2 ___

Emma tells us about The Llangollen International Music Festival that takes place every July in a small town in Wales. 'Each year people come from many different countries. There's lots of choral music, folk singing and dancing as well as classical music. The concerts and competitions take place inside an enormous marquee. My school choir's going to compete in the youth choir competition. It will be tough but we hope to get to the semi-finals.'

3 ___

Sanjay is the lead singer in rock band Tin Heads. 'People don't usually think we have rock and heavy metal in India, but there are millions of people who are into this type of music,' he says. This year Sanjay's band is competing on day one of the Independence Rock Festival in Mumbai. I-Rock is the oldest and the biggest rock festival in India. 'If you win, you get a cash prize and expensive music gear. We rehearse a lot and we want to win.'

A

B

C

4 ___

Farrokh lives in Zanzibar City, which has one of the most important music festivals on the African continent. The festival takes place in an old fort in the historical centre of the city, called Stone Town. 'It's an amazing African party', Farrokh tells us. 'You can hear all types of music here: traditional, fusion, reggae, jazz and hip-hop. The musicians come from all over Africa. During the festival I help backstage with food and drinks so I get to meet many of the famous bands!'

D

> **NEW** WORDS
> * perform * take place * choral
> * marquee * choir * compete * tough
> * semi-finals (of a competition)
> * be into (something) * cash * gear
> * rehearse * fort * fusion * backstage

Speak

4 **Work in pairs. Answer the questions.**

1 Which of the festivals in the photos would you like to go to? Why?/Why not?
2 Do you know any music festivals or competitions in other countries?
3 Can you play a musical instrument?

Listen

5 🎧 **Listen to two conversations. Choose the correct options.**

1 There are more than 150 / 50 music festivals in the UK every year.
2 Len mentions rock, jazz and **dance / hip-hop** festivals.
3 Len thinks the 'Big Chill' music festival is much **bigger / better** than Glastonbury.
4 Robert is playing in **a rock band / an orchestra** this weekend.
5 Robert thinks performing at the Royal Albert Hall is **a bit scary / exciting**.

> ## Project
>
> **6** **Imagine you are going to organise a youth music festival in your home town. Write a paragraph for the school website about your plans.**
>
> * Where is it going to be?
> * What type of competitions/awards are there going to be? (Best Singer, Best Rock Band, etc.)
> * What are the prizes going to be?
> * Are you going to invite any famous musicians?
>
> *We are going to organise …*

19

Exercise 5
2 dance 3 better 4 an orchestra 5 a bit scary

Extension ▬▬▬
Ss work in pairs to roleplay a radio interview with one of the teenagers from the article in Exercise 2. In their pairs they decide who will take the role of the interviewer and who will be the interviewee, say Sanjay. Help Ss to get started by writing two or three example Q&A on the board, e.g.:

Interviewer:	*Hi, Sanjay. Tell me about the festival you're performing in.*
Sanjay:	*It's the I-Rock Festival in Mumbai.*
Interviewer:	*And what's the name of your band?*
Sanjay:	*We're called the Tin Heads.*

Encourage Ss to ask no more than five or six questions and to use some of the new words from the list on page 19. Monitor the activity and provide help where necessary.

Exercise 1

It's from Sam, Jo's friend. He wants to invite her to a concert on Saturday night.

Exercise 2

1 town hall
2 Saturday
3 8
4 £10

Exercise 3

2 E 3 D 4 A 5 C

Exercise 4

1 Hello 2 How are things with you?, How's it going?
3 Bye for now, Love

1e The concert

SKILLS FOCUS: WRITING AN INFORMAL EMAIL

Get ready to write

1 Read the email. Who is it from and what is it about?

To: joanne_98@emailme.com

Subject: Saturday night!

1 ¹Hi Jo,

2 ²How are you? I hope you're having a good break after your exams.

3 Do you like The Indigoes? A group of my school friends are going to see them on Saturday. Do you fancy coming with us? Danny's got flu so he wants to sell his ticket (it's £10).

4 The concert starts at eight in the town hall. We're meeting at 6.30 and we're going to have a pizza first. I think it finishes at about half past ten. My dad can give us a lift home.

5 It's going to be a really good evening – I hope you can make it!

³Speak soon,

Sam

---

2 Complete the missing words.

The **INDIGOES**

Live concert
at the ¹___ on
² ___ 3rd November
at ³___ p.m.

Tickets cost ⁴___.

3 Read the email again and match the sections in the email (1–5) to the correct headings (A–E).

1 – B

A Details and arrangements
B Greeting
C Summary and conclusion
D Main message
E Introduction

WRITING TIP: INFORMAL EMAILS

You can start an informal email with *Dear (John)*, … but you can also start it with *Hi!* or *Hello!* End it with a friendly expression, for example: *See you soon, Bye for now, Speak soon, Love* or even just a *x* after your name.
Now do Exercise 4.

4 Look at the email in Exercise 1. Replace the words and phrases in red (1–3) with a word and phrase from the box (there are two choices for each). Then compare with a partner.

- Bye for now   • Dear   • Hello
- How are things with you?
- How's it going?   • Love

1 Dear Jo …

Write

5 Look at the information below. Write an email to a friend. Invite him/her to join you and Carl on Friday evening. Use the headings in Exercise 3 as a guide.

C U @ Benji's café @ 6 – Let's have a snack before it starts!
Carl

TALENT SHOW

On Friday 14th March at Seldon High School.
7.30–9.30
Adults £5
Students £3

20

1 Language Revision

Grammar (15 marks)

1 Choose the correct options.

0 We'll go / **'re going** to the cinema tomorrow. Do you want to come?

1 In the future robots **will / are going to** play musical instruments.

2 They're planning their holidays. They**'re going to go / 'll go** to Italy.

3 Are you coming out with us tomorrow night? Sorry, I**'ll go / 'm going** to a concert.

4 I really like that music. I think I**'m going to / 'll** download it right now.

5 We can't come to the party. We**'ll stay / 're staying** with my uncle this weekend.

6 I feel nervous. I think I**'ll practise / 'm practising** my audition song again.

7 It probably **won't rain / isn't raining** today.

.../7

2 Complete the sentences so they mean the same.

0 *Batman* is more exciting than *Spider-Man*. *Spider-Man* isn't as exciting as *Batman*.

1 The first film wasn't as good as the second one.
The second film was ___ the first one.

2 Jessica is more intelligent than Emma.
Emma ___ as Jessica.

3 This film is better than all the others.
This is ___ film.

4 *Toy Story 2* isn't as funny as *Toy Story 3*.
Toy Story 3 is ___ *Toy Story 2*.

.../8

Vocabulary (16 marks)

3 Write the musical instrument.

0 efutl *flute*
1 oenphxoas ___
2 arnietcl ___
3 noiap ___
4 turiga ___
5 elolc ___
6 oybkedar ___
7 sumdr ___
8 utemptr ___

.../8

4 Complete the adjectives.

0 I fell asleep because the film was very b<u>oring</u>.
1 I didn't understand the story. It was c___d and c___g.
2 I was really frightened. It was a very s___ film.
3 The photography was aw__e, but the plot was d__g and d__l.
4 Well done! Your project on the Romans was ex___ and very f___y!

.../8

Phrases/Use your English (9 marks)

5 Complete with phrases from the box.

• hang on! • What's up? • can't make it!

A: Hi, Sarah. ¹___
B: I'm organising my party. Are you coming?
A: When is it?
B: Next Friday.
A: Oh no! I ²___ I'm going to Adel's party.
B: That's a shame!
A: Oh, ³___ I can come after all. Adel's party is on Saturday.

.../3

6 Look at the jumbled conversation. Number the lines in the correct order.

☐ a) What about going on Sunday afternoon?
☐ b) Great! What time does the film finish?
☐1 c) Would you like to see the new *Batman* film with me on Saturday afternoon?
☐ d) I'd like to, but I'm babysitting my brother in the evening.
☐ e) Good idea! I love pizza.
☐ f) Yes, Sunday's better. Do you fancy going for a pizza after the film?
☐ g) It finishes at 7 p.m., a perfect time to go for a meal!

.../6

(1/12) LISTEN AND CHECK YOUR SCORE	
Grammar	.../15
Vocabulary	.../16
Phrases/Use your English	.../9
Total	**.../40**

ROUND-UP 1

ROUND-UP 2

eText
Games
Boat Game
Hangman
Pelmanism

Exercise 1
1 will 2 're going to go 3 'm going 4 'll 5 're staying 6 'll practise 7 won't rain

Exercise 2
1 better than 2 isn't as intelligent 3 the best 4 funnier than

Exercise 3
1 saxophone 2 clarinet 3 piano 4 guitar 5 cello 6 keyboard 7 drums 8 trumpet

Exercise 4
1 complicated, confusing 2 scary 3 awesome, disappointing, dull 4 excellent, funny

Exercise 5
1 What's up? 2 can't make it! 3 hang on!

Exercise 6
2 d) 3 a) 4 f) 5 e) 6 b) 7 g)

Look forward ›››

Play the sit down/ stand up game with the class about household jobs that they do at home. Get the class to stand up. Say *Sit down if you ...* (e.g. *do the washing up / tidy your room / take the rubbish out).*

Ss for whom the first statement is true sit down. Continue with different statements until only one or two Ss are still standing. Do they help with any other household jobs?

Background note

Charity shop:
A shop which sells mostly second-hand clothes and household goods which are given by members of the public. The sales help to raise money for different charities such as Oxfam. Most high streets in UK towns and cities have charity shops.

Exercise 1
Jodie needs her calculator for her Maths homework.

Exercise 2
2 DS 3 F 4 T 5 DS

2a I've just told you.

Grammar Present perfect simple with time adverbials *ever, never, already, just, yet*

Vocabulary Household jobs

Dialogue

1 🎧 Listen and read. Why does Jodie need her calculator?

Luke:	Have you been in my room, Jodie?
Jodie:	Yes, I was looking for my calculator.
Luke:	I've already looked. It isn't in there.
Jodie:	How do you know? Your room's a mess. Have you *ever* made your bed?
Luke:	Of course I have. Anyway, yours isn't much better. I've never seen it tidy.
Jodie:	Actually, I'm sorting it out right now.
Luke:	Well, good for you! Have you found the carpet yet?
Jodie:	Oh, ha ha, very funny. I'm going to take some old clothes to a charity shop in a minute.
Luke:	OK, you do that and I'll finish my Maths homework. I bet you haven't started yours yet.
Jodie:	True, I haven't. But that's because I can't.
Luke:	Why? What do you mean?
Jodie:	I've just told you. I can't find my calculator.

Phrases
• How do you know?
• good for you!
• ha ha, very funny
• you do that

Comprehension

2 Answer true (T), false (F) or doesn't say (DS).

1 Jodie can't find her calculator. *T*
2 Luke had it yesterday.
3 Jodie's room is always tidy.
4 They've both got Maths homework.
5 Luke has got the calculator.

22

Vocabulary: Household jobs

3 (2/02) **Recall Complete the phrases with the words from the box. Then check the Word bank on page 111. Listen and repeat.**

- do (x 7) • empty • lay • make (x 2) • take
- tidy • wash

1 _make_ breakfast	8 ___ the vacuuming
2 ___ the bed	9 ___ the washing
3 ___ the car	10 ___ the washing-up
4 ___ the cleaning	11 ___ your room
5 ___ the ironing	12 ___ the cooking
6 ___ the rubbish out	13 ___ the shopping
7 ___ the table	14 ___ the dishwasher

Grammar

Present perfect simple with time adverbials *ever, never, already, just, yet*

I've already looked.
Have you **ever made** your bed?
I've never seen it tidy.
I've just told you.
Have you **found** the carpet **yet**?
You **haven't started** yours **yet**.

Note
The verb *go* has two past participles, *gone* and *been*.
He's gone *to his room.* (He's in it now.)
He's been *in his room.* (He was there but isn't there now.)

Complete the rules.
The words ¹___, ²___, ³___ and ⁴___ usually come between the auxiliary and the main verb.
The word ⁵___ usually comes at the end of a sentence.

Practice

4 **Recall Write the past participle form of the verbs. Then check the irregular verb list on page 118.**

be – been   buy – bought

- be • buy • come • do • eat • find • get
- go • have • hear • lose • make • meet
- put • read • run • say • see • sing • sit
- spend • take • think

5 **Write sentences with the present perfect form of the verbs and *just, yet, already* or *never*.**

1 she/see/the film
She's already seen the film.

4 he/see/a tiger before

2 I/not make/the bed

5 the train/not arrive

3 you/finish/that book?

6 he/have/a bath

6 **Put the word in brackets in the correct place in the sentence. Then ask and answer in pairs.**
1 Have you ⁄cooked a meal? (ever) *ever*
  Have you ever cooked a meal?
  Yes, I have./No, I haven't.
2 Have you had your sixteenth birthday? (yet)
3 Have you broken a bone? (ever)
4 Have you had lunch? (just)
5 Have you performed in a concert? (ever)
6 Have you learnt to drive? (yet)

Write and speak

7a **Work in pairs. Write three more *Have you ever ... ?* questions.**

b **Find a new partner. Take turns to ask and answer the new questions.**

Extra practice

▶ For more practice, go to page 103.

2 Have you had your sixteenth birthday yet?
3 Have you ever broken a bone?
4 Have you just had lunch?
5 Have you ever performed in a concert?
6 Have you learnt to drive yet?

Extension ◼▶
Ss play 'participle tennis' by saying the forms of the verb in turn, e.g.:
A: *do*
B: *did ... play*
C: *played ... ,* etc.
If they need to, they can use the irregular verb list on page 118 for reference.

Extra practice
Page 123

eText
😊 **Video and Animation**
Grammar: Present perfect simple with *ever, never, not ... yet, already, just*

MOTIVATOR 2a

Exercise 3
2 make 3 wash 4 do 5 do 6 take 7 lay 8 do 9 do 10 do 11 tidy 12 do 13 do 14 empty

Grammar
1–4 just, already, ever, never
5 yet

Exercise 4
See irregular verb list on page 118 of the Students' Book.

Exercise 5
2 I haven't made the bed yet.
3 Have you finished that book yet?
4 He's never seen a tiger before.
5 The train hasn't arrived yet.
6 He's just had a bath.

2b He asked me out.

Grammar	Present perfect simple and past simple
	Time adverbials
Vocabulary	Relationship words and phrases
Function	Talk about problems: suggestions and advice

Read

1 🎧 2/03 Listen and read the problem page. Who's got the worst problem? Why do you think so?

PROBLEMS?
TAMSIN IS HERE TO HELP.

HOME **ADVICE**

My girlfriend often borrows money from me, but she doesn't always give it back. Yesterday she borrowed £10 because she wanted to buy me a present – crazy! I don't want to break up with her, but I've lent her quite a lot over the past few months and I'm getting a bit annoyed. Help!

Mike, 16

I go around in a group of three. Most of the time we get on well, but a few weeks ago the other two had a big argument. They haven't made up yet – it's going on and on and I hate it. I don't know what to do, it's driving me mad.

Jules, 15

I'm worried about my best friend. He's missed a lot of school recently, in fact last week he stayed away for three days. I don't think his parents know. I haven't told my mum and dad because I don't want to get him into trouble. What should I do?

Luke, 16

Up to now, the boy next door has been one of my best friends. We've always been like brother and sister. Then last weekend he asked me out. I was really shocked. I don't think of him like that. I said 'No' and now he doesn't speak to me. I feel terrible.

Josie, 15

Comprehension

2 **Answer the questions in pairs. Who ...**

1 bought Mike a present? *his girlfriend*
2 paid for it?
3 has two best friends?
4 doesn't go to school every day?
5 surprised a friend?
6 has upset a friend?

Vocabulary: Relationship words and phrases

3 🎧 2/04 **Listen and repeat. Which ones are positive and which are negative?**

Positive: *ask somebody out, ...*
Negative: *argue (with), ...*

- argue/have an argument (with)
- ask somebody out   • be/get annoyed (with)
- be friends (with)   • break up (with)
- fall in love (with)   • fall out (with)
- get divorced (from)   • get engaged/married (to)
- get on well (with)   • go out (with)   • make up

24

Look back ‹‹‹

Household jobs

Ss play a game in groups about household jobs. The first student makes a sentence, starting with *Every Saturday, I ...* Each student in the group then adds one more household job, continuing for as long as they can. (Point out that this doesn't have to be true of the household jobs that they do in real life!) Demonstrate the game first with one

or two students, e.g.:

Teacher: *Every Saturday, I make my bed.*
Student A: *Every Saturday I make my bed and do the ironing.*
Student B: *Every Saturday I make my bed, do the ironing and wash the car.*

For less confident Ss who need help with the vocabulary, you could write a selection of household jobs from the Word bank for Lesson 2a on page 111.

Exercise 2
2 Mike 3 Jules 4 Luke's friend 5 Josie's friend 6 Josie

Exercise 3
Positive: be friends (with), fall in love (with), get engaged/married (to), get on well (with), go out (with), make up

Negative: have an argument (with), be/get annoyed (with), break up (with), fall out (with), get divorced (from)

44

Grammar

Present perfect simple and past simple

Name the tenses.

1 She **wanted** to buy me a present.
2 I**'ve lent** her quite a lot.
3 He **stayed** away for three days.
4 I **haven't told** my mum and dad.

Complete the rules.

We use the ¹___ tense to refer to finished time.
We use the ²___ tense when the past still affects the present.

Practice

4 **Make five true sentences using the time adverbials in the box.**

I started school eight years ago.
I've just had lunch.

- ago • already • at one o'clock • ever
- in 2013 • just • last night • never
- on Saturday • recently • so far • yet
- this morning • up to now • yesterday

5 **Write sentences. Use the present perfect or the past simple.**

1 when/they/start/going out?
 When did they start going out?
2 you/ever/fall in love?
3 they/not/make up/yet
4 he/phone/her/yet?
5 when/they/break up?
6 she/never/argue/with him
7 they/meet/last year
8 my parents/get married twenty years ago

Speak

6 **Ask and answer about the things in the box.**

A: Have you ever been to a wedding?
B: Yes, I have. I went to one last year.
A: Whose wedding did you go to?
B: I went to my cousin's wedding. It was fun.

- go to a wedding • lose something important
- have flu • be on a plane • see an elephant
- meet a famous person

Use your English: Talk about problems: suggestions and advice

7 Listen and repeat. Then practise the conversation in pairs.

A: You look fed up. What's the matter?
B: I'm a bit worried about my homework.
A: Why? Is it difficult?
B: No, not really. But I haven't got time to do it.
A: Well, why don't you talk to your teacher? Perhaps you can do it tomorrow.
B: Yes, good idea. Thanks.

Ask about a problem
You look a bit miserable/worried/fed up.
What's the matter/What's up?

Respond
I'm a bit worried about my homework.
I don't know what to do about my homework.

Suggest and advise
I see. Well, why don't we study together?
Maybe you should stay in and revise this weekend.
I don't think you should worry too much.

8 **Work in pairs. Look again at the problems in Exercise 1. Then roleplay conversations with Mike, Jules, Luke and Josie. Use the ideas in the box or your own ideas.**

A: Hi, Mike, you look fed up. What's the matter?
B: I don't know what to do about …

- explain how you feel • say 'No!'
- forget your wallet • talk to him/her/them
- discuss it with an adult • relax
- forget about it

Write

9 **Choose one of the conversations from Exercise 8. Write the conversation. Use Exercise 7 to help you.**

Extra practice

For more practice, go to page 103.

eText

Video and Animation

Use your English: Talk about problems: suggestions and advice

MOTIVATOR 2b

25

Grammar

1 past simple 2 present perfect

Exercise 5

2 Have you ever fallen in love?
3 They haven't made up yet.
4 Has he phoned her yet?
5 When did they break up?
6 She's never argued with him.
7 They met last year.
8 My parents got married twenty years ago.

Extension

Relationship words and phrases
Ss describe the relationship of a well-known celebrity couple such as Brad Pitt/Angelina Jolie or describe the relationship development in a film such as *Shrek*.

Extra practice

Page 123

Write on the board a selection of time adverbials, e.g. *never, in 2013, just, on Saturday,* etc.

Then ask Ss to make a statement, based on one of the time adverbials, and provide a prompt for another S to make a statement, e.g.:

T: *never*

A: *I've never broken my arm. … in 2013 …*

B: *In 2013, I … ,* etc.

Remind Ss that they need to use either the present perfect simple or the past simple, as appropriate.

Exercise 3

2 They sometimes feel unimportant.
3 Because they dislike arguments and they are good peacemakers.
4 To share their things.
5 When there are stepbrothers or stepsisters.

2c People who you can trust.

Grammar Defining relative clauses with *who, which, that, whose, where*
Vocabulary Family

Get started

1 Which would you prefer – to have lots of brothers and sisters, or to be an only child? Why?

Read

2 🔊 Listen and read the article. Do you think this article is true about you and your family?

Comprehension

3 **Work in pairs. Answer the questions according to the article.**

1 When do oldest children become anxious?
   When the second child arrives.
2 What negative feelings do youngest children sometimes have?
3 Why do middle children often have lots of friends?
4 What do only children need to learn?
5 How can the only child in a family become the youngest?

KNOW **YOUR** PLACE!

Are you an only child? Or perhaps you are the oldest, the youngest, or a middle child. Does it matter? Well, yes, it does! The place **where** you are in your family affects your personality.

Oldest children are confident people and natural leaders – but they are sometimes anxious, too. Why? The first child gets lots of attention from parents, grandparents, aunts and uncles. Then the second child arrives. It's a major event that changes everything.

Youngest children are usually easy-going people who love parties and fun. They often have more freedom than their brothers and sisters. On the other hand, they sometimes think their parents don't care about them. They feel unimportant: they often get clothes and toys which the others have used before them.

Middle children make friends easily. They dislike arguments and are good peacemakers (they have to be!). They are people who you can trust. However, children that are in the middle often feel less special than their brothers and sisters. Things don't always seem fair.

Only children spend a lot of time alone or with adults. This means they are often confident, independent and successful at school. They never have to share their things – that's a lesson they have to learn.

Of course, things change. For example, when the oldest child moves out, the middle child 'moves up'. Perhaps she'll finally get the bedroom that she's always wanted! Or think about an only child whose parents get divorced. Perhaps he will have  stepbrothers and stepsisters one day – then he will suddenly become the oldest, the youngest or a middle child.

Oldest, youngest, middle or only child, it's part of the reason you're you!

26

Vocabulary: Family

4a **Recall** Name as many family words as you remember. Then check the Word bank on page 111.

b 🔊 **Extension** Listen and repeat. Then complete the sentences with the words from the box.

> • daughter/son-in-law • fiancée/fiancé
> • married • mother/father-in-law • single
> • sister/brother-in-law • stepmother/father
> • stepsister/brother

1 My brother's wife is my _sister-in-law_ and she's my parents' ___.
2 My mum got married again. Her second husband is my ___ and his daughter is my ___.
3 My sister is going to marry her ___ next year. Then she won't be ___ anymore.

Grammar

Defining relative clauses: who, which, that, whose, where

who/that
Youngest children are usually easy-going people **who/that** love parties. (subject)
They are people (**who/that**) you can trust. (object)

which/that
It's a major event **which/that** changes everything. (subject)
Perhaps she'll finally get the bedroom (**which/that**) she's always wanted! (object)

whose
Think about an only child **whose** parents get divorced.

where
The place **where** you are in your family affects your personality.

Complete the rules.
We use ¹___ or ²___ for people and ³___ or ⁴___ for things.
We use ⁵___ for places and ⁶___ for possession.
We can omit ⁷___, ⁸___ or ⁹___ when they refer to the object of the sentence.

Practice

5 Join the sentences. Use _who, which, where_ or _whose_. Then, when possible, write a second sentence omitting the relative pronoun.

1 They're the people. I met them last night.
They're the people who I met last night.
They're the people I met last night.
2 That's the house. I was born there.
3 They're the toys. I gave them to my sister.
4 She's the girl. She's got four brothers.
5 He's the boy. His brother's just got married.
6 It's a problem. It causes arguments.
7 There's the girl. We were talking about her.
8 This is the book. I need it.

6 Make true sentences. Then compare with a partner.

1 I don't like people who ...
2 I like going on holiday to places where ...
3 I've got some friends who ...
4 I like films which ...
5 I prefer food which ...

Pronunciation: /æ/ family, /ɑː/ father

7 🔊 Go to page 116.

Listen

8 🔊 Listen to the conversation and answer true (T) or false (F).

1 Harry is the youngest child in his family. _T_
2 He's got a sister who is married.
3 His niece was born two years ago.
4 His niece's name is Alice.
5 He's got three sisters.
6 Harry's sister Jackie is married to Andy.

SOLVE IT!

9 Listen again. How old is Alice's mum?

Extra practice

For more practice, go to page 103.

Exercise 8
2 T 3 F 4 T 5 F 6 T
Exercise 9
She's 25.

Extension
Family
Write the word _Family_ on the board. In pairs, Ss write down eight family words. Then put two pairs together and get each pair to take it in turns to describe their family words. They mustn't use the actual words. The other pair has to guess the words.

Extra practice
Page 123

eText
😊 **Video and Animation**
Pronunciation: /æ/, /ɑː/

MOTIVATOR 2c

Exercise 4b
1 daughter-in-law 2 stepfather, stepsister 3 fiancé, single

Grammar
1 who 2 that 3 which 4 that 5 where 6 whose 7 who 8 which 9 that

Exercise 5
2 That's the house where I was born.
3 They're the toys (which/that) I gave to my sister.
4 She's the girl who/that has got four brothers.
5 He's the boy whose brother's just got married.
6 It's a problem which/that causes arguments.
7 There's the girl (who/that) we were talking about.
8 This is the book (which/that) I need.

Exercise 7
/æ/ anxious, exam, family, hand, have, married, matter, natural
/ɑː/ argument, aunt, father, last, part, party, start

2d   The Rock Roses

SKILLS FOCUS: LISTENING and SPEAKING

'Hey, Ian, what are you doing next Saturday?'

'I don't know. Why?'

'I've got a spare ticket for The Rock Roses concert. My cousin's just dropped out. Do you want to come?'

'You bet I do. Fantastic. Oh, but how much is it?'

'That's just it, it's free. My dad works at the theatre, so he's got a couple of free tickets. How good is that?'

'It's excellent. I can't wait. Thanks, James.'

'No problem. It'll be a blast. See you tomorrow at school.'

Ian put his phone down and went to find his mother.

'Guess what, Mum, James has got me a free ticket for The Rock Roses. Isn't that amazing!'

'That sounds wonderful. Hang on, when is it?'

'This Saturday evening. Why? What's the matter?'

'Ian, that's the day of Danny's birthday party. Don't tell me you've already forgotten?'

Danny was Ian's next-door neighbour. He was three years younger than Ian and he hero-worshipped the older boy. He often called round to visit and he even copied Ian's taste in music and TV programmes. Ian found him quite annoying. It didn't usually matter too much, but this time it mattered a lot.

'Oh no! I don't believe it. I can't miss The Rock Roses! I can see Danny any time!'

'Don't be mean. He's really looking forward to Saturday and I don't think he's invited many people. And you *have* already accepted the invitation, you know.'

'I know, but they're my favourite band. I've always wanted to see them. Are you saying I can't go?'

'Well, Ian, I suppose it's up to you.'

28

NEW WORDS
- Hey • spare • drop out • That's just it.
- a couple of • blast • guess what
- hero-worship • taste (in music, etc.)
- mean (= unkind)
- look forward to • it's up to (you)

Get started

1 Imagine you can have a free ticket to a concert. Who would you most like to see?

Read

2 Read the story about Ian. Why is he upset?

Comprehension

3 Choose the correct options.
1 The spare ticket was James's dad's / cousin's.
2 At first, Ian's mother was pleased / worried about the concert.
3 Ian is the same age as / older than Danny.
4 Danny is planning a big / small party.
5 Ian's mother says he must go to the party / decide.

Speak your mind!

> **SPEAKING TIP:** SPEAK AS MUCH AS POSSIBLE
>
> Get as much practice as possible. Always try to join in conversations and discussions in English. Make sure you always say something.
> Now do Exercise 4.

4a Work in pairs (AA and BB).

Students A: Think of three reasons why Ian should go to the concert, not the party. Make notes.

Students B: Think of three reasons why Ian should go to the party, not the concert. Make notes.

b Make new pairs (AB). Use your notes to roleplay a discussion about what Ian should do.

A: He should go to the concert because …
B: No, I don't agree. I think …

Write

5 Read Ian's message and write your reply. Give reasons for your advice.

> This is tough. I really want to go to the concert – they're my favourite band of all time! I don't want to upset Danny but I see him every day. I mean, he lives next door. What do you think I should do?

> *Hi Ian.*
> *I can see your problem.*
> *I think …*

Listen

> **LISTENING TIP:** LISTEN FOR GIST
>
> Listen to the whole recording first, to get a general idea of the meaning. Then listen again for detail.
> Now do Exercise 6.

6a Listen to Ian talking to James the next day at school. Choose the correct options.
1 Ian is going to go to ___.
   a) the party   b) the concert
2 James is ___.
   a) surprised   b) upset
3 James says it's ___.
   a) a problem   b) fine

b Listen again and answer the questions.
1 At first, what does James suggest?
2 What two reasons does Ian give for his decision?
3 What does James say about his dad?
4 What does he say about The Rock Roses?

Speak

7 Do you think Ian was right? Why?/Why not? Tell the class.

Extension

Tell the Ss they are going to work in pairs to write their own situation, similar to Ian's, where someone has to make a difficult decision, and they need advice from their friends. Ss can record this in brief notes. Monitor Ss as they discuss, giving help where necessary.

When they have written their notes, they pass them on to one or two other pairs, who should write an answer, giving advice. The notes should then be returned to the original pair. They can decide who has given the best advice on the situation.

Exercise 2
Ian is upset because he wants to go to the concert but has already agreed to go to Danny's party.

Exercise 3
2 pleased 3 older than 4 small 5 decide

Exercise 6a
1 a) 2 a) 3 b)

Exercise 6b
1 He suggests Ian explains about the concert.
2 He's already said he'll go. There aren't many people going.
3 He can get them other tickets.
4 They are on tour.

Exercise 1

1 I've already done my homework.
2 Robert hasn't read the book yet.
3 I've never been to Ireland before.
4 She's just had lunch.
5 Has Jackie's boyfriend ever met her parents?

Exercise 2

1 Have you ever been 2 went 3 did you stay 4 stayed 5 've never been 6 visited

Exercise 3

1 whose 2 which 3 who 4 who 5 sentence 4

Exercise 4

1 lay 2 do 3 do 4 make
1 d) 2 a) 3 e) 4 b)

Exercise 5

1 son-in-law
2 engaged
3 husband
4 have, get
5 out

Exercise 6

1 How do you know?
2 Ha ha, very funny
3 Good for you.
4 do that

Exercise 7

1 c) 2 a) 3 b)

2 Language Revision

Grammar (16 marks)

1 Write sentences. Use the present perfect form of the verbs and the words in brackets.

0 Have/perform/in a play? (ever)
Have you ever performed in a play?
1 I/do/my homework (already)
2 Robert/not read/the book (yet)
3 I/go/to Ireland before (never)
4 She/have/lunch (just)
5 Jackie's boyfriend/meet/her/parents? (ever)

.../5

2 Complete the conversation with the present perfect or past simple form of the verbs.

A: Hi, Joe. How are you?
B: Fine, thanks. ⁰*I've just come* (just come) back from the USA. ¹___ (you/ever/go) there?
A: Yes, I ²___ (go) two years ago. Where ³___ (you/stay)?
B: We ⁴___ (stay) with some friends in Hollywood.
A: I ⁵___ (never go) to Hollywood! Did you meet anybody famous?
B: No, we didn't. But last week, we ⁶___ (visit) Universal Film Studios.
A: Lucky you!

.../6

3 Choose the correct options.

0 This is the place where / which I was born.
1 She's the girl who / whose brother is on TV.
2 I don't like films who / which are sad.
3 It's my sister Jane whose / who is the actress.
4 They are the people who / whose we met last year.
5 Which sentence doesn't need a relative pronoun? ___

.../5

Vocabulary (14 marks)

4 Complete the phrases (0–4). Then match them to the definitions (a–e).

0 – c

0 *do* the washing — a) wash dirty cups and plates
1 ___ the table — b) prepare the first meal of the day
2 ___ the washing-up — c) wash dirty clothes
3 ___ the vacuuming — d) arrange things ready to eat a meal
4 ___ the breakfast — e) clean the carpet

.../8

5 Complete the sentences.

0 The opposite of 'get married' is 'get *divorced*'.
1 Meg is my mum's mother. My dad is Meg's ___.
2 Before you get married, you get ___.
3 John and Helen are married. They are ___ and wife.
4 If you ___ arguments, you don't ___ on well.
5 If a boy likes a girl, he asks her ___.

.../6

Phrases/Use your English (10 marks)

6 Complete with phrases from the box.

- How do you know? • Good for you.
- Ha ha, very funny. • do that.

A: Have you bought a new phone, Terry?
B: Yes, I have. ¹___
A: Because you're speaking on it all the time!
B: ²___
A: I'm going to buy a new phone, too.
B: ³___
A: I'll phone you every hour.
B: You ⁴___ But I won't always answer!

.../4

7 Match the sentences (0–3) to the sentences (a–d) to make a conversation.

0 – d

0 You look miserable.
1 What's the matter?
2 When did that happen?
3 Maybe you should call him and make up.

a) It was last Friday night. I really regret it.
b) Maybe I should. I miss him!
c) My boyfriend Philip and I have split up.
d) I am.

.../6

LISTEN AND CHECK YOUR SCORE	
Grammar	.../16
Vocabulary	.../14
Phrases/Use your English	.../10
Total	**.../40**

30

ROUND-UP 1

ROUND-UP 2

eText

Games

Boat Game

Hangman

Pelmanism

2 Skills Revision

1 _____
2 _____

My mum always asks me to do a lot of things around the house. I do the vacuuming, the washing-up and make the beds. This annoys me because my twin brother Mark doesn't do any jobs. I've told my mum that it's not fair, but she just doesn't listen. Last Tuesday we had a big argument when I refused to take out the rubbish. At the moment we're not speaking to each other and last weekend I stayed with Grandma. She's the only person who listens to me. What should I do?

—————————— *Trisha 14*

3 _____

I'm worried about my best friend, Denise. I think she really likes my boyfriend, Nick. Every time I've met up with him recently, Denise always seems to be there, too. Last Friday I met Nick at a café. Denise was in the café when I arrived! Denise isn't as attractive as me, but she is very funny and Nick laughs at all her jokes! I haven't spoken to her about this yet because I am afraid of falling out with her. I don't know what to do.

—————————— *Kimberly 15*

Read

1 Read the text quickly and match the headings (A–D) to the gaps (1–3). There is one extra heading.

A He's my boyfriend, not yours!
B I've just broken up with him.
C Ask Annie – the problem page for teens
D I'm fed up with household jobs.

2 Read the text again. Answer true (T), false (F) or doesn't say (DS).

0 Trisha does a lot of household jobs. *T*
1 Trisha lives with her grandmother.
2 Trisha isn't speaking to Mark.
3 Denise is going out with Nick.
4 Denise is more attractive than Kimberly.
5 Kimberly doesn't want to have an argument with Denise.

Listen

3a Listen and choose the correct option.

The listening is about ... .
a) shopping   b) a music event   c) a rock concert

b Listen again and choose the correct options.

0 The workshop is about the history of music / musical instruments.
1 At the end of the workshop everybody **performs / listens to** a concert.
2 Danny **has / hasn't** been to the event before.
3 At first, Erica thinks it sounds **dull / exciting**.
4 Erica thinks Tom Sutherland is **cool / boring**.
5 On Saturday Erica is **going shopping / visiting a relative**.
6 Erica and Danny are going to the workshop in the **morning / afternoon**.

Write

4 Write an email to a friend inviting him or her to an event (for example, a concert or a party). Use the headings as a guide.

- greeting
- introduction
- main message
- details and arrangements
- summary and conclusion

Dear Miriam,
How are things with you?

NOW I CAN		
Read	understand letters about problems.	☐
Listen	understand gist and detail in a conversation.	☐
Write	write an invitation.	☐

31

Exercise 1
1 C 2 D 3 A
B is the extra heading.

Exercise 2
1 F 2 T 3 F 4 F 5 T

Exercise 3a
b)

Exercise 3b
1 performs 2 has 3 dull 4 cool 5 going shopping
6 morning

eText
🔌 Additional video lesson

To watch a vlog about jobs for cash, go to Students' eText, page 31.

For the worksheets and teaching notes go to the Teacher's Resource Materials folder.

Look forward 〉〉〉

Write *City life* on the board and tell the Ss that Unit 3 looks at different aspects of living in a town or city. In pairs get the Ss to discuss and write down ten key words that they associate with city life, with the focus on getting around (Lesson 3a) and places (Lesson 3b). Monitor Ss as they talk, checking for relevance and spelling.

Now ask Ss to share their list with the rest of the class and record their words on the board. How many of the lists had the same words? Were there many differences?

Exercise 1

The webpage mentions five types of transport: Tube, bus, rickshaw, boat (river bus), cable car

Exercise 2

1 by cable car 2 a rickshaw 3 river buses 4 double-decker buses and the cable car 5 the Tube

Exercise 3

2 Rickshaws aren't big enough to carry lots of people.

3 I don't dance well enough to perform in public.

4 You're too young to get married.

5 David doesn't study/hasn't studied hard enough to pass his exams.

3 CITY LIFE

3a Too big to see it all on foot.

Grammar	*too* + adjective/adverb + *to*
	(not) + adjective/adverb + *enough to*
Vocabulary	Adjectives and nouns of measurement
	Transport

Read

1 🔊 **Listen and read the webpage. How many types of transport does it mention?**

GETTING AROUND

THE CITY *in style*

So, you have a weekend in London. Lucky you! Here's some advice: plan carefully and decide what you want to do. The city's too big to see it all on foot, so what's the best way to get around?

The Tube is quick and easy, but it's often too crowded to find a seat. Some people prefer to catch a bus and of course there's a great view from the top of a double-decker!

If buses aren't stylish enough to tempt you, how about a rickshaw? The rickshaw rider will take you wherever you want to go. Sit back and enjoy the greenest way to travel! Or, if you want to avoid the traffic, go by boat. River buses are popular and they move slowly enough to see the sights along the river.

Back on dry land, you can use one of the many bridges to cross the river – or if you're too tired to walk, use the cable car! The London cable car goes over the Thames at a height of 90 metres. The river there is only one kilometre wide so it's a short trip. At busy times of the day the cable car goes too fast to take good photos. At other times the ride is slower and long enough to enjoy the view.

Comprehension

2 **Answer the questions in pairs.**

Find ...

1 two ways of crossing the river. *by bridge, ...*

2 an unusual kind of taxi.

3 a slow way to enjoy the sights along the river.

4 two ways to look down on London.

5 a fast but sometimes uncomfortable way to get about.

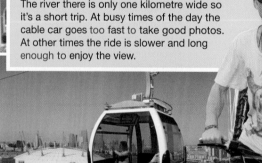

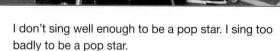

32

6 Jack isn't strong enough to carry that box.

7 Are you clever enough to solve the puzzle?

8 Maisie ran too slowly to win the race.

Exercise 4

Suggested answers:

I run too slowly to be in the Olympics. I don't run fast enough to be in the Olympics.

I don't get up early enough to get to school on time. I get up too late to get to school on time.

I don't sing well enough to be a pop star. I sing too badly to be a pop star.

I'm not fit enough to run a kilometre. I'm too unfit to run a kilometre.

I'm not confident enough to make a speech. I'm too shy to make a speech.

Grammar

too + adjective/adverb + to

The city's **too big to** see it all on foot.
The car goes **too fast to** take photos.

(not) + adjective/adverb + enough to

It's (isn't) **long enough to** enjoy the view.
They (don't) move **slowly enough to** see the sights.

Practice

3 Make sentences. Use the prompts and *too ... to* or *(not) ... enough to*.

1 it/be expensive/travel by taxi
   It's too expensive to travel by taxi.
2 rickshaws/not be big/carry lots of people
3 I/not dance well/perform in public
4 you/be young/get married
5 David/not study hard/pass his exams
6 Jack/not be strong/carry that box
7 you/be clever/solve the puzzle?
8 Maisie/run slowly/win the race

4 Write sentences about you with *too ... to* or *(not) ... enough to*. Use the ideas in the box or your own ideas.

I'm (not) old enough to have a job.
I'm too young to have a job.

- be old/young – have a job
- run fast/slowly – be in the Olympics
- get up early/late – get to school on time
- sing well/badly – be a pop star
- be fit/unfit – run a kilometre
- be confident/shy – make a speech

Vocabulary: Adjectives and nouns of measurement

5 🔊 Listen and repeat. Then match the nouns to the adjectives.

age – old

age cost depth distance height length
size speed width

big deep expensive far fast high long
old wide

Listen

6 🔊 Listen to the talk about the Docklands Light Railway. Complete the notes.

- DLR = *Docklands Light Railway*
- opened in ²_____
- unusual because ³_____
- started with ⁴_____ stations and was ⁵_____ km long
- now ⁶_____ stations and ⁷_____ km long
- 200,000 passengers every ⁸_____
- goes ⁹_____ ground (mostly)
- speed: ¹⁰_____ km per hour

Vocabulary: Transport

7a Look at the types of transport in Exercise 1 again. Write the advantages and disadvantages of each one.

The Tube: quick, easy, often crowded

b Recall How many more types of transport can you name? Check the Word bank on page 112.

car, tram, ...

Speak and write

8 Discuss the questions in pairs or small groups. Then write some travel advice to tourists in your town or city.

- What are the different ways of travelling around your town or city?
- Which ways are the slowest, fastest, cheapest and most expensive?
- Which form of transport do you prefer? Why?
You can travel around our town by tram, ...

Extra practice

➤ For more practice, go to page 103.

33

cable car: at busy times goes too fast to take good photos, but at other times is slower and long enough to enjoy the view

Extension ▮▬

too ... to, (not) ... enough to

Ask Ss in pairs to think of four ideas which could go with *too ... to* or *(not) ... enough to*. (They can refer back to the prompts and ideas in Exercises 3 and 4 if they need help to get started.) Encourage them to think up silly or over-the-top ideas, e.g. *lift a bus*, *swim the Atlantic Ocean.*

They then swap ideas with another pair, who have to think up appropriate sentences using *too ... to* or *(not) ... enough to*, e.g. *I'm not strong enough to lift a bus. / I'm too weak to lift a bus.*

Ss feed back to the class the funniest/most interesting sentences.

Extra practice
Page 123

MOTIVATOR 3a

Background note

While the UK has had a metric system of measurement since the early 1970s many British people are more familiar with the old imperial system of feet/miles, etc. and you will frequently see this used.

Exercise 5
cost – expensive, depth – deep, distance – far, height – high, length – long, size – big, speed – fast, width – wide

Exercise 6
2 1987 3 there are no drivers
4 15 5 13 6 45 7 34 8 day 9 above 10 80

Exercise 7a
bus: great view, not stylish

rickshaw: will take you wherever you want to go, greenest way to travel, slow, lots of traffic

river bus: moves slowly enough to see the sights along the river, popular so might be crowded

Get the Ss to stand up. Write a sentence on the board, e.g. *I usually go to school by bus.* Students for whom this statement is true sit down. Write the next sentence on the board, e.g. *I usually go to school on foot.*

Continue with different forms of transport until only one student (the winner) is still standing.

Exercise 1

1 sports centre
2 petrol station
3 museum 4 art gallery 5 restaurant
6 library 7 park
8 café 9 square
10 tourist information centre 11 cinema
12 music shop
13 pharmacy
14 newsagent
15 police station 16 bank
17 supermarket
18 car park
19 swimming pool
20 hotel

Exercise 2

Emma lives in the block of flats opposite the playground.

Exercise 3

He phones *her* because he's late. She gives him directions from the *department store* to her flat. He knows when he gets to the right place because *she* sees *him*.

Exercise 4

1 park
2 restaurant

3b You can't miss it.

Vocabulary	Places in town
Function	Ask for and give directions

Vocabulary: Places in town

1 Recall **List all the places in town on the map. Then check the Word bank on page 112.**

Martin: Hey, Emma. Sorry, I'm late. I'm a bit lost.
Emma: Oh no, where are you? Stupid question! I mean, what can you see?
Martin: I'm standing in front of Davidson's department store. It's next to a bank.
Emma: OK, that's Joyner Street. No problem, you aren't too far away. Go right, down Joyner Street to the traffic lights.
Martin: OK, hang on … right, I've done that!
Emma: Good. Now go past the cinema. Then take the second turning on the left into West Street.

Martin: OK, what now?
Emma: Go straight on until you see a children's playground on your left. You can't miss it. I live opposite the playground … Oh, nice hoodie!
Martin: How do you know?
Emma: Look up! Hi there!
Jodie: Hi, Martin!

Phrases
- I'm a bit lost. • I mean, …
- what now?

Dialogue

2 🔊 **Listen and read. Where does Emma live? Find it on the map.**

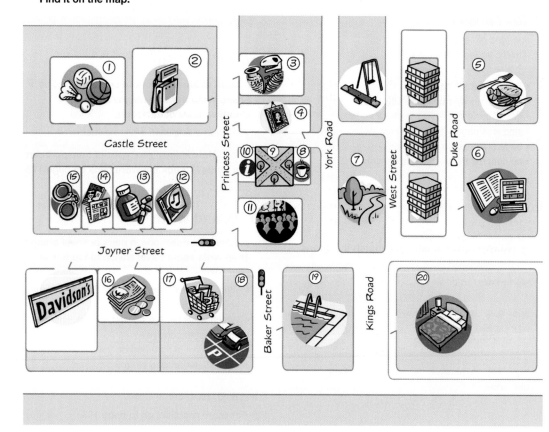

34

Exercise 5

1 tourist information centre
2 swimming pool

Exercise 6

1 Can you <u>tell</u> me the <u>way</u> to the <u>hospital, please</u>?
2 <u>How</u> do I <u>get</u> to the <u>park</u>?
3 Turn <u>left</u> and go <u>straight on</u>.

Extension ▰▰▰

Ask for and give directions

Ask the Ss to choose a destination in the local area (cinema, sports centre, etc.) and to write it on a slip of paper. Collect the papers and redistribute them. Each S should now move around the room to ask for directions to this place from the school. Introduce the phrase *I'm sorry, I'm afraid I don't know.*

This should preview the writing in Exercise 9.

Comprehension

3 **Rewrite the summary, correcting the mistakes.**

Martin is on his way to see Jodie. She phones him because he's late. She gives him directions from the library to her flat. He knows when he gets to the right place because he sees her.

Martin is on his way to see Emma …

Practice

4 **Look at the map on page 34. Then complete the directions with the places in the box. There are three extra places.**

> • cinema   • park   • playground   • restaurant
> • supermarket

1 Go left out of the sports centre. Cross Princess Street and go straight on, past the square on your right and the art gallery on your left. Turn right and you'll see the ___ on your left.

2 From the bank, cross over the road and turn right. Take the fourth turning on the left. Go past the library and you'll see the ___ on your right.

Listen

5 Look at the map again and listen to two phone conversations. Where are the two people going?

Pronunciation: Sentence stress and rhythm

6 Go to page 116.

Use your English: Ask for and give directions

7 **Find Davidson's on the map. Listen and repeat. Then practise the conversation in pairs.**

A: Excuse me. Can you tell me the way to the art gallery, please?

B: Yes, sure. Go down Joyner Street until you get to the traffic lights, then turn left. Go straight on, past the tourist information centre. Cross over the road and you'll see it on the right opposite the petrol station. You can't miss it.

A: Thanks very much.

B: No problem. You're welcome.

Ask for directions

Excuse me./Sorry to bother you …

Can you tell me the way to the theatre, please?

How do I get to the theatre?

Where's the nearest theatre, please?

Give directions

Go left out of the library. Turn right at the corner. It's next to the bank.

Take the second/third turning on the left.

See Exercise 4 for other directions.

---

8 **Work in pairs. Take turns to ask for and give directions to four places on the map.**

Write

9 **Write directions from your home to the nearest shop, station or bus stop.**

Extra practice

For more practice, go to page 104.

Extra practice
Page 124

eText
Video and Animation

Pronunciation: Sentence stress and rhythm
Use your English: Ask for and give directions

Places in town

Play a quickfire 'Guess the place' game. Start by drawing a simple icon on the board to represent a place in town (e.g. for *supermarket* draw a shopping trolley). The first S to guess the correct place comes to the board and draws a different icon, and so on until the Ss have drawn and guessed all the vocabulary.

If Ss need help with ideas for icons, they can refer to the map on page 34 of the Students' Book.

3c We throw away too many things.

Grammar   *too many, too much, not enough*
    Pronouns *some-, any-, no-, every-* + *thing, where, one, body*
Vocabulary   Countable and uncountable nouns

Read

1 🎧 ³/₀₈ **Listen and read the webpage. Which is the correct summary?**

a) Do more recycling.   b) Eat less food.   c) Don't throw things away.

TALKBACK: YOU ASK, WE ANSWER. TODAY, WE'RE TALKING … RUBBISH!

Home | News | **Articles**

> I know I should recycle things, but why? The refuse collectors collect our rubbish every week. So what's the problem? ben15

Of course we can't recycle everything, but we throw away far too many things. Each year the average British family throws away about 100 kg of glass, 40 kg of plastic and 260 kg of paper (that's about five trees). That's an awful lot of rubbish! And believe it or not, we throw away about one third of all the food we buy (so we waste a lot of money, too).

Not enough people recycle and too much rubbish goes to landfill sites (enormous holes in the ground). As everything lies there year after year, it poisons the land. It also creates methane (a greenhouse gas that increases global warming). These days, there isn't enough space for all the landfill sites we need – we have to send some of our rubbish overseas!

> It doesn't matter if I recycle or not. One person can't change anything. nonamegirl

Not true! Change has to start somewhere – why not with you? And remember this – if nobody does anything, nothing will change!

Comprehension

2 **Answer true (T), false (F) or doesn't say (DS) according to the webpage.**

1 *Ben15* thinks recycling is a waste of time. *DS*
2 The UK uses 260 kg of paper per person every year.
3 British people waste most of the food that they buy.
4 Rubbish in landfill sites pollutes the earth and the air.
5 Some of our rubbish goes to landfill sites in other countries.
6 *nonamegirl* wants to change things.

S🔍LVE IT!

3 Joe is 16. How much glass (approximately) has his family thrown away in his lifetime?

36

Exercise 1

a)

Exercise 2

2 F 3 F 4 T 5 T 6 DS

Exercise 3

1,600 kg

Vocabulary: Countable and uncountable nouns

4a 🔊 3/09 **Listen and repeat. Put the words from the box in the table.**

• family • food • glass • holes • money • people
• plastic • problem • rubbish • things

Countable	Uncountable
family	food

b 🔊 3/10 **Listen and repeat. Now add these words to the table in Exercise 4a.**

• air • children • cities • garden • information
• litter • luggage • music • news • pollution
• school • shop • snow • street • traffic • woman

Grammar

too many, too much, not enough

We throw away far **too many** things.
Too much rubbish goes to landfill sites.
Not enough people recycle.
There **isn't enough** space.

Practice

5 **Choose the correct options in sentences (1–4). Then complete the sentences with the correct form of the verb be.**

1 There 's too (much)/ many pollution in our towns.
2 There ___ too much / many rubbish in the streets.
3 There ___ too much / many traffic on the roads.
4 There ___ too much / many people in the city.
5 There ___ (not) enough parks and playgrounds.
6 ___ there enough food for us?
7 There ___ (not) enough places where we can recycle.
8 There ___ (not) enough clean air.

Grammar

Pronouns some-, any-, no-, every- + thing, where, one, body

	some-	any-	no-	every-
thing	something	anything	nothing	everything
place	somewhere	anywhere	nowhere	everywhere
person	somebody	anybody	nobody	everybody
	someone	anyone	no one	everyone

Practice

6 **Complete the sentences with words from the grammar box.**

1 A: What will the Earth be like in a thousand years' time?
  B: _Nobody_ knows.
2 A: What shall we do with these old newspapers?
  B: Let's find ___ to recycle them.
3 A: I don't know ___ who grows their own food. Do you?
  B: Yes, my aunt grows vegetables in her garden.
4 A: Let's do ___ about the litter in the playground.
  B: OK, I'll get some rubbish sacks.
5 A: Is there ___ in that bottle?
  B: No, ___. It's empty.
6 A: What a terrible place. There's rubbish ___.
  B: Yes, and there's ___ to sit down.

Listen

7 🔊 3/11 **Listen to Della talking about her town. Read the summaries (1–6) and tick (✓) the ones that are correct.**

1 I live here.   ☑
2 There's nothing to do here.   ☐
3 My friends and I don't go to the sports club.   ☐
4 I like expensive clothes shops.   ☐
5 There aren't enough cafés.   ☐
6 The streets are dirty.   ☐

Speak

8 **Work in pairs or small groups. Talk about your town, and the things you would like to change (traffic, pollution, rubbish, noise, etc.). Then tell the class.**

There's too much traffic. There's nowhere to go in the evenings.

Extra practice

▶ **For more practice, go to page 104.**

Exercise 6
2 somewhere
3 anyone/anybody
4 something
5 anything, nothing
6 everywhere, nowhere

Exercise 7
Correct summaries:
3, 5 and 6

Extension ▰

Countable and uncountable nouns

Ss write *countable* and *uncountable* on separate cards/slips of paper. Call out different countable and uncountable nouns, including nouns not covered in this lesson, for example food related nouns such as *banana, milk*. Ss hold up the appropriate card. Individual Ss could take turns to do the calling out.

Extra practice

Page 124

eText

⏎ **Video and Animation**

Grammar: *too many, too much, not enough*

MOTIVATOR 3c

Exercise 4a
Countable: holes, people, problem, things
Uncountable: glass, money, plastic, rubbish

Exercise 4b
Countable: children, cities, garden, school, shop, street, woman
Uncountable: air, information, litter, luggage, music, news, pollution, snow, traffic

Exercise 5
2 There's too much rubbish in the streets.
3 There's too much traffic on the roads.
4 There are too many people in the city.
5 There aren't enough parks and playgrounds.
6 Is there enough food for us?
7 There aren't enough places where we can recycle.
8 There isn't enough clean air.

Exercise 2a

Hong Kong, Edinburgh and Sydney

boat/traditional junk, rickshaw and helicopter

Exercise 2b

2 noun: streams of light

3 adjective: amazing, breathtaking

4 noun: criminals, bad characters in stories

5 noun: a type of sweet, toffee

6 noun: a barbecue

Exercise 3

2 A multimedia show of lights and music.

3 In Edinburgh's underground city.

4 Holyrood Palace and Edinburgh Castle.

5 Sydney Opera House and Sydney Harbour Bridge.

6 You can go surfing, relax on the beach and have a barbecue.

Exercise 4

2 90

3 24 / 48

4 Sydney Opera House, Bondi Beach

5 English

6 Central Station bus stop

7 34

ACROSS CULTURES

3d Sightseeing – by land, sea or air!

SKILLS FOCUS: READING

Get started

1 Look at the photos. Which place looks a) the most interesting b) the most exciting?

Read

> **READING TIP: HOW TO GUESS THE MEANING OF NEW WORDS**
>
> Use clues to guess the meaning of new words. First, decide what part of speech the word is (e.g. verb, noun or adjective). Then guess what it means from the context (what comes before and after). You can check the meaning in a dictionary later.
>
> Now do Exercise 2.

2a (3/12) Read the travel guide quickly. What three cities can you visit? What are the three exciting ways to see them?

b Read the guide again and find these new words. Guess the meaning.

1 junk (line 5)
'junk' is a noun. I think it is a traditional Chinese boat.
2 beams (line 11)
3 stunning (line 11)
4 villains (line 15)
5 fudge (line 20)
6 barbie (line 33)

Comprehension

3 Answer the questions.

1 What is the best way to see Hong Kong's high buildings?
From a boat on the harbour.
2 What is the 'Symphony of Lights'?
3 Where can you find ghosts in Edinburgh?
4 What sights can you see in Edinburgh's Royal Mile area?
5 What sights can you see on the helicopter ride?
6 What can you do on Bondi Beach?

38

TEEN TRAVEL: GUIDE

THREE EXCITING WAYS TO SEE THREE EXCITING CITIES

HONG KONG, CHINA

Did you know that Hong Kong is actually 260 small islands? This city is famous for its skyline. Hong Kong's skyscrapers are too tall to appreciate from the street, so the best way to see them is from
5 a boat on the harbour. Travel in a traditional junk once used by Chinese fishermen and pirates. You can take a night cruise around Victoria Harbour to see the incredible 'Symphony of Lights'. This is a multimedia light and music show where you can see
10 Hong Kong's highest buildings. They are illuminated with coloured lights and laser beams – it's stunning!

EDINBURGH, SCOTLAND

If you don't fancy walking, a fun way to see Edinburgh is by rickshaw. You can fit two or three people in this unusual taxi and the driver gives you
15 a guided tour. Learn about the villains and heroes that lived in the old town. Your guide can also tell you tales about the ghosts in Edinburgh's forgotten underground city. If this is too scary, take a break and visit one of Edinburgh's traditional sweet shops –
20 try some home-made fudge, it's delicious! Finish your tour in the area called the Royal Mile, in the old part of the city. At the bottom you can see Holyrood Palace and at the top, Edinburgh Castle.

SYDNEY, AUSTRALIA

Have you ever been in a helicopter? Take a
25 twenty-minute ride over the city and its beaches. It's amazing to see Sydney's skyscrapers and waterways from the air. The pilot gives a commentary and you can see Sydney Harbour Bridge and Sydney Opera House. The helicopter
30 ride ends at Bondi Beach. This is a popular place for surfers. But if you are not brave enough to go surfing you can relax on the golden beach. And if you're hungry, why not enjoy an Australian 'barbie'? Watch out in January though, because it is summer
35 here and the beach is often too crowded to do anything.

Extension

Write the following sentences on the board. Play the recording again for Ss to decide if they are true or false or it doesn't say (answers in brackets).

1 *The local city buses don't have many passengers.* (False – They are too crowded to find a seat.)

2 *You can ask the hop-on hop-off bus to stop when you want to get off.* (Doesn't say)

3 *You can see all the main sights of Sydney from the bus.* (True)

4 *You can buy a ticket for one day or two days.* (True)

5 *There are six buses an hour.* (False – There are buses every 15 minutes, i.e. four an hour.)

6 *The tour starts and ends at Central Station.* (Doesn't say that it ends there.)

They then compare their answers in pairs before checking as a class. When checking answers, ask Ss to correct the false sentences.

Listen

4 🎧 Listen to the information about the Sydney 'Hop-on hop-off bus tour'. Complete the notes in the table.

Bus type:	[1] _Open-air double-decker_
Duration of tour:	[2] ___ minutes
Ticket types:	[3] ___ / ___-hour tickets
Sights:	[4] ___, ___
Language of tour commentary:	[5] ___
Place to start tour:	[6] ___ bus stop
Number of bus stops:	[7] ___

Speak

5 Work in pairs. Make a list of the places, activities and sights in the guide in Exercise 2. Decide which ones you would recommend for teenagers, older people, or for young children.

Project

6 Write a travel blog about a place you went to last summer. Use the ideas below. Include a photo you took, or download one from the internet.

- Where you went
- Who you went with
- How you got there (means of transport)
- Something exciting that happened
- Your opinion of the place

Last summer I went to London …

NEW WORDS

- skyline • skyscraper • appreciate
- harbour • pirates • cruise • illuminated
- fit • hero • tales • underground
- home-made • waterways • commentary

39

Exercise 1

2 d) 3 a) 4 e)

Exercise 2

2 in Phoenix Park
3 at Temple Bar
4 in the city centre
5 at Temple Bar

Exercise 3

Paragraph 1:
Walking around the
town – The best
way to see the city
is on foot.

Paragraph 2:
Entertainment –
There's plenty of
entertainment on
offer.

Paragraph 3:
Shopping –
Shoppers will love
the city centre.

Paragraph 4:
Open spaces –
You're never far
from a park in
Dublin.

3e A great city

SKILLS FOCUS: WRITING A BROCHURE

DUBLIN A GREAT CITY

Are you a music-lover, a shopper or do you just want to relax? Dublin offers it all!

[1]__ Walk around the historic streets of Temple Bar and explore the wide variety of shops and market stalls. Relax in a riverside café and watch the world go by. This part of the city is a 'must' for tourists – there's something there for everyone!

[2]__ Check out the many music venues or get tickets for a show or film in one of Dublin's great theatres and cinemas. There are lots of museums and galleries to choose from too, including the very popular Wax Museum Plus, with life-size models of celebrities past and present.

[3]__ Its shops sell everything from high fashion to paperbacks and pencils. And for something a little bit different, go to the Dublin flea market (you'll need plenty of time!).

[4]__ The most famous one is Phoenix Park – it's one of the biggest city parks in Europe. It's home to many animals and birds, including a magnificent herd of deer. You can see more exotic animals as well, because Dublin Zoo is there, too!

Get ready to write

1 Read the text from a tourist brochure. Complete it with the sentences (a–e). There is one extra sentence.

1 – b

a) Shoppers will love the city centre.
b) The best way to see the city is on foot.
c) Visit one of Dublin's many beautiful beaches.
d) There's plenty of entertainment on offer.
e) You're never far from a park in Dublin.

2 In pairs, answer the questions.

Where can you:

1 see models of famous people?
   At the Wax Museum Plus.
2 see wild creatures?
3 sit by the river?
4 buy designer clothes?
5 see an old part of town?

> **WRITING TIP: PARAGRAPHS AND TOPIC SENTENCES**
>
> Organise your writing in paragraphs with different topics. You can start each new paragraph with a 'topic sentence' (see a–e above). This tells the reader the main topic of the paragraph.
> Now do Exercise 3.

3 Read the text in Exercise 1 again. Match the paragraphs to the topics in the box. There is one extra topic.

> • Entertainment • Open spaces • Shopping
> • Transport • Walking around the town

Write

4a Work in pairs. You are going to write a text for a tourist brochure about a town or city.

1 Choose a town or city you both know.
2 Choose four topics from the box in Exercise 3 and note down your ideas.

Entertainment: four cinemas, skating rink, theatre
Shopping: market, …

b Now write the brochure. Think of a title and then write four paragraphs. Start each paragraph with a topic sentence.

Oxford: my city
If you're looking for entertainment, Oxford is the place to go. There are four cinemas and they show a wide range of films. There's also …
You can buy almost anything in Oxford! There's a …

40

3 Language Revision

Grammar (14 marks)

1 Complete the sentences. Use *too ... to* or *(not)
... enough to* and the words in brackets.

0 Billy didn't catch the bus. (run fast)
Billy *didn't run fast enough to* catch the bus.
1 They can't get married. (be young)
They ___ get married.
2 We don't go on expensive holidays. (be rich)
We ___ go on expensive holidays.
3 I didn't have breakfast. (get up late)
I ___ have breakfast.
4 She didn't pass the exam. (work hard)
She ___ pass the exam.

.../4

2 Complete the sentences with one word.

I don't like big cities because there are ⁰*too*
many people. There's also too ¹___ pollution
and ²___ enough clean air. I think there are too ³___
buildings and there aren't ⁴___ parks.

.../4

3 Complete the words.

0 Is there *any*thing in this bag?
1 I can't find my watch. I've looked every___.
2 The film was boring. ___body enjoyed it.
3 This shop is fantastic. I like every___ in it!
4 I think there's ___thing in my shoe.
5 The school is closed. Every___ has gone home.
6 I'd like to go ___where hot for my holiday.

.../6

Vocabulary (14 marks)

4 Complete the words.

0 How *deep* is this pool? What's its *depth*?
1 What's the s___ of the train? How f___ is it?
2 How h___ is the building? What's its h___?
3 What's the w___ of the river? How w___ is it?
4 What's the l___ of the bridge? How l___ is it?

.../8

5 Write the correct place in town.

0 buy a book? *bookshop*
1 see a painting?
2 post a letter?
3 buy some food?
4 go swimming?
5 drink a coffee?
6 borrow a book?

.../6

Phrases/Use your English
(12 marks)

6 Look at the jumbled conversation. Number the
lines in the correct order.

☐ a) Yes, very stupid!
☐1 b) Hi, Jerry. I'm a bit lost!
☐ c) Oh great. 'Flicks' is just opposite my block
of flats.
☐ d) Sorry. Can you see anything? I mean, a
shop or a park?
☐ e) Oh dear! Where are you? I suppose that's a
stupid question.
☐ f) Yes, a cinema called 'Flicks'.

.../5

7 Complete with words and phrases from the
box.

• welcome • miss it • turn left • past • Sorry to
• along • Take • ~~Excuse me~~

A: ⁰ *Excuse me*. How do I get to the post office?
B: ¹___ this road and then go ²___ Chester Road.
Go ³___ the bank and then you'll see it.
A: Thanks.
B: You're ⁴___.

A: ⁵___ bother you, can you tell me where the
station is?
B: No problem. Go down the road, then ⁶___. You
can't ⁷___!

.../7

LISTEN AND CHECK YOUR SCORE	
Grammar	.../14
Vocabulary	.../14
Phrases/Use your English	.../12
Total	**.../40**

41

Exercise 7
1 Take 2 along
3 past 4 welcome
5 Sorry to 6 turn left
7 miss it

ROUND-UP 1

ROUND-UP 2

eText
Games

Boat Game

Hangman

Pelmanism

Exercise 1
1 are too young to 2 aren't rich enough to 3 got up
too late to 4 didn't work hard enough to

Exercise 2
1 much 2 not 3 many 4 enough

Exercise 3
1 -where 2 No- 3 -thing 4 some- 5 -body/-one
6 some-

Exercise 4
1 speed/fast 2 high/height 3 width/wide 4 length/long

Exercise 5
1 art gallery 2 post office 3 supermarket
4 swimming pool 5 café 6 library

Exercise 6
2 e) 3 a) 4 d) 5 f) 6 c)

Look forward >>>

Introduce the Ss to the unit topic *Time passes* and read out the introduction to the school webpage. Ask the class what it might be like to be a new student, like Martin, in an unfamiliar town or country. Share your own experiences with the Ss: what did you like/not like when you first arrived, did you change your mind as time passed, what did you miss most about your home town/ country?

Ss who have had similar experiences can share them with the rest of the class.

Exercise 2
French and (British) history

Exercise 3
2 DS 3 F 4 F 5 DS

4 TIME PASSES

Grammar   Present perfect simple with *for* and *since*
Vocabulary Collocations with *make* and *do*

Get started

1 Would you like to study abroad for a year? Why?/Why not?

Read

2 Listen and read the school webpage. Which subjects are a problem for Martin?

Comprehension

3 Answer true (T), false (F) or doesn't say (DS).

1 Martin is from London. *F*
2 He prefers California to London.
3 He likes the British weather.
4 Maths and Science are different at his new school.
5 He doesn't enjoy French.

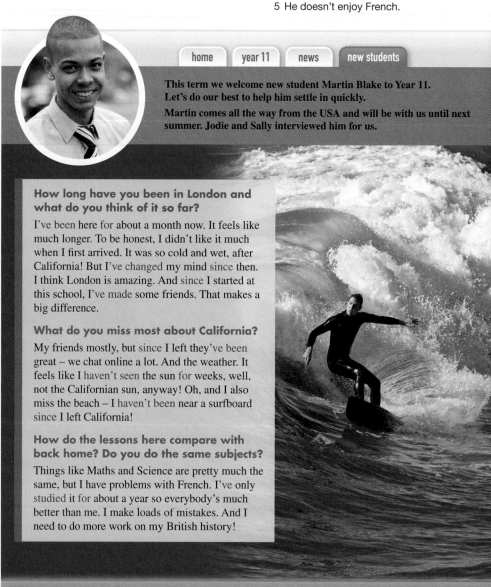

home | year 11 | news | **new students**

This term we welcome new student Martin Blake to Year 11. Let's do our best to help him settle in quickly.

Martin comes all the way from the USA and will be with us until next summer. Jodie and Sally interviewed him for us.

How long have you been in London and what do you think of it so far?

I've been here for about a month now. It feels like much longer. To be honest, I didn't like it much when I first arrived. It was so cold and wet, after California! But I've changed my mind since then. I think London is amazing. And since I started at this school, I've made some friends. That makes a big difference.

What do you miss most about California?

My friends mostly, but since I left they've been great – we chat online a lot. And the weather. It feels like I haven't seen the sun for weeks, well, not the Californian sun, anyway! Oh, and I also miss the beach – I haven't been near a surfboard since I left California!

How do the lessons here compare with back home? Do you do the same subjects?

Things like Maths and Science are pretty much the same, but I have problems with French. I've only studied it for about a year so everybody's much better than me. I make loads of mistakes. And I need to do more work on my British history!

42

Exercise 4a
2 made some friends 3 makes a big difference
4 Do you do the same subjects? 5 make loads of mistakes 6 do more work

Exercise 4b
2 made a difference 3 do my best 4 made an appointment with 5 made a decision 6 make some money 7 doing 8 do the shopping

Grammar
1 *for* 2 *since*

Exercise 5
For: ages, half an hour, a long time, six months, three seconds, two weeks, a thousand years, a day

Since: we started at this school, I was twelve, last July, 2000, my birthday, New Year's Eve, this morning, I got up, yesterday, the spring

Vocabulary: Collocations with *make* and *do*

4a 🔊 **Listen and repeat. Then find six of the expressions in the webpage on page 42.**

do our best

- do a subject • do nothing/something
- do some exercise • do some/the shopping
- do your best
- do your homework/some work/the housework
- make a decision • make a difference
- make a drink/a cake/a sandwich/a meal
- make a mess • make a mistake
- make a noise • make an appointment (with)
- make friends (with) • make (some) money

b **Replace the underlined words with the correct form of expressions from Exercise 4a.**

1 We have become friends with our new neighbours. *made friends*
2 Congratulations, your hard work changed the situation.
3 I will do everything I can.
4 I've arranged to see the doctor.
5 We weren't sure, but now we've decided.
6 I need to earn some cash.
7 Jack's studying Art History at college.
8 Can you go to the shops and buy some food?

Grammar

Present perfect simple with *for* and *since*

I've been here **for** about a month.
I **haven't seen** the sun **for** weeks.
I've changed my mind **since** then.
Since I started at this school, I've made some friends.

Complete the rules with *for* or *since*.

We use ¹___ to talk about a period of time.
We use ²___ to talk about a point in the past.

Practice

5 **Put the words and phrases in the lists.**

- 6 p.m. • a few minutes • ages
- half an hour • we started at this school
- I was twelve • last July • a long time
- six months • 2000 • my birthday
- New Year's Eve • this morning
- three seconds • two weeks • I got up
- yesterday • a thousand years • the spring
- a day

for	since
a few minutes	6 p.m.

6 **Read the situations and write two sentences for each one. Use the present perfect form of the verbs with *for* and *since*.**

1 Tom and Sylvie got married in 2010. (be)
   They've been married for … years.
   They've been married since 2010.
2 Jackie had her first pair of glasses when she was eight. She's fifteen now. (wear)
3 The last time I saw Ben was at his birthday party three months ago. (not see)
4 Cathy and Ted met on their first day of college. That was two years ago. (know)
5 The last time I had a break was at eleven o'clock. It's half past three now. (not have)
6 Della has flu. It's Friday. She became ill on Saturday. (have)

Speak

7a **Ask and answer the questions in pairs. Note down your partner's answers.**

- Where do you live?
- How long have you lived there?
- What's your favourite band?
- When did you first like him/her/them?
- What's your favourite TV programme?
- When did you first watch it?
- What's your least favourite food?
- When did you last eat it?

b **Now tell the class about your partner.**

Nikos lives in/at … He's lived there for/since …

Extra practice

➤ **For more practice, go to page 104.**

Extra practice
Page 124

eText

📺 **Video and Animation**

Grammar: Present perfect simple with *for* and *since*

MOTIVATOR 4a

43

Exercise 6

2 She's worn glasses for seven years. She's worn glasses since she was eight.
3 I haven't seen Ben for three months. I haven't seen Ben since his birthday party.
4 They've known each other for two years. They've known each other since their first day of college.
5 I haven't had a break for four and a half hours. I haven't had a break since eleven o'clock.
6 Della has had flu for six days. Della has had flu since Saturday.

Extension

Collocations with make and do

Ss write *make* and *do* on separate cards/slips of paper. Call out part of a collocation, e.g. … *some exercise*, … *an appointment*. Ss hold up the appropriate card to complete the collocation.
Individual Ss could take turns to do the calling out.

Present perfect simple with *for* and *since*

Ask the Ss to write down on a card two statements about themselves, using the present perfect and *for* or *since*, e.g. *I've worn glasses since I was 10* and *I've lived in this town for four years.* Collect in the cards, then ask each Ss to pick up one and to mingle, asking questions to match the card to the correct person.

Finally, Ss report back to the class, but without saying the name of the person, e.g. *Student X has worn glasses since he/she was 10* and *He/she has lived in this town for four years.*

Can the other Ss correctly guess the identity of Student X?

Background note

Brixton Academy: A popular music venue in south London.

4b You've been talking for ages.

Grammar	Present perfect continuous with *for* and *since*
Vocabulary	Phrasal verbs with *look*

Dialogue

1 🎧 **Listen and read. Why did Jodie need to speak to Martin?**

Martin: Hi, Jodie.

Jodie: Hi, Martin, at last! You've been talking on the phone for ages.

Martin: Oh sorry. How long have you been trying?

Jodie: Since five o'clock. Have you been talking to the States?

Martin: Yes, I have, but I haven't been talking to the same person for three hours! The last one was Sophie.

Jodie: Who's Sophie? Your girlfriend?

Martin: Let's just say she's a friend. She's been diving in Hawaii for a week. It's not fair! Anyway, what's up?

Jodie: It's about that concert at the Brixton Academy next month. Luke and I have been searching online for tickets since lunchtime and …

Martin: Don't tell me you've got some!

Jodie: Yes, we have, but they're £30 each. What do you think?

Martin: Well, I've been saving for a bike since I arrived, but that can wait – I'm in!

Jodie: Great. We're on it!

Phrases
- at last! • for ages • Let's just say … • It's about …
- Don't tell me … • I'm in! • We're on it!

Comprehension

2 Choose the correct options.

1 Martin has had one conversation / several conversations.
2 Sophie is **Martin's** / **Jodie's** friend.
3 Jodie wanted to tell Martin about a **holiday / concert**.
4 Jodie and Luke **are looking for / have found** some tickets.
5 Martin is saving for a **ticket / bike**.

44

Vocabulary: Phrasal verbs with *look*

3a Match the phrases (1–5) to the correct endings (a–e).

1 – d

1 look at
2 look up
3 look forward to
4 look for
5 look after

a) something exciting
b) something you've lost
c) a baby
d) a picture
e) a difficult word in a dictionary

b Complete the sentences with *at, up, forward to, for* or *after*.

1 I don't understand this word. I'm going to look it *up.*
2 I'm looking ___ the concert next week.
3 Wow! Look ___ that sunset!
4 That plant is dying. You don't look ___ it well enough.
5 John's lost his wallet. Can you look ___ it, please?

SOLVE IT!

4 Look at the dialogue in Exercise 1 again. What time does Jodie speak to Martin?

Exercise 1
She wants to tell Martin they've got tickets for a concert.

Exercise 2
2 Martin's 3 concert 4 have found 5 bike

Exercise 3a
2 e) 3 a) 4 b) 5 c)

Exercise 3b
2 forward to 3 at 4 after 5 for

Exercise 4
Jodie speaks to Martin at 8 o'clock.

Exercise 5b
B: No, we're nowhere near.
A: Look! Her hair isn't really fair!
B: Ssh, dear. Don't stare!
A: Come and sit here, Claire
B: Where? On that chair?

Pronunciation: /ɪə/ we're, /eə/ where

5 🎧 (4 04) **Go to page 116.**

Grammar

Present perfect continuous with *for* and *since*
Affirmative
You**'ve been talking** on the phone **for** ages.
I**'ve been saving** for a bike **since** I arrived.
Negative
I **haven't been talking** to the same person **for** three hours.
Questions
How long **have** you **been trying**?
Have you **been talking** to the States?
Short answers
Yes, I **have**./No, I **haven't**.

Practice

6 **Complete the questions and answers. Write the present perfect continuous form of the verbs in brackets or short forms.**

1 A: You look tired. How long *have you been travelling* (you/travel)?
   B: We ___ (drive) since six o'clock this morning.
2 A: ___ (Tom/do) his homework this morning?
   B: No, he ___. He ___ (play) basketball since 9 a.m.
3 A: Hi. You look fed up!
   B: You're right, I am. I ___ (stand) at this bus stop for half an hour.
4 A: Look at this mess. What ___ (you/do)?
   B: Sorry. We ___ (sort) out our old clothes for the last two hours.
5 A: How long ___ (Amy/prepare) for the half marathon?
   B: She ___ (train) every morning for weeks now – she's very fit!
6 A: Sorry I'm late. ___ (you/wait) for ages?
   B: No, I ___, don't worry.

7 **Complete the postcard. Choose *for* or *since* and write the present perfect continuous form of the verbs.**

Hi Martin,
This is the last day of our holiday ☺ I ¹*'ve been carrying* (carry) this postcard around ²**for / since** days, but I haven't had time to write it. There's lots to tell you!
On our second day here I made friends with a girl called Kirstie, and ³**for / since** then we ⁴___ (go) around together. Right now we're in a café on the beach. We ⁵___ (sit) here ⁶**for / since** hours and I've had two ice creams!
Guess what – I'm learning to dive! I ⁷___ (only learn) ⁸**for / since** a week so I'm just a beginner, but Kirstie's really good. She ⁹___ (dive) ¹⁰**for / since** she was twelve.
How's London? What ¹¹___ (you/do) ¹²**for / since** the last time we spoke?
I'll call soon,
Love, Sophie xxx

Listen

8 🎧 (4 05) **Martin and Emma are at the sports centre. Listen and complete the sentences.**

1 Emma has been playing badminton *since she was about eight.*
2 Martin first played basketball ___ ago, when he was ___.
3 Emma has been a member of the sports centre for about ___.
4 She has been playing hockey since ___.
5 Martin has been playing football since ___.

Speak

9 **Talk about you. Ask and answer in pairs, then tell the class.**
- What's your favourite sport or hobby?
- How did you become interested in it?
- How long have you been doing it?

Write

10 **Look at Exercise 7 again. Imagine you are on holiday. Write a postcard to a friend back home. Say what you and your family and friends have been doing.**

Extra practice

🠖 **For more practice, go to page 105.**

45

Exercise 8
2 ten years, about six 3 six months 4 last May 5 he arrived in the UK

Extra practice
Page 125

eText
📺 **Video and Animation**
Pronunciation:
/ɪə/, /eə/

MOTIVATOR 4b

Extension ▰▰

Pronunciation: /ɪə/ *we're*, /eə/ *where*
Ask Ss to repeat chorally the sentences from Exercise 5b, as quickly as they can. Put Ss in pairs to write their own sentences, using one or both of the sounds as often as possible. Ss should then practise saying their sentences with their partner. This will help reinforce the lack of sound/spelling relationship in English. Ask a few Ss to read theirs aloud and 'teach' the other students.

Exercise 6
1 've been driving 2 Has Tom been doing, hasn't, 's been playing 3 've been standing 4 have you been doing, 've been sorting 5 has Amy been preparing, 's been training 6 Have you been waiting, haven't

Exercise 7
2 for 3 since 4 've been going 5 've been sitting 6 for 7 've only been learning 8 for 9 's been diving 10 since 11 have you been doing 12 since

Phrasal verbs with *look*

Ask the Ss to work in pairs to make up a conversation between two people. They should use two, or if possible three, of the phrasal verbs from Exercise 3 in Lesson 4b. They should try to make the conversation flow as naturally as possible. Monitor the pairs as they work, giving help where necessary.

When Ss are happy with their conversation, they put it down on paper. More confident pairs could then act it out for the class. The rest of the class could vote on whose conversation is the best/sounds the most natural.

Background note

Goths: The Goth subculture began in the UK in the 1980s. Goths like to look dark and mysterious: they often wear black clothes, colour their hair black, and wear white or very pale make-up. Goth music refers to a particular style of rock music which often explores dark themes.

Exercise 1

Luke doesn't like the photo.

4c   She used to be a Goth.

Grammar	*used to*
	Echo questions
Function	Show interest

Dialogue

1 🎧 **Listen and read. Who doesn't like the photo?**

Jodie: Hey, have a look at this. Guess who the girl is.

Martin: I've no idea. Why? Who is she?

Jodie: It's our mum when she was fifteen!

Martin: Is it? Really?

Jodie: Yes. She used to be a Goth.

Martin: Did she? That's so cool.

Luke: Cool? I think it's weird.

Martin: Did she use to wear the make-up and clothes at school?

Jodie: No, she didn't. But she and her friends used to dress up like this at weekends.

Martin: How amazing!

Jodie: Yes, I know. She says it used to take hours to put on her make-up and then take it off again.

Martin: What about your dad?

Jodie: Well, he didn't use to dress up like that. But he was in a band!

Martin: Was he? Wow! Your parents are so interesting!

Luke: Are they? I think they're embarrassing!

Comprehension

2 **Answer the questions in pairs.**

1 Who is the girl in the photo?
Jodie and Luke's mother
2 How old is she in the photo?
3 Did she look like that every day?
4 Who played in a band?
5 What does Martin think about his friends' parents?
6 Does Luke agree?

46

Exercise 2

2 Fifteen
3 No, she didn't, only at weekends.
4 Luke and Jodie's dad was in a band.
5 He thinks they are cool and interesting.
6 No. He thinks they're embarrassing.

Grammar

used to	
Affirmative	
She **used to** be a Goth.	
It **used to** take hours.	
Negative	
He **didn't use to** dress up like that.	
Questions	
Did she **use to** wear the make-up and clothes at school?	
Short answers	
Yes, she **did**./No, she **didn't**.	

Practice

3a **Complete the questions with the correct form of *used to* and the verbs in brackets.**

1 What money _did they use to_ have (they/have) in Italy before the euro?
2 ___ (your grandparents/use) computers at school?
3 What ___ (people/do) before they had mobile phones?
4 ___ (some people/believe) the world was flat, not round?
5 ___ (you/go) to school when you were five?

b **Now match the questions (1–5) in Exercise 4a to the answers (a–e). Then complete the answers.**

_1 – e_

a) Yes, they ___. They were frightened of falling off!
b) No, I ___. I started when I was six.
c) They ___ (use) landlines.
d) No, they ___ (not have) anything like that. Just books!
e) They _used to have_ (have) the lira.

Speak and write

4a **In pairs, talk about you as a child. Use the topics below and *used to/didn't use to*.**

When I was five, I used to love the colour pink. I used to wear pink tops, pink skirts, everything pink but I hate the colour now!

• clothes • food • games • hobbies • TV

b **Now write about your partner.**

When Tomas was little he used to wear the same hat every day.

Grammar

Echo questions	
Affirmative	
A: She used to be a Goth.	B: **Did she?**
A: He was in a band!	B: **Was he?**
A: You look great.	B: **Do I?**
A: We've made dinner.	B: **Have you?**
Negative	
A: I don't like pizza.	B: **Don't you?**
A: They didn't use to like sport.	B: **Didn't they?**
A: She wasn't very nice.	B: **Wasn't she?**
A: He hasn't got up yet.	B: **Hasn't he?**

5 🔊 4 07 **Listen and respond. Complete the echo questions. Then listen and check.**

1 _Have_ I?   4 ___ it?   7 ___ she?
2 ___ we?   5 ___ she?   8 ___ they?
3 ___ it?   6 ___ you?

Pronunciation: Rising intonation (to show interest)

6 🔊 4 08 **Go to page 116.**

Use your English: Show interest

7 🔊 4 09 **Listen and repeat. Then practise the conversation in pairs.**

A: I didn't go online at all last week.
B: Didn't you? Why not?
A: We had no connection.
B: Really? How awful.

Show interest
Echo questions: _Are/Aren't you? Did/Didn't you?_, etc.
Really?
How awful/exciting/amazing …
Why?/Why not?

8 **Practise similar conversations in pairs. Then invent other situations.**

1 I'm going to be on TV tonight. (They're showing the football match I went to.)
2 I need some dollars. (I'm going to New York.)
3 I'm not coming to school tomorrow morning. (I'm going to the dentist's.)

Extra practice

➤ For more practice, go to page 105.   **47**

Extension ◼
used to
Ss work in small groups. Each S thinks of three things to tell the others in their group that they, or someone they know, used to do. Two of the statements should be true and one should be false. The Ss take it in turns to make their statements and guess which are true/untrue. The Ss who are guessing can ask questions to test the 'truth', starting with _Did you use to …?_

Extra practice
Page 125

eText
📹 **Video and Animation**
Grammar: _used to_
Pronunciation: Rising intonation
Use your English: Show interest

MOTIVATOR 4c

Exercise 3a
2 Did your grandparents use to use 3 did people use to do 4 Did some people use to believe 5 Did you use to go

Exercise 3b
2 d) didn't use to have 3 c) used to use 4 a) did 5 b) didn't

Exercise 5
2 Are 3 Isn't 4 Is 5 Won't 6 Can't 7 Is 8 Didn't

Exercise 6a
Interested: 1, 4, 5

Exercise 2

Ned's choices are to do nothing or to tell a teacher.

Exercise 3

2 e) 3 b) 4 a) 5 c)

Exercise 7a

2 excellent – Mr Benson

3 together – Ned

4 copied, the internet – Mr Benson

5 same – Ned

6 understand – Mr Benson

Exercise 8

Chrissy and Ned are going to stay behind after school and repeat the work.

4d Right or wrong?

SKILLS FOCUS: LISTENING AND SPEAKING

REAL LIFE **ISSUE**

Get started

1 When you need some information, which do you prefer to use – a library or the internet? Why? Tell the class.

Read

2 🎧 Read the online problem page. What are Ned's two choices?

IN A FIX?

Here's your chance
to share your problems and say what you think.

Home   About us   Stories

My friend and I often copy stuff from the internet for our homework. Basically we just change some words round to make it look a bit different. I know we shouldn't, but I never really understand why. If the information is correct, why is it wrong to copy it? Anyway, the teachers have caught her, but not me. I actually got a really good mark and she's in big trouble. I don't know how or why it happened because we both use the same websites. We've been doing it for ages! Obviously I've felt a bit bad since it happened, but what can I do? My friend says she won't tell on me and nobody else knows. The thing is, we aren't the only people who do it. I don't really know what to do.

Ned, Oxford

▷ I don't think you should do anything. What's the point? It just means two people get into trouble instead of one. And as you say, everyone does it!   *timbo, Sheffield*

▷ I think you should explain everything to your teacher and talk it through. You shouldn't get into trouble if you're honest about it this time and you don't do it again.   *northernboy, Leeds*

▷ I agree with you, Ned. I don't think it's wrong to copy from the Net. But it IS wrong to abandon your friends! That's why I think you should tell your teacher. Go on, you know I'm right. 😊   *amy15, Lincoln*

48

Extension

Working in the same pairs as in Exercise 9, Ss choose one of the situations A–D. They then improvise a phone conversation between one of the people (Sam, Bella, Frankie or David) and their best friend. They should decide what the person says, the advice the friend might give – and the person's response(s) to that advice.

Monitor the Ss' discussion, giving help as necessary. More confident Ss could act out their phone conversations for the class, sitting on chairs back to back so that the phone chat feels more real.

NEW WORDS
• stuff • basically • copy
• in (big) trouble • obviously
• tell on somebody • nobody else
• the thing is, … • What's the point?
• instead of • as you say
• talk something through • abandon

Comprehension

3 Match the beginnings (1–5) to the correct endings (a–e) to make true sentences.

1 – d

1 Ned's friend has been cheating for some time
2 The teachers have caught her,
3 *timbo* thinks Ned should do nothing,
4 *northernboy* thinks Ned has done wrong
5 *amy15* thinks Ned should do something

a) and he thinks he should tell a teacher.
b) but the other two don't agree.
c) because his friend is in trouble.
d) and Ned has been doing the same.
e) but they haven't caught him.

Speak

4 Ned says, 'If the information is correct, why is it wrong to copy it?' What do you think? Did Ned do anything wrong? What about his friend? Discuss with your partner, then tell the class.

5 Work in pairs. What do you think Ned should do? Why? Tell your partner.

Write

6 Read the advice in Exercise 2 again. Then write your advice to Ned. Give reasons.

I think/don't think you should …

Listen

> **LISTENING TIP:** LISTEN FOR KEY WORDS
> Listen to the words which are stressed. These are the key words and they tell you the most important information.
> Now do Exercise 7.

7a Listen to the conversation. Complete the missing words and say who is speaking (Mr Benson or Ned).

1 You know, the *History* project. *Ned*
2 That was ___.
3 Chrissy and I did it ___.
4 But Chrissy just ___ from ___.
5 I did the ___ thing.
6 Did you ___ it?

b What do you think Mr Benson is going to do?

8 Listen to Ned and Chrissy. What is going to happen tomorrow? Do you think it is fair?

Speak your mind!

> **SPEAKING TIP:** STRESS THE IMPORTANT WORDS
> Try to stress the most important words in each sentence.
> Now do Exercise 9.

9 Work in pairs. Read the situations (A–D) and discuss the questions (1–3). Then tell the class what you think.

A Sam took his friend's homework out of his bag and copied it. His friend didn't know.
B Bella's dad did her Maths homework for her while she was watching TV.
C Frankie showed Jack his exam answers while the teacher wasn't looking.
D David's mother helped him with his Geography homework and checked his work.

1 Who was cheating?
2 Who should get into trouble?
3 Whose behaviour was the worst?

49

Exercise 1

1 hasn't rained, for
2 haven't seen, for
3 has lived, since
4 haven't visited, since

Exercise 2

1 We've been cooking since 4 o'clock.
2 They've been searching for information online for hours.
3 Henry's been playing computer games since lunchtime.
4 Have you been waiting a long time?

Exercise 3

1 used to play 2 did you use to wear
3 didn't use to like
4 used to cry

Exercise 4

1 Are you? 2 Didn't she? 3 Do you?
4 Wasn't it?

Exercise 5

1 made 2 make
3 doing 4 do 5 do
6 made 7 make

Exercise 6

1 after 2 for 3 up
4 forward to

Exercise 7

1 for ages. 2 Don't tell me, 3 Let's just say 4 It's about
5 I'm in! 6 We're on it!

Exercise 8

2 b) 3 g) 4 c) 5 a)
6 f) 7 d)

Grammar (20 marks)

1 Complete with the present perfect simple form of the verbs. Then choose the correct options.

0 My mum *has been* ill (be) for / since last week.
1 It___ (not rain) for / since a week.
2 I___ (not see) him for / since a long time.
3 Anne ___ (live) in her flat for / since July.
4 They ___ (not visit) us for / since my birthday.

.../8

2 Write sentences. Use the present perfect continuous form of the verbs and *for* or *since*.

0 I/save/for a new phone/ages
  I've been saving for a new phone for ages.
1 We/cook/4 o'clock
2 They/search/for information online/hours
3 Henry/playing/computer games/lunchtime
4 you/wait/a long time?

.../4

3 Complete the sentences with the correct form of *used to*.

0 My parents *used to live* (live) in London when they were children.
1 Dad ___ (play) football in school.
2 What ___ (you/wear) when you were eight?
3 I ___ (not like) make-up, but I do now.
4 My brother ___ (cry) a lot when he was a baby.

.../4

4 Write the echo questions for these statements.

0 I've just found some money! *Have you?*
1 We're going on holiday tomorrow!
2 Anna didn't go to school yesterday.
3 I live in Manchester.
4 It wasn't very funny.

.../4

Vocabulary (11 marks)

5 Choose the correct options.

0 Don't make / do a noise.
1 He hasn't made / done a decision yet.
2 I'll make / do an appointment with the vet.
3 In fact, I'm doing / making nothing.
4 I'm going to do / make a course.
5 She should make / do some exercise.
6 My brother made / did a mess in his bedroom.
7 Will you do / make a cake on Friday?

.../7

6 Complete the extracts from a dictionary.

0 look *at* : to turn your eyes towards something or someone in order to see them
1 look ___ : to do things to make sure that someone or something is safe and well (same meaning as *take care of*)
2 look ___ : to use your eyes to find something
3 look ___ : to find information in a book, on a computer, etc.
4 look ___ : to think about something exciting that is going to happen

.../4

Phrases/Use your English (9 marks)

7 Complete with phrases from the box.

• Don't tell me, • We're on it! • Let's just say
• for ages. • I'm in! • It's about • at last!

A: Pete, ⁰*at last!* I've been looking for you ¹___
B: ²___ you've won something!
A: ³___ I've had a bit of luck.
B: Well. Come on, tell me.
A: I'm in the final of an online game. I need help for the second round. ⁴___ sport. Can you help me?
B: Yes! ⁵___
A: Great. ⁶___

.../6

8 Number the lines of the conversation in the correct order.

☐ a) She's the detective. She studied drama.
☐ b) Are you? What are you going to see?
☐ c) Really? Who's she playing?
☐ d) Did you? Why don't you come with me?
1 e) I'm going to the theatre tonight.
☐ f) Did she? I did drama at university, too.
☐ g) *Murder Mystery*, my sister's in the play.

.../3

LISTEN AND CHECK YOUR SCORE	
Grammar	.../20
Vocabulary	.../11
Phrases/Use your English	.../9
Total	**.../40**

50

ROUND-UP 1

ROUND-UP 2

eText

Games

Boat Game

Hangman

Pelmanism

4 Skills Revision

Read

1 Read the text about Anna's Eco School. Find the underlined words. What do they mean?

1 survey – a questionnaire or project

ANNA'S ECO SCHOOL

| ABOUT | BLOG | CONTACT |

At our school we have learnt that everybody can do something to help the environment. My class did a ¹**survey** on how much rubbish we throw away every day. We checked all the rubbish bins in the school. You can't imagine how much waste 2,500 ²**pupils** and 150 teachers can produce! There was far too much plastic, paper and even uneaten food. And all that rubbish went to landfill sites. So we decided to take action!
We ³**set up** a school recycling scheme. Everybody does something, teachers and students. We put plastic boxes with ⁴**stickers** next to the bins in all the classrooms and in the school yard. The stickers tell you what type of rubbish you must put into the boxes. At the end of the week someone from each class empties the boxes. Then we send all the rubbish to a recycling ⁵**plant**. Since we started we have been sending 187 kg less paper to the landfill sites every week! What do you do at your school?

2 Answer true (T), false (F), or doesn't say (DS).

  0 Anna is writing about a school survey. *T*
  1 Anna's class looked at the contents of all the school bins.
  2 All the school rubbish went to a big hole in the ground.
  3 Only the students recycle rubbish.
  4 You get a sticker every time you use a recycling box.
  5 Today, pupils at the school don't throw away food.

Listen

3 🎧 4 14 Listen to a London bus tour guide talking about a famous street, The Strand. Listen for key words and complete the notes.

  0 The Strand is one of London's *oldest* roads.
  1 'Strand' means river ___ in old English.
  2 Today Somerset House is an ___ and ___ centre.
  3 On the left is Waterloo ___.
  4 The Savoy is a ___ for the rich and famous.
  5 There are over ___ theatres in London's West End.

Write

4 Write about a famous street in your country. Write three paragraphs. Start each paragraph with a topic sentence:

  1 The most famous street in town
  2 Things to see and do there
  3 How to get there

NOW I CAN		
Read	identify specific information in a text.	☐
Listen	understand a tour guide and complete notes.	☐
Write	write a short description of a place.	☐

51

Exercise 1
2 students 3 started 4 small pieces of paper you can write on and put onto something 5 a factory

Exercise 2
1 T 2 T 3 F 4 F 5 DS

Exercise 3
1 bank 2 arts, cultural 3 Bridge 4 hotel 5 forty

eText
🖳 Additional video lesson

To watch a vlog about jobs for cash, go to Students' eText, page 31.

For the worksheets and teaching notes go to the Teacher's Resource Materials folder.

Look forward >>>

Ask Ss to work in pairs to talk about what they're wearing and other items they have with them in the classroom such as bags, wallets, smartphones and/ or books. Do they know what materials they are made of? Do they know where any of the items were made?

Pairs then feed back to the rest of the class about their partner, e.g.: *[Sam's] T-shirt is made of cotton. It was made in China.* Ss could also look at the photo on page 52 if they need ideas.

Exercise 1

Luke has bought an old record player and he is going to buy an old record.

Exercise 2

2 the scarves
3 Luke 4 Jodie
5 Martin

Exercise 3

Five pounds

Exercise 4a

cardboard (box), cotton (shirt, etc.), denim (jeans), fur (collar on jacket), leather (jacket), metal (record player), paper (tablecloth), plastic (record player lid), rubber (boots), silk (scarves), silver (bracelets), suede (bag), wool (sweater)

5 AROUND THE WORLD

5a They were made in Thailand.

Grammar Present simple passive
Past simple passive
Vocabulary Materials

Dialogue

1 🔊 5/01 **Listen and read. What has Luke bought and what is he going to buy next?**

The four friends are at a market.

Emma: Let's look at this stall. It's run by my aunt.
Jodie: These scarves are beautiful. What are they made of? Are they cotton?
Emma: No, they're silk. They're made in Thailand.
Jodie: Oh no, what on earth has Luke bought?
Luke: Look at this! It was only a fiver.
Jodie: That's because it's junk. How old is it?
Luke: Well, I think record players like this were produced in the sixties.
Martin: Cool! Things aren't designed to last fifty years these days!
Jodie: True, but does it work? Are the things on sale here checked before they're sold?
Luke: Yes, they are. I asked. They're all tested by an electrician. This one was tested last week.
Martin: Now you need an old record. Have you got any money left?
Luke: Yes, I only spent half of it on this. Come on.

52

Comprehension

2 Answer the questions.

Who or what …
1 wants to look at a stall? *Emma*
2 comes from Thailand?
3 has bought something old?
4 thinks Luke has made a mistake?
5 agrees with Luke?

3 How much money has Luke got left?

Phrases
● Oh no ● what on earth …?
● a fiver ● True, but …

Exercise 4b

Suggested answers:

glass/plastic bottle, cardboard/metal/plastic/wooden box, metal/plastic/wooden chair, denim/fur/leather/ suede/woollen coat, paper envelope, cotton/fur/silk/ suede gloves, denim jeans, gold/metal/silver key, glass/metal/paper/wooden plate, cotton/silk/woollen scarf, cotton/woollen socks, gold/metal/plastic/silver/ wooden spoon, cotton/silk T-shirt

Exercise 6

2 Portuguese is spoken in Brazil.
3 Koala bears are found in Australia.
4 Silk is produced in Thailand.
5 Kimonos are worn in Japan.

Exercise 7

2 The first man was sent into space in 1961.
3 The Pyramids were built thousands of years ago.
4 The *Mona Lisa* wasn't painted by Picasso.
5 The first Olympic Games were held in Greece.
6 *Hamlet* wasn't written by JK Rowling.

Vocabulary: Materials

4a 🎧 **Listen and repeat. Which of these materials can you see in the photo?**

cardboard

> • cardboard • cotton • denim • fur • glass
> • gold • leather • metal • paper • plastic
> • rubber • silk • silver • suede
> • wood (*adj* wooden) • wool (*adj* woollen)

b **What other things can you see or think of?**

rubber boots, plastic plates, leather gloves

Pronunciation: /kl/ clothes, /pl/ player

5 🎧 **Go to page 117.**

Grammar

Present simple passive	Past simple passive
Affirmative	
It**'s run** by my aunt. They**'re** all **tested**.	It **was tested** last week. Record players **were produced** in the sixties.
Negative	
It **isn't made** of cotton. They **aren't sold** here.	It **wasn't tested**. They **weren't made** in Italy.
Questions	
What**'s** it **made** of? **Are** they **checked**?	When **was** it **tested**? **Were** they **tested**?
Short answers	
Yes, they **are**. No, they **aren't**.	Yes, they **were**. No, they **weren't**.

Note

When we want to say who or what causes an action, we use *by* + noun: *It's/was run **by** my aunt.*

Practice

6 **Write sentences from the prompts in the present simple passive.**

1 coffee/grow/Kenya
   Coffee is grown in Kenya.
2 Portuguese/speak/Brazil
3 koala bears/found/Australia
4 silk/produce/Thailand
5 kimonos/wear/Japan

7 **Rewrite the sentences in the past simple passive.**

1 Sir Walter Raleigh brought potatoes to Europe.
   Potatoes were brought to Europe by Sir Walter Raleigh.
2 They sent the first man into space in 1961.
3 They built the Pyramids thousands of years ago.
4 Picasso did not paint the *Mona Lisa*.
5 They held the first Olympic Games in Greece.
6 JK Rowling did not write *Hamlet*.

8 **Read the conversations, then complete them. Write the present or past simple passive form of the verbs, or short answers.**

1 A: What*'s your hat made* (your hat/make) of?
   B: Cotton, I think.
2 A: Where in Greece ___ (that photo/take)?
   B: It ___ (not take) in Greece. We were in Spain.
3 A: When ___ (this film/make)?
   B: About five years ago.
4 A: How much ___ (you/pay) for this job?
   B: I ___ (not pay) anything. I'm a volunteer.
5 A: ___ (your rubbish/collect) every week?
   B: Yes, it ___. They collect it every Monday.

Speak and write

9a **Think about an object that is in your home. Choose from the box, or use your own ideas. Don't tell your partner what it is. Then ask and answer in pairs. Can your partner guess?**

> • a table or chair • a radio • a carpet
> • a clock • a bike • a mirror • a toy

> • What's it made of?
> • When/Where was it made?
> • Where is it kept?
> • How often is it used?

b **Write sentences about your object. Change partners. Can he or she guess?**

It's made of wood. It was made about fifty years ago but I don't know …

Extra practice

▶ For more practice, go to page 105.

53

They can start another round with a different short passive sentence.

Extra practice Page 125

eText
📺 Video and Animation

Grammar: Present simple passive and past simple passive

Pronunciation: /kl/, /pl/

MOTIVATOR 5a

Exercise 8

2 was that photo taken, wasn't taken
3 was this film made 4 are you paid, 'm not paid
5 Is your rubbish collected, is

Extension ▰▰▰

Present simple/past simple passive

In small groups, Ss take turns trying to add to a short passive sentence like *The T-shirts were sold*, e.g. to *The T-shirts were sold on a market stall,* then *The T-shirts were sold on a market stall in London*, etc. They can add ideas but they can't change what the first S says. If the last S in the chain gives up or forgets the previous sentence, the person who spoke before them wins that round.

Materials/
Present simple
passive

Ss work in pairs.
Each S thinks of
something they
can see in the
classroom, or an
item from the photo
of the market stall
in Lesson 5a. Their
partner has to
guess the object
using only *Yes/No*
questions, e.g.:
*Is it made of
cotton? Is it red?*

Exercise 2
Because the pilot
lost control of the
balloon.

Exercise 3
2 F 3 T 4 DS 5 F 6 F

Exercise 4
2 take off 3 trip
4 push 5 slip 6 sink
7 lift 8 float

Exercise 6
2 could/was able
to 3 were able to
4 couldn't/wasn't
able to 5 could/
was able to 6 was
able to

Exercise 7
2 in the north of
England 3 £2 4 his
name and address
5 the south of
France 6 his
balloon on a beach
7 His balloon won
the competition.

5b I couldn't sleep.

Grammar Past ability: *could* and *was/were able to*
Vocabulary Verbs of action

Get started

1 Would you like to go up in a
   hot-air balloon? Why?/Why not?
   Tell the class.

Read

2 🔊 5 04 Listen and read Julia's story.
   Why was she frightened?

Comprehension

3 **Answer true (T), false (F) or doesn't say (DS).**

   1 Julia went in the hot-air balloon with her parents
      and her aunt. *F*
   2 The ride was noisy all the time.
   3 The weather changed.
   4 There was something wrong with the balloon.
   5 They landed well.
   6 She definitely wants to do it again.

Write a story that begins 'I'll never forget … '

I'll never forget the day I went up in a hot-air balloon. It
was a birthday present from my aunt. She knows I like
adventures! Well, it was certainly that!

I had to get up really early, but it wasn't a problem – I
couldn't sleep anyway, I was so excited!

My parents and my aunt came to watch. They waved as I
got into the balloon. There were five other passengers and
the pilot, of course! When we took off it was quite noisy
and I couldn't hear anything except the roar of the flames.
Then it became much quieter. I can't describe the feeling.
It was like a dream. The sky was bright blue and clear.
Everything was calm. I could see all the people below us.
They were getting smaller and smaller as we floated
higher and higher.

Then the storm began! It came from nowhere. The balloon
dropped suddenly and it started raining hard. The pilot
decided to land as quickly as possible, but he couldn't
control the balloon. The wind was carrying us towards the
sea. I'm telling you, it was very scary!

Luckily, the wind changed direction and we were finally
able to land in the middle of a field. There was an
enormous bump as we hit the ground and I fell out of the
basket. We were all a bit shocked, but luckily nobody was
hurt. I was able to walk back to my family and show them
I was OK.

Was I frightened? Yes, very. Will I ever do it again? Not sure!

Julia Brooke

54

Extension ▰▰▰

could and *was able to*
Ask the Ss to write (on card or a slip of paper) one
true statement about themselves to describe things
they could or couldn't do when they were young, e.g.:
When I was eight I could swim 50 metres.
*When I was at primary school I couldn't speak French,
but I can now.*

Collect and redistribute the papers so that each S has
a statement, but at this stage they don't know who
has written it. Ss then mingle and find the person who
made the statement by asking questions.

Finally, Ss report back to the class, e.g. *When Sasha
was eight she could …*

Vocabulary: Verbs of action

4 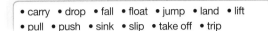 Listen and repeat. Then match the pictures (1–8) to the verbs in the box. There are five extra words.

- carry • drop • fall • float • jump • land • lift
- pull • push • sink • slip • take off • trip

drop

5 Work in pairs. Take turns to mime verbs in Exercise 4. What's your partner doing?

A: *You're lifting something.*
B: *Yes. OK, your turn. You've dropped your phone.*

Grammar

could and was/were able to
Affirmative
General ability
I **could/was able to** see all the people.
Specific event
We **were able to** land in the middle of a field.
Negative
General ability and specific event
I **couldn't/wasn't able to** sleep.
He **couldn't/wasn't able to** control the balloon.
Questions
Could you sleep?
Was he **able to** control it?
Short answers
Yes, I **could**./No, I **couldn't**.
Yes, he **was**./No, he **wasn't**.

Practice

6 Choose the correct options. If both are correct, circle both.

1 Last Sunday I lost my key but I **could / was able to** climb through a window.
2 Mozart **could / was able to** read and write music when he was four.
3 We used a satnav so we **could / were able to** find the right place.
4 The singer had a sore throat so he **couldn't / wasn't able to** perform.
5 My grandmother **could / was able to** cook and sew when she was ten.
6 It was dark, but I **could / was able to** open the door.

Listen

7  Listen to the story and answer the questions in pairs. Then listen and check.

1 When did this story happen?
last summer
2 Where does Thomas live?
3 How much did a balloon cost?
4 What did Thomas write down?
5 Where did he go on holiday?
6 What did he find and where was it?
7 What was his second surprise?

Write

8 Now write the story. Use your answers from Exercise 7 to help you. Remember to use linking words (*and*, *but*, *however* and *then*).

> The Grand Balloon Race
> Last summer, Thomas Clark went to a summer fair ...

Extra practice

▷ For more practice, go to page 106.

55

Extra practice
Page 126

MOTIVATOR 5b

eText
😊 Video and Animation

Grammar: Past ability, *could* and *was/were able to*

Verbs of action

Divide the class
into two teams to
play a simple game
of charades. Make
game cards with
verbs of action and
an object. Ask one
S to take a card
(without showing it)
and act out in mime
what the card says,
e.g. *lift a heavy
suitcase, fall off a
ladder.*
The first S to guess
the answer scores
a point for their
team and picks up
the next card to
mime the action.

Background notes

Plato (c 428–348
BCE): A famous
philosopher and
mathematician
from ancient
Greece. Plato's
best-known work
is the *Republic*, in
which he sets out
his ideas for good
government. He set
up the Academy in
Athens, probably
the first institution
of higher education
in the Western
world.

**Loch Ness
monster:** A large,
mysterious creature
which is said to live
in Loch Ness, one
of the largest and
deepest lochs (or
lakes) in Scotland.
The existence
(or otherwise) of
'Nessie' has never
been conclusively
proved.

5c Plato, who was born in Athens, …

Grammar	Non-defining relative clauses: *who, whose, which, where*
Vocabulary	Landscape and environment
Function	Give and react to opinions

Read

1 🔊 5/07 **Listen and read the article. Choose the best title:**

A Fact or Fiction?
B Adventures under the sea
C Stories from long ago

Everyone's heard of the Loch Ness Monster, which is supposed to live at the bottom of a long, deep lake (a 'loch') in Scotland. Some people believe in it, some don't. Here are two more 'underwater mysteries' … what do you think?

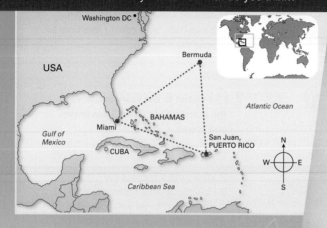

The Bermuda Triangle

This area of the Atlantic Ocean, which covers the area between Bermuda, Miami and Puerto Rico, is famous for the mysterious disappearance of more than 1,000 sailors and pilots. In 1945, five American aeroplanes took off but never landed. A sixth plane, which was sent to find them, also disappeared.
Some people say that hurricanes, which are common in this region, were the cause. Others think something in this area affected the pilots' compasses. Some even say that the pilots, whose planes were never found, were taken by aliens.

THE LOST CITY OF ATLANTIS

About 2,500 years ago the Greek philosopher and writer Plato, who was born in Athens, described a wonderful island city. There were fantastic buildings, fountains with hot and cold water and statues made of gold. The city, which was called Atlantis, was surrounded by five rings of water. Ships passed from the harbour through tunnels to the centre, where a fantastic palace stood on a hill.
Plato says that Atlantis sank into the sea. It's possible – perhaps there was a huge tsunami – but where is the evidence? There have been many 'discoveries' of Atlantis, but they have all been false. Maybe it will always be a mystery.

Comprehension

2 **Match the beginnings (1–6) to the correct endings (a–f).**

1 – e

1 A *loch* is
2 Ships and planes have disappeared in
3 Some people think the pilots were carried away in
4 Atlantis was on
5 In the centre of Atlantis was
6 Atlantis disappeared into

a) spaceships.
b) the sea.
c) an island.
d) the Bermuda Triangle.
e) a Scottish lake.
f) a palace.

56

UFOs: There have been many sightings of UFOs (unidentified flying objects) since the mid twentieth century. To date, none of these sightings have been identified as objects known to humans, but many people believe in their existence as evidence of extraterrestrial life.

Exercise 1

A

Exercise 2

2 d) 3 a) 4 c) 5 f) 6 b)

Vocabulary: Landscape and environment

3a **Recall** What landscape words do you know? Check the Word bank on page 112.

lake, island, …

b  **Extension Listen and repeat. Then use words from the box to complete the sentences. There are three extra words.**

- bush • cliff • coastline
- desert • harbour • hill
- path • rock • stream • valley
- waterfall • wood(s)

1 From the top of the *cliff* you can see the beach and the sea.
2 We walked through the ___ to learn the names of the trees.
3 There's a small village in the ___ between the two mountains.
4 We sailed out of the ___ and followed the island's ___.
5 It doesn't often rain in a ___.
6 Walk along that little ___ until you get to the cottage.
7 Near our house there's a small ___ that runs into the river.
8 We swam out to a big ___ and then sat on it to sunbathe.

Grammar

Non-defining relative clauses: who, whose, which, where

Plato, **who** was born in Athens, described a wonderful island city.
The pilots, **whose** planes were never found, were taken by aliens.
A sixth plane, **which** was sent to find them, also disappeared.
Ships passed from the harbour through tunnels to the centre, **where** a fantastic palace stood.

Choose the correct option.

We use non-defining relative clauses to give **essential / extra** information.

Practice

4 **Add the extra information using *who, whose, which* or *where*. Remember the commas.**

1 Every year thousands of tourists visit Loch Ness. (They hope to see the monster there.)
Every year thousands of tourists visit Loch Ness, where they hope to see the monster.
2 Many people are frightened of the Bermuda Triangle. (It's an area of the Atlantic Ocean.)
3 People think the pilots lost their way. (They were training.)
4 Plato wrote about Atlantis thousands of years ago. (His books are read all over the world.)
5 Some people believe that a tsunami destroyed Atlantis. (It's a huge wave.)

Use your English: Give and react to opinions

5  **Listen and repeat. Then practise the conversation in pairs.**

A: In my opinion, the Loch Ness Monster is just a stupid story.
B: I don't agree. I think it's possible. We don't know everything!
A: I know, but nobody's seen it. I think the photos are fakes.
B: Well, I'm not sure. I think there's something there. And I love reading the stories about it.

Give opinions
I (don't) think …
In my opinion, …
I love/can't stand …

React to opinions: agree
I know, …
Yes, you're right/that's true.
I agree.
I think so, too.

React to opinions: disagree
I don't think so.
(I'm afraid/sorry, but) I don't agree/I disagree.
I know/see what you mean, but …
Actually, I think you're wrong.

6 **Work in pairs. Discuss the statements. One agree and the other disagree.**

1 I don't think the Bermuda Triangle exists.
2 I think some stories about UFOs are true.

Extra practice

▶ **For more practice, go to page 106.**

Extension ▮▮
Landscape and environment
Write *Landscape and environment* on the board. In pairs, Ss write down eight words connected with landscape and environment. Then put two pairs together and get each pair to take it in turns to describe their words. They mustn't use the actual words. The other pair has to guess the words.

Extra practice
Page 126

eText
🖥 Video and Animation
Use your
English: Give and react to opinions

MOTIVATOR 5c

Exercise 3b
2 wood(s) 3 valley 4 harbour, coastline 5 desert 6 path
7 stream 8 rock

Grammar
extra

Exercise 4
2 Many people are frightened of the Bermuda Triangle, which is an area of the Atlantic Ocean.
3 People think the pilots, who were training, lost their way.
4 Plato, whose books are read all over the world, wrote about Atlantis thousands of years ago.
5 Some people believe that a tsunami, which is a huge wave, destroyed Atlantis.

Exercise 1
a) 3 b) 1 c) 2

Exercise 2
1 d) 2 a) 3 c)

Exercise 3
2 F 3 DS 4 F 5 DS
6 T

Exercise 5
2 stalactites
3 orchestra 4 boat
5 torches 6 need

ACROSS CULTURES

5d   Wonders of nature

SKILLS FOCUS: **READING**

Get started

1 **Look at the photos (1–3) and answer the question.**

Which photo shows:
a) caves?   b) a waterfall?   c) a mountain?

Read

> **READING TIP:** HOW TO MATCH
> SENTENCES TO GAPS IN THE TEXT
> Look for words in the sentences that match
> the words in the text. Then read the sentences
> before and after the gap in the text.
> Now do Exercise 2.

2 (5/10) **Read the article and complete it with the sentences (a–d). There is one extra sentence. Then listen and check.**

a) This strange animal, which looks like a guinea pig, is also known as a rock rabbit.
b) The valley, which is ten kilometres long, has many streams and woods.
c) When you enter, light comes from millions of glow worms on the ceiling of the cave.
d) On the way up, you can dive into the pools or take photos of water falling around you.

Comprehension

3 **Read the article. Answer true (T), false (F) or doesn't say (DS).**

1 The Dunn's River Falls are on the coast. *T*
2 You can walk up the Dunn's River Falls without help.
3 Table Mountain has 2,200 species of wild flowers.
4 The 'dassie' is only found on Table Mountain.
5 There are millions of bats inside the Waitomo Glowworm caves.
6 Glow worms generate light to get something to eat.

> **NEW** WORDS
> • end up   • on your own   • slippy
> • hand in hand   • chain   • overlook
> • endangered species   • cave   • stalactite
> • stalagmite   • luminous   • torch
> • glow worm   • creatures   • regret

58

Wonders of NATURE to visit ▶

Extension ▮▮▮

When the Ss have completed their project in Exercise 6, they could work in small groups to find out about the different landscape feature that each S has chosen. In their groups they should decide which landscape feature is the most interesting and the one that they would recommend to visitors.

Monitor Ss as they talk, giving help where needed. Groups present their chosen landscape feature to the rest of the class. Finally, the class could vote on the one they would most like to visit.

Nicole

Dunn's River Falls is our wonder of nature in Jamaica. The falls are like giant rock steps that end up in the Caribbean Sea. You can climb up them, but not on your own because they're very slippy! You have to go up hand in hand and make a long human chain. It's great fun! Special shoes are provided to help you walk through the water. ¹___ The Falls are really beautiful, but it's not just tourists who visit. Scenes from *Dr No*, which was the first ever James Bond movie, were filmed here.

Kevin

Did you know that Table Mountain was made one of the *New Seven Wonders of Nature* in 2011? Table Mountain is the famous flat-topped mountain that overlooks my home town, Cape Town, in South Africa. It's also a national park with a large number of plants and animals. Five of the world's most poisonous snakes are found here. But don't worry, they're rarely seen! If you're lucky, another animal you can see is the 'dassie', which is only found in Africa. ²___ Years ago you could also find leopards on the mountain, but now they are an endangered species in South Africa.

Irene

I love the Waitomo Glowworm Caves, which are one of New Zealand's most amazing natural wonders. They were formed over 30 million years ago and are famous for stalactites and stalagmites and for their luminous worms. Yes, luminous! You won't need a candle or a torch inside the cave. ³___ These small creatures make light to attract insects for food. It's weird! Take a guided tour and experience this amazing wonder of nature – you won't regret it!

Speak

4 **In pairs, answer the questions.**

1 Which of the places in the photos would you most like to visit?
2 Which of the places is the most scary or the most dangerous? Why?
3 What natural landscape features can you find in your country?
4 Is there a place in your country that could be a *New Natural Wonder of Nature*?

Listen

5 🔊 **Read the tour brochure for the Glowworm caves. Guess the missing words in the text. Then listen and complete (1–6).**

New Zealand Tours for Teens:
WAITOMO CAVES

Discover a secret underground world on our guided tour.

CATHEDRAL
We will walk through underground tunnels to the Cathedral. The Cathedral, which is the biggest ¹*cave*, has huge stalagmites and ²___. It's enormous inside and the acoustics are incredible. On one occasion, a whole symphony ³___ was able to perform here!

GLOWWORM CAVES
Next we will take an underground ⁴___ trip along the Waitomo River. It's mysterious, but it's also dark and wet inside – we'll provide ⁵___ and waterproof jackets. Next, we will enter the Glowworm Caves. You don't ⁶___ your torches here! Above your head there will be millions of glow worms, which light the way.

Project

6 **Do a project about a landscape feature in your country. Answer the questions. Download a photo of it from the internet.**

- What is the feature?
- Where is it?
- Why did you choose it?
- What is it like?
- What can you do/see there?

Mount Etna is a volcano in Sicily …

59

Exercise 1

2 that 3 then 4 Next
5 After 6 Then
7 Finally 8 before

Exercise 2

2 F 3 T 4 DS 5 F 6 T

5e   A day out

SKILLS FOCUS: WRITING A BLOG

Get ready to write

1 **Read the blog and complete it with the correct words.**

> • After • before • Next • Finally • first • that
> • then • Then

This is MANDY'S BLOG

Monday 13th June

Last Saturday was my friend Jack's birthday. A group of us went with him and his parents to the seaside. It was an awesome day.

¹*First*, we went for a walk along the pier. We could see the sea through the gaps in the wood under our feet. It was a weird feeling.

After ²__ we went to a fun fair and had a ride on a gigantic rollercoaster. It's 60 metres high! While we were queuing I got really scared – I think Jack did, too – and when it was our turn his mum couldn't even watch! The train carried us up quite slowly – and ³__ WHAM we dropped straight down. It was terrifying, but also amazing fun. I wanted to do it again, but the queue was too long.

⁴__ we went on a water ride round a big lake. That was brilliant, too. We got very wet, but luckily it wasn't a cold day!

⁵__ that we were quite hungry, so we went into a park and had a picnic.⁶ __ we all went for a walk along the beach.

⁷__, it was time to go home, but ⁸__ that we went shopping. I just bought a cap for my brother. It was one of my best days ever.

2 **Answer true (T), false (F) or doesn't say (DS).**

1 The friends had a day out to celebrate Mandy's birthday. *F*
2 They took a boat out to sea.
3 She thought the rollercoaster was scary.
4 It was a sunny day.
5 They had a picnic on the beach.
6 She took a present home.

60

WRITING TIP: A NARRATIVE

When writing a narrative, use sequencers *first, then, next, after (that)/afterwards, before (that), finally*. This helps the reader understand the order of events.

Note

We went climbing and ~~next~~ then we had lunch.
First, we went climbing. Next, we had lunch.

Write

3a **Think about a day out which you really enjoyed. Use the ideas below to help you. Make notes.**

1 A wildlife park (a safari drive/the animals/lunch in the café/an exhibition)
2 The beach (swimming/bat and ball game/picnic lunch/sunbathing/the weather)
3 The mountains (skiing or hiking/lunch by a lake/taking photos)
4 Caves (guided tour/boat trip/gift shop)

b **Now write a blog, describing the day. Use the guide below and remember to use sequencers.**

- Opener: Say when the trip was, where you went and who you went with.
- Main narrative (one or more paragraphs): Describe what you did, what you enjoyed the most and what was not so good.
- Ending: Say how you felt at the end of the day.

Last summer I went with my friends to …

5 Language Revision

Grammar (13 marks)

1 Complete the sentences so they mean the same. Use a correct form of the passive.

0 Shakespeare wrote *Hamlet*.
Hamlet <u>was written</u> by Shakespeare.
1 Einstein didn't discover the first antibiotic.
The first antibiotic ___ by Einstein.
2 They didn't grow grapes in England in the past.
In the past, grapes ___ in England.
3 Volunteers run the charity shop.
The charity shop ___ by volunteers.
4 They checked passports at the border.
Passports ___ at the border.
5 People make shoes out of leather.
Shoes ___ of leather. .../5

2 Complete the sentences with the correct form of *could* or *was able to*.

0 Sorry I *couldn't/wasn't able to* come to the picnic.
1 She was clever. She ___ write by the age of three.
2 ___ they ___ reach the top of the mountain?
3 Tony took a map, so he ___ find the hotel later.
4 When I was young I ___ ski, but now I can. .../4

3 Choose the correct options.

0 Mount Everest, <u>b</u> is the highest mountain in the world, is 8,848 metres high.
a) who   b) which   c) where
1 David Berry, ___ is from London, is an artist.
a) whose   b) where   c) who
2 Javier Bardem, ___ uncle was a film director, is a famous actor.
a) who's   b) who   c) whose
3 The Niagara Falls, ___ are three waterfalls, are on the US and Canadian border.
a) who   b) which   c) where
4 Jamaica, ___ the sun often shines, is a top tourist destination.
a) where   b) whose   c) which   .../4

Vocabulary (18 marks)

4 Complete the words to make materials.

0 pa*per* plates
1 pl ___ bottle
2 su ___ shoes
3 wo ___ table
4 le ___ jacket
5 ca ___ box
6 co ___ shirt   .../6

5 Match the first half of a word in A to the second half in B to make landscape words.

0 – e

A	*0 str* 1 val 2 bu 3 co 4 vol 5 hi 6 isl 7 water 8 for
B	a) fall b) sh c) and d) ley *e) eam* f) ll g) cano h) est i) ast

.../8

6 Circle the word that is different.

0 (valley) climb jump drop
1 bush harbour skip path
2 push design pull lift
3 drop fall invite dive
4 survive trip slip jump   .../4

Phrases/Use your English (9 marks)

7 Complete with phrases from the box.

• Oh no!   • a fiver.   • True, but

Adam: 0*What* are you wearing? It's so unusual.
Brenda: 1___ many women wear them. It's Indian and it's made of silk.
Adam: How much did it cost?
Brenda: A thousand pounds.
Adam: 2___ That's very expensive.
Brenda: Ha ha, I'm joking. It only cost 3___   .../3

8 Complete the conversation.

A: I hate fast food. I 0*think* it's bad for you.
B: You're 1___. It isn't healthy, but it is nice.
A: I don't think 2___. I never eat it.
B: Sorry, 3___ I'm sure I've seen you eating a burger in the café down the road!
A: 4___, but I've only done it once. Never again!
B: I know what you 5___ – their food isn't great.
A: That's 6___. In fact, it's disgusting.   .../6

5 12	LISTEN AND CHECK YOUR SCORE	
Grammar		.../13
Vocabulary		.../18
Phrases/Use your English		.../9
Total		**.../40**

61

Exercise 7
1 True, but 2 Oh no!
3 a fiver.

Exercise 8
1 right 2 so 3 but
4 Yes 5 mean 6 true

ROUND-UP 1

ROUND-UP 2

eText
 Games

Boat Game

Hangman

Pelmanism

Exercise 1
1 wasn't discovered 2 weren't grown 3 is run 4 were checked 5 are made

Exercise 2
1 could/was able to 2 Were, able to 3 could/was able to 4 couldn't/wasn't able to

Exercise 3
1 c) 2 c) 3 b) 4 a)

Exercise 4
1 plastic 2 suede 3 wood/wooden 4 leather
5 cardboard 6 cotton

Exercise 5
1 d) valley 2 b) bush 3 i) coast 4 g) volcano 5 f) hill
6 c) island 7 a) waterfall 8 h) forest

Exercise 6
1 skip 2 design 3 invite 4 survive

Ask if any Ss have
had a holiday in the
UK and what they
remember about it.
They tell a partner
where they stayed
and what they did.
Ss who have not
visited the UK can
tell their partner
why they would like
to go there, and if
there is anything
they think they
won't like (e.g. the
weather).
Ss can feed back
to the rest of the
class on anything
interesting or
unusual that their
partner told them.

Background notes

**Buckingham
Palace:** See
Background note
for Welcome
Lesson c.

The London Eye:
A huge Ferris wheel
with 32 'pods'
or capsules for
passengers. It was
opened on the
South Bank of the
River Thames at
the beginning of
the millennium and
is one of London's
most popular
tourist attractions.

West End show:
See Background
notes for Lesson
1a.

6 THINGS TO REMEMBER

6a It might snow.

Grammar	*will/won't/may/might* for predictions
Vocabulary	Holidays
Function	Reminders, promises and offers

🧳 LEISURE TIME
Holidays in the UK

Are you taking a tent, staying in a country cottage or relaxing in a five-star hotel? Make sure you read our travellers' tips!

I'm not sure about the weather. What clothes should I pack?
You don't say when you are going, but you can be sure the weather will be different every day. It'll probably rain, so take an umbrella and take some comfortable shoes for sightseeing. In the summer, you'll need sunglasses and sun cream, but take a jumper, too because it might not be very warm in the evenings. In the winter, you might have sunny days, but it will be cold and it may even snow. ➡

It sounds boring, but British people love talking about the weather. Conversations often include phrases like 'It's a lovely day, isn't it?' or even 'Nice weather for ducks!' So, if you want to start a conversation there's always something to discuss!

My family and I are staying in a B & B. What will the food be like?
'B & B' means 'bed and breakfast'. You won't get lunch or an evening meal, but you'll enjoy a good breakfast, usually a choice between 'continental' or 'full English'. You certainly won't be hungry after a 'full English' of eggs, sausages, beans, tomatoes and mushrooms, as well as toast and marmalade! ➡

A lot of cafés offer 'All day breakfast' on their menus. As well as the eggs, sausages, etc. look out for something called 'bubble and squeak'– it's fried cabbage and mashed potato!

Read

1 🔊 6 01 Listen and read the travel webpage. What's a 'B & B'?

Comprehension

2 **Choose the correct options.**
1 British weather [often] / sometimes changes.
2 You **should take / won't need** warm clothes in the summer.
3 British people are usually **interested in / bored with** the weather.
4 In the UK it's possible to have a 'full English' **in the morning / at any time.**

Vocabulary: Holidays

3a **Recall** **Name as many holiday activities as you can remember. Then check the Word bank on page 112.**

go sightseeing, ...

b 🔊 6 02 **Extension** **Listen and repeat. Which words can you see in the photos (1–3)? Where would you like to stay?**

cottage

- B & B (bed and breakfast) • campsite
- caravan • cottage • (self-catering) flat
- hostel • hotel • motor home • tent
- villa

62

Exercise 1
'B & B' is a bed and breakfast.

Exercise 2
2 should take 3 interested in 4 at any time

Exercise 3b
B & B (bed and breakfast), campsite, caravan, cottage, tent

Exercise 4
2 won't go 3 will need 4 may/might stay 5 may/might go 6 will visit 7 may not/might not be 8 may/might have 9 will spend 10 won't have 11 may/might manage

Exercise 5b
1 English, mushroom, special, station, cash, machine
2 casual, measure, unusual

Grammar

will/won't/may/might for predictions

Affirmative

It **will be** cold. (definite)

It **may/might** snow. (possible)

Negative

You certainly **won't be** hungry. (definite)

It **may/might not be** very warm. (possible)

Note

We often use these adverbs with *will* or *won't*: *certainly/definitely, probably, perhaps/maybe*

Practice

4 Read about tourists in the UK and complete the sentences with *will* (✓), *won't* (✗), *may/might* (?) or *may not/might not* (? ✗) and a verb from the boxes.

• go (x 2) • need • stay • visit

Next year, about twenty-eight million tourists ¹*will visit* (✓) the UK. Some ²___ (✗) to London of course but many of them ³___ (✓) accommodation in the capital city. These tourists ⁴___ (?) in one of the many London hotels, or they ⁵___ (?) to a B & B or a hostel.

• be • have (x 2) • manage • spend
• visit

A lot of them ⁶___ (✓) famous places like Buckingham Palace, although the royal family ⁷___ (? ✗) there. They ⁸___ (?) a ride on the London Eye and perhaps they ⁹___ (✓) time in one of the museums. They certainly ¹⁰___ (✗) enough time to do everything, but they ¹¹___ (?) to go to a concert or a West End show.

Pronunciation: /ʒ/ leisure, /ʃ/ shoes

5 (6 03) Go to page 117.

Speak

6 Work in pairs. Ask and answer about the future. Use the prompts and *will, won't* and *may/might (not)*.

1 What/watch/on TV tonight?
   A: *What will you watch on TV tonight?*
   B: *I think I'll watch …, but I might watch … What about you?*
2 What/wear/tomorrow?
3 go out/on Saturday?
4 do/any housework at the weekend?
5 go/shopping at the weekend?

Use your English: Reminders, promises and offers

7 (6 04) Listen and repeat. Then practise the conversation in pairs.

A: Don't forget to pack your passport. Remember, we won't have much time in the morning.

B: It's OK. I won't forget it.

A: And make sure you set your alarm. I'll do it for you if you like.

B: Don't worry. There's no need. I'll set it in a minute.

Reminders

Don't forget to pack your passport.

Remember, we won't have much time in the morning.

Make sure you set your alarm.

Promises

Don't worry. I will/I won't.

It's OK. I'll remember.

I promise I won't forget.

Offers

I'll do it for you if you like.

Shall I call you?

Would you like me to call you?

Responses

Yes, please. That would be great.

Don't worry. There's no need.

8 Work in pairs. Practise similar conversations. Use the prompts or your own ideas.

Reminders: we're going on holiday/to a party …

Offers: lend you my camera/give you a lift …

Extra practice

For more practice, go to page 107.

Extension ▰▰▰

Pronunciation: /ʒ/ leisure, /ʃ/ shoes

Say the words from Exercise 5a and b in random order. Ask Ss to raise their left or right hand according to the sound that they hear.

Extra practice

Page 127

eText

🔲 Video and Animation

Grammar: *will/won't/may/might* for predictions

Pronunciation: /ʒ/, /ʃ/

Use your English: Reminders, promises and offers

MOTIVATOR 6a

Holidays

Ss play a game in groups about what they did on holiday. The first S makes a sentence, starting with *On my holiday, I …* Each S in the group then adds one more holiday phrase or activity, continuing for as long as they can.

Demonstrate the game first with one or two Ss, e.g.:

Teacher: *On my holiday, I went camping.*

Student A: *On my holiday, I went camping and windsurfing.*

Student B: *On my holiday, I went camping and windsurfing and I stayed in a tent.*

For less confident Ss who need help with the vocabulary, you could write the holiday vocabulary from Exercise 3b and the Word bank on page 111 on the board.

6b If she's here, we'll invite her.

Grammar First conditional with *if/unless*
will future with *when/as soon as*

Vocabulary Adjectives with prefixes: *un-, in-* and *im-*

Dialogue

1 🔊 6 05 **Listen and read. Why do they want to hide the list?**

Jodie:	What time's Martin coming?
Emma:	He'll be here at four unless he gets lost again!
Jodie:	Unlikely, but not impossible, knowing him! Right, who else shall we invite to his surprise party?
Luke:	What about his friend, Sophie?
Jodie:	Why? Is she coming over from the States? I didn't know that.
Luke:	Yes, she is, but I'm not sure when exactly. She'll probably come when her school breaks up.
Jodie:	Well, if she's here for his birthday, we'll invite her, obviously.

The doorbell buzzes.

Emma:	Oh no, that's him! He's twenty minutes early. That's a bit inconvenient! Hi, come on up … Quick, hide the list, or he'll see it as soon as he walks in … Hi! How are you doing?
Martin:	Hey guys, what's up? You look a bit uncomfortable, Jodie. Are you OK?

Phrases

• knowing (him) • who else • obviously
• that's (him)! • come on up • Quick
• How are you doing?

64

Exercise 1

Because they are planning a surprise party for Martin.

Exercise 2

2 DS 3 T 4 DS 5 T 6 F

Exercise 3

Twenty minutes to four.

Exercise 4

2 If, say 3 If, brings 4 won't know, unless 5 When, knocks 6 'll jump, as soon as 7 'll be, when 8 When, is

Comprehension

2 Answer true (T), false (F) or doesn't say (DS).

1 Luke, Emma and Jodie are planning a party for Martin. *T*
2 Emma thinks Martin will get lost again.
3 Sophie is going to visit Martin.
4 Martin is usually on time.
5 They are surprised when he arrives.
6 Martin sees the list immediately.

SOLVE IT!

3 What time does Martin get to Emma's flat?

Grammar

First conditional with *if/unless*

If she**'s** here, we**'ll invite** her.
He**'ll be** here at four **unless** he **gets** lost.

will* future with *when/as soon as

She**'ll** probably **come when** her school **breaks up**.
He**'ll** see it **as soon as** he **walks** in.

Practice

4 Complete the sentences with the correct form of the verbs and choose the correct options.

1 We *'ll have* (have) the party at Emma's place **if** / when her parents agree.
2 Unless / If they ___ (say) 'no', we'll ask Luke and Jodie's parents.
3 If / As soon as everyone ___ (bring) some food to share, we'll have plenty to eat.
4 Martin ___ (not know) anything about it **if /** unless someone tells him.
5 If / When he ___ (knock) on the door, we'll hide.
6 We ___ (jump) out and shout 'surprise!' **as soon as / if** he comes in.
7 He ___ (be) surprised **if / when** he sees everyone.
8 If / When the party ___ (be) over, we'll all help to clear up.

Vocabulary: Adjectives with prefixes: *un-, in-* and *im-*

5a 🎧 Listen and repeat.

1 likely – unlikely
2 convenient – inconvenient
3 possible – impossible

b 🎧 Write the opposite form of the adjectives. Add *un-, in-* or *im-*. Then listen, check and repeat.

1 *un*likely
2 *in*convenient
3 *im*possible
4 ___attractive
5 ___comfortable
6 ___dependent
7 ___experienced
8 ___fit
9 ___formal
10 ___friendly
11 ___happy
12 ___healthy
13 ___interesting
14 ___kind
15 ___necessary
16 ___patient
17 ___pleasant
18 ___polite
19 ___popular
20 ___practical
21 ___tidy
22 ___usual

6 Complete the sentences with words from Exercise 5b.

1 His room is always a mess. He's *untidy*.
2 I slept through the film. It was really ___.
3 Don't eat fast food every day. It's ___.
4 It isn't cold, so coats are ___.
5 Nobody can solve the puzzle. It's ___.
6 My feet hurt. My new shoes are ___.
7 I've never done this before. I'm ___.
8 Stay calm. Don't be ___.

Speak and write

7a Work in pairs. Plan a surprise goodbye party for a friend who is moving away. Use the questions to help you.

- How will you make it a surprise? What are you going to tell him/her? What will you do when he/she comes in?
- What food/music will you have?
- What sort of present will you give him/her?

b Now write your plan. Then tell the class.

We'll say we're going out for a pizza and we'll tell him to meet us at …

Extra practice

For more practice, go to page 107.

Extension

Adjectives with prefixes

Put Ss into groups of three. Each group member should take a different prefix: *un-, in-* or *im-* and write a word beginning with that prefix. They write the word on card with slight space between the prefix and the rest of the adjective, then cut the card in two. Groups shuffle their six cards and swap their cards with another group. Ss then move around the class to find a partner who has the prefix or adjective which matches theirs. How long will all the partners take to be matched? To finish, partners come to the front of the class and announce their combined word.

Extra practice
Page 127

eText
😊 **Video and Animation**

Grammar: First conditional with *if/unless*; *will* future with *when/as soon as*

Exercise 5b
4 unattractive 5 uncomfortable 6 independent
7 inexperienced 8 unfit 9 informal 10 unfriendly
11 unhappy 12 unhealthy 13 uninteresting 14 unkind
15 unnecessary 16 impatient 17 unpleasant
18 impolite 19 unpopular 20 impractical 21 untidy
22 unusual

Exercise 6
2 uninteresting 3 unhealthy 4 unnecessary
5 impossible 6 uncomfortable 7 inexperienced
8 impatient

MOTIVATOR 6b

Adjectives with prefixes

In pairs, give Ss 30 seconds to write down as many adjectives with prefixes -un, in- and im- as they can remember.

The pair with the most correct adjectives wins.

6c The two men hadn't met before.

Grammar Past perfect simple
Vocabulary Collocations with *lose*

Get started

1 **What is it like to be a twin? Tell your partner what you think (or what you know!).**

Read

2 🔊 6 08 **Listen and read the article. Did the twins meet while they were growing up?**

Comprehension

3 **Answer the questions in pairs.**

1 How many people called James are mentioned?
a) two   b) three   c) four

2 Who married someone called Linda and then someone called Betty?
a) both twins   b) the twins' sons   c) nobody

3 How many dogs were called 'Toy'?
a) one   b) two   c) it doesn't say

4 Did the brothers work at the same places at the same time?
a) yes   b) no   c) it doesn't say

5 Did they weigh the same?
a) yes   b) no   c) it doesn't say

SOLVE IT!

4 **How old were the brothers when they met?**

Vocabulary: Collocations with *lose*

5 🔊 6 09 **Listen and repeat. Then complete the sentences with the phrases from the box.**

- lose a match   • lose interest
- lose sight (of something)
- lose touch (with someone)   • lose weight
- lose your memory   • lose your temper
- lose your way

1 We didn't win. We lost the *match*.
2 He forgets everything. He's lost his ___.
3 My brother doesn't collect stamps any more. He's lost ___.
4 Tom looks thin. Has he lost ___?
5 I haven't seen Jo for ages. We've lost ___.
6 Calm down! Don't lose ___.
7 The car turned a corner and we lost ___ of it.
8 Use your satnav. Then you won't lose ___.

Stranger than fiction:

the amazing story of James and James

Identical twins look and often behave exactly the same. It's not surprising – they share the same genes and they grow up together. But what happens when they're separated and lose touch? When he was nine, James Lewis discovered he had an identical twin. Different families had adopted the babies when they were one month old. The hospital hadn't told them their new sons were twins. Thirty years later, James managed to find his brother. Amazingly, they had grown up only forty-five miles apart. James's brother was also called James – but that was just the first of many weird coincidences. When they finally met, these are some of the things they discovered:

- Both men had married women called Linda.
- Both men had then got divorced and had married women called Betty.
- One man had named his son James Alan, the other had named his son James Allan.
- James Lewis had once owned a dog called 'Toy' – and his brother had given his dog the same name.
- Both men had worked at a petrol station and a burger bar.
- They had had the same illnesses and they had gained and lost weight at the same points in their lives.
- They enjoyed the same sports and hobbies, drove the same kind of car and went on holiday to the same place.

Remember, the two men hadn't met before. Was it all chance, or had the brothers communicated in some strange way before they met? Nobody really understands it.

66

Exercise 2
No, they never met while they were growing up.

Exercise 3
2 a) 3 b) 4 c) 5 c)

Exercise 4
They were 39 years old when they met.

Exercise 5
2 memory 3 interest 4 weight 5 touch 6 your temper
7 sight 8 your way

Grammar
before

Exercise 6
2 2 were, 1 'd had 3 2 met, 1 had grown up
4 1 had always felt, 2 understood 5 2 told, 1 had told

Exercise 7
2 hadn't studied, did 3 had lost, couldn't 4 Had you read, saw 5 were, hadn't packed 6 Had they been, went

Grammar

Past perfect simple

Affirmative and negative

Different families **had adopted** the babies.

The two men **hadn't met** before.

Questions and short answers

Had they **communicated** before they met?

Yes, they **had**./No, they **hadn't**.

Choose the correct option.

We use the past perfect to describe a past event that happened **before / after** another past event.

Practice

6 **Work in pairs. Read the sentences and say which action happened first.**

1 James <u>found out</u> about his twin. They <u>had lived</u> in the same area all their lives.

2 They <u>were</u> surprised. They<u>'d had</u> very similar lives.

3 They <u>met</u> as adults. They <u>had grown up</u> in different families.

4 They <u>had always felt</u> something was missing in their lives. They finally <u>understood</u>.

5 Somebody <u>told</u> his parents about the other baby. Nobody at the hospital <u>had told</u> them.

Many twins attend annual conferences where they can meet other twins and share their experiences.

7 **Complete the sentences. Write the past perfect or past simple form of the verbs in brackets.**

1 Toby <u>was</u> (be) late for school because he <u>'d missed</u> (miss) the bus.

2 I ___ (not study) hard enough before I ___ (do) the exam.

3 Annie ___ (lose) her key so she ___ (can't) get into the flat.

4 ___ (you/read) the book before you ___ (see) the film?

5 We ___ (be) cold because we ___ (not pack) any warm clothes.

6 ___ (they/be) to France before they ___ (go) last week?

Listen

8 Listen to the story and answer the questions in pairs. Make notes.

1 How old was Rob Jones? Which race did he take part in? Who went to watch the race?

2 What did Rob do before the race started? What did Rob's dad do? What did Jenny do?

3 How long did Rob take to complete the race? When did he look at his photo? Whose picture had he taken?

4 Who was in Jenny's photo? What was he doing?

Write

9 **Look at your notes from Exercise 8 again. Imagine you are Rob and complete the description of what happened.**

What a race! I was really tired at the end but I finished in five hours – not too bad!
I went home with Mum and Dad and Jenny and we … Then, a few days later, …
That wasn't the only coincidence. Jenny …

Extra practice

For more practice, go to page 108.

67

Extra practice
Page 128

eText
Video and Animation

Grammar: Past perfect simple

MOTIVATOR 6c

Exercise 8

1 He was 22 years old. The London Marathon. His mum, dad and sister.

2 Rob took a photo. Rob's dad put Jenny on his shoulders. Jenny took a photo.

3 About five hours. A few days later. Jenny's.

4 Rob. He was taking a photo.

Extension

Past perfect simple

Ss tell each other stories of strange or funny things that have happened to them. They can make up a story if they need to. Monitor and then ask Ss who told good stories to feed back to the class.

87

Exercise 2

There was a fire at his parents' shop.

Exercise 3

2 Don and his friends went to Italy.

3 There was a fire at Don's parents' shop.

4 Sarah received a text.

5 Sarah was worried about Don.

6 Sarah told Harry about the fire.

6d The ski trip

SKILLS FOCUS: LISTENING AND SPEAKING

REAL LIFE ISSUE

'Have a wonderful time and don't come back with a broken leg.'

'Don't worry, Mum, I'll be fine. I'll text you when we get there. Byeee … '

Don waved to his family as the coach drove away from the school. Then he turned to his friend Harry.

'I can't believe it, after all this time. It feels like I've been saving for this ski trip forever!'

'I know. I dream about washing-up! But it's worth it. This is going to be awesome.'

They had both worked hard to pay for the trip. Harry had found a Saturday job in a local restaurant and Don had worked for his parents in their corner shop. This was their first ski trip and they were very excited. Their friend Sarah leant forward from the seat behind.

'Not long now. A whole week in the Italian Alps! I can't wait!'

The friends soon discovered that skiing wasn't as easy as it looked. By the end of the fourth day they were aching all over and exhausted – but happy. That evening Harry was talking to Don and Sarah.

'You're a natural, Don. You'll be in the advanced class soon!'

'I don't think so, but I'm having a fantastic time. Anyway, I'm off to bed now. I'm so tired!'

Sarah followed Don to the door.

'Are you OK?'

'Yeah, why?'

'Oh, nothing. Sleep well, then.'

'What was that about?'

'Surely he's told you? There's been a fire at the shop. Nobody was hurt, but lots of stuff was damaged. I think it was quite serious.'

'How do you know that?'

'My parents live in the same road. My sister texted me.'

'Oh, how awful! I'm sure nobody's told him. I guess they don't want to spoil his week. He'll want to go home if he finds out.'

'Oh no. Now what? Are you going to tell him?'

'I don't know.'

NEW WORDS
- forever • corner shop • lean (leant)
- ache • exhausted • (You're) a natural.
- (I'm) off to bed • spoil • Now what?

Get started

1 Imagine the perfect trip abroad. Where are you going? How are you going to get there? What are you going to do?

Read

2 🎧 6/11 Read the story. What happened while Don was away from home?

Comprehension

3 Put the sentences in the correct order (1–6).

☐ Sarah was worried about Don.

☐ Don and his friends went to Italy.

☐ Sarah received a text.

7 Don and Harry saved enough money to pay for the ski trip.

☐ Sarah told Harry about the fire.

☐ There was a fire at Don's parents' shop.

68

Speak your mind!

4 **Work in pairs. Read the sentences. Then complete each one with one or two more ideas.**

1 If he does nothing, *Don will probably be angry and upset later, because Harry didn't tell him.*
2 If he tells Don, *it'll spoil the holiday.*

SPEAKING TIP: ASK FOR MORE EXPLANATION

If you don't understand something, ask the person to explain. Use expressions like:
Sorry, I'm not sure what you mean./What do you mean?/Are you saying … ?
Now do Exercise 5.

5a **Work in pairs. Match the opinions (1–3) to reasons from the box and your own ideas.**

I think Harry should tell Don because Don will want to support his family. Another reason is, …
1 Harry should tell Don.
2 Harry shouldn't do anything.
3 Harry should talk to somebody else.

- It's none of Harry's business.
- Don will want to support his family.
- It isn't fair on Harry – he needs to share the problem.
- Don's parents will tell him when he gets home.
- Harry needs some advice.
- You shouldn't keep secrets from your friends.
- (*Your own ideas*)

b **Now work in groups. What do you think Harry should do? Discuss in your group and give reasons.**

A: Harry shouldn't do anything because it's none of his business.
B: What do you mean? Are you saying you shouldn't be interested in your friends?
A: No, I mean …
B: I don't agree. I think he should tell Don, because …
C: Perhaps he should discuss the problem with someone else. I mean, …

Listen

LISTENING TIP: PREPARE TO LISTEN

Before you listen, look at the task. This will help focus your listening.
Now do Exercise 6.

6a 🎧 **Listen to the whole conversation, then answer the question.**

Who told Don about the fire?

b 🎧 **Listen again, then answer the questions in pairs. Note down your answers.**

1 What did Harry do?
2 What did Harry's dad do?
3 How is Don's family?
4 What is Don going to do?

Write

7 **Write a paragraph describing what happened. Use your notes from Exercise 6b.**

Harry phoned his parents and …

69

Extension ▰

Write the following sentences on the board. Explain to the Ss that there is one mistake in each sentence. Play the recording from Exercise 6 again for Ss to identify the incorrect word/ phrase and to write down the correct word/phrase.

1 *Harry told Don about the fire.* (told > didn't tell)
2 *Harry phoned Don's parents.* (Don's > his)
3 *Harry's parents didn't know about the fire.* (didn't know > knew)
4 *Don's mum phoned him a few minutes ago.* (a few minutes > about an hour)
5 *They're all going home in a week's time.* (a week's > three days')

They then compare their answers in pairs before checking as a class. When checking answers, ask Ss to say the full correct sentences.

Exercise 5a

1 … you shouldn't keep secrets from your friends.
2 It's none of Harry's business. Don's parents will tell him when he gets home.
3 It isn't fair on Harry – he needs to share the problem. Harry needs some advice.

Exercise 6a

Don's parents

Exercise 6b

1 Harry phoned his parents.
2 Harry's dad went to speak to Don's parents.
3 They are fine.
4 Don's going to stay in Italy.

Exercise 1
1 may/might
2 won't
3 may/might
4 might not/may not

Exercise 2
1 arrives, 'll start
2 When 3 unless
4 Will, see

Exercise 3
1 hadn't had
2 hadn't realised
3 had forgotten
4 had worked

Exercise 4
1 Go 2 campsite
3 tent 4 caravan
5 motor home

Exercise 5
1 f) 2 d) 3 c) 4 a)
5 e)

Exercise 6
1 impatient
2 independent
3 unfit
4 inexperienced

Exercise 7
1 That's 2 Quick
3 Come 4 on 5 else

Exercise 8
2 b) Shall
3 e) would
4 a) if
5 d)

6 Language Revision

Grammar (14 marks)

1 Complete the sentences. Use *will/won't*, *may/might* (*not*) and the information in brackets.

0 The weather _will_ definitely be sunny.
1 We're not sure. We ___ go skiing.
2 It ___ be cold, it's always hot there!
3 You ___ need a jacket in the evening, sometimes it's cold.
4 We ___ see anything at the top of the mountain, sometimes it's cloudy.

.../4

2 Choose the correct options.

0 If / Unless you study, you will pass the exam.
1 When everybody **will arrive / arrives**, we'll start / start dinner.
2 **When / If** school finishes, we'll go to the shopping centre.
3 He'll get here on time **unless / as soon as** he misses the train.
4 **Do / Will** you tell Tom the news when you **see / will see** him?

.../6

3 Complete the sentences with the past perfect form of the verbs in the box.

• forget • not realise • ~~steal~~ • work • not have

0 Danny was angry. Somebody _had stolen_ his bike.
1 Jenny was hungry. She ___ any lunch.
2 I arrived late. I ___ the time!
3 Was your friend upset because you ___ her birthday?
4 They passed their exams. They ___ really hard.

.../4

Vocabulary (14 marks)

4 Complete the sentences.

Holiday ideas

> Pay for a room and have breakfast at a ⁰_B & B_.
> ¹___ camping at a ²___ and sleep in a ³___ .
> Pull a ⁴___ behind your car, or drive a ⁵___ and sleep in it, too.

.../5

5 Match the phrases (0–5) to the correct meanings (a–f).

_0 – b_

0 lose sight   a) become angry
1 lose interest   b) not see anymore
2 lose weight   c) forget
3 lose your memory   d) get thin
4 lose your temper   e) not win
5 lose a match   f) get bored   .../5

6 Complete the adjectives with *un-*, *in-* or *im-*.

0 I can't do this crossword. it's _im_possible!
1 Be calm and wait. Don't be ___patient.
2 Sarah doesn't need help. She's very ___dependent.
3 I must do some exercise. I'm really ___fit.
4 He can't do the job yet. He's too ___experienced.   .../4

Phrases/Use your English (12 marks)

7 Complete the phrases in the dialogue.

Steve: Where's Gina?
Vicky: ⁰_Knowing her_, she's got lost.
Steve: Someone's at the door.
Vicky: ¹T___'s her. ²Q___! Hide.
Gina: Hi, Vicky, it's Gina.
Vicky: Oh, Gina. ³C___ ⁴o___ up.
Gina: Hi, Vicky. How are you doing?
Vicky: I'm fine. I've got a surprise for you.
Gina: Is it Steve?
Vicky: Who ⁵e___!   .../5

8 Look at the jumbled conversation. Number the lines in the correct order. Then write the missing words.

☐ a) I'll do that for you ___ you like.
☐ b) Don't worry. ___ I invite Jake, too?
1 c) Don't _forget_ to invite Sue to the party.
☐ d) It's OK, I'm going to the supermarket this afternoon.
☐ e) Yes, please. That ___ be great. Jake's cool. Oh. I need to buy a cake.   .../7

 LISTEN AND CHECK YOUR SCORE

Grammar	.../14
Vocabulary	.../14
Phrases/Use your English	.../12
Total	**.../40**

70

ROUND-UP 1

ROUND-UP 2

eText

Games

Boat Game

Hangman

Pelmanism

90

6 Skills Revision

My big jump! 》》

I will never forget my first big bungee jump. I had done some bungee jumping indoors, but I'd never tried it outdoors. I'd also watched people on TV jump off big cliffs, waterfalls and bridges but I thought it was too scary for me. ¹__ So we went to Middlesbrough, which has a famous bridge, for my first big bungee jump. The bridge, which crosses the river Tees, was opened in 1911 and is made of iron. I had to climb 122 steps to get to the top. ²__ A jump officer helped me put on my kit and then it was my turn to jump. Suddenly I was very scared. I wasn't able to breathe; I couldn't move. ³__ It was awesome. I jumped 50 metres down to the water. I could see my mum and dad waving from the river bank as I was falling. I felt great!

Read

1 Read about Matt's bungee jump. Match the sentences (A–D) to the gaps (1–3) in the text. There is one extra sentence.

A The officer shouted '1, 2, 3 … ' and I jumped!
B The water was cold and very deep.
C When I arrived I couldn't look down.
D But in 2013, I changed my mind.

2 Answer the questions.

1 Why did Matt think he couldn't do an outdoor jump?
2 Where did Matt do his first outdoor jump?
3 What is the Middlesbrough bridge like?
4 How did Matt feel just before he jumped?
5 How high is the bridge?

Listen

3 🎧 ⁶/₁₄ Listen to five people talking about their holidays. Match the speakers (1–5) to the places to stay (a–g). There are two extra places.

1 – b

Speaker 1
Speaker 2
Speaker 3
Speaker 4
Speaker 5

a) old countryside hotel
b) caravan
c) hostel
d) campsite
e) bed and breakfast
f) self-catering flat
g) city hotel

Write

4 Write about an outdoor experience. Use linking phrases (*first of all, then, finally,* etc.). Use the questions to help you.

- Where did you go?
- Who did you go with?
- What did you do?
- What was exciting about the experience?

I remember when …

NOW I CAN		
Read	follow an article and find specific information.	☐
Listen	identify the main topic in short monologues.	☐
Write	write about an experience.	☐

71

Exercise 1

1 D 2 C 3 A

Exercise 2

1 He was afraid because he had seen people on TV jump off cliffs and bridges.
2 On a bridge in Middlesbrough
3 It is over 100 years old and it's made of iron.
4 He felt he couldn't breathe or move.
5 The bridge is 50 metres high.

Exercise 3

2 d) 3 g) 4 a) 5 e)

eText
📺 Additional video lesson

To watch a vlog about a trip to the Lake District, go to Students' eText, page 71.

For the worksheets and teaching notes go to the Teacher's Resource Materials folder.

Look forward ⟫⟫

Tell the Ss to look at the photos from the Edinburgh Festival Fringe on page 72 of the Students' Book and describe what they think is happening in each photo.

Have any Ss watched street performers like these? Have they been to any similar festivals, or indeed to the Edinburgh Festival itself? If not, what would they like to see?

Background note

Edinburgh Festival Fringe: Takes place every August in Scotland's capital, as part of the Edinburgh Festival. The Fringe is the largest arts festival in the world and showcases the performing arts, including comedy, theatre, music and dance. There are also many street performers on the Royal Mile.

Exercise 2

He was throwing balls to people and catching them when they threw them back.

Exercise 3

2 T 3 DS 4 F 5 T 6 T

7a He told her to throw it.

Grammar Reported requests and commands
Vocabulary Adjective word order

Get started

1 Have you ever seen a magic trick? Do you know how it was done? Tell the class.

Read

2 🎧 Listen and read the webpage. What was the man doing while he was on his unicycle?

Comprehension

3 Answer true (T), false (F) or doesn't say (DS).

1 Ray White is in Scotland. *T*
2 There are lots of shows to choose from.
3 Ray hasn't seen many shows yet.
4 He knows how the magic trick was done.
5 The cyclist caught every ball.
6 Ray is going to see another show now.

YouthPress 🔍 [SEARCH] 🏠 ENTERTAINMENT MUSIC SPORTS

EDINBURGH FESTIVAL FRINGE

Ray White is spending a week at that amazing Scottish festival, the Edinburgh Fringe. Here's his first *YouthPress* report.

I've never seen so many people and all of them are having fun! Everywhere you go, performers in weird and wonderful costumes approach you. They all tell you to go to their show, which of course is the best in town. You couldn't possibly go to all of them.

So far, my favourite is Mickey's Marvellous Magic Show, which I saw yesterday. It was in a huge old theatre, but there were only about thirty people in the audience. Never mind, Mickey was brilliant! He asked someone to write down a number on a card and told him not to show anyone. Then he pulled out a card from his pocket and there was the same number. Of course I thought it was a fix – but then he asked me to write down a name. I couldn't believe it when he had the same name in his pocket. Spooky!

Outside, lots of people were watching a man on a unicycle. He was cycling backwards and forwards inside a big square area in the street. He threw a little red rubber ball to a girl in the crowd and told her to throw it back. He caught it, then he did the same with two balls, then three, then four, then five – it was awesome.

I'm off to see the Fearless Flying Grannies now. (Sounds interesting? I'll tell you later!)

Exercise 4

2 Harry asked Joe to carry a bag for him.
3 A police officer told us to get off our bikes.
4 Julie asked Tom to help her with the washing-up.
5 Ben asked Sam not to tell anyone.
6 The dentist told his patient to relax.

Exercise 5

2 to pass her the sugar
3 to look at the whiteboard
4 to listen to her
5 to take the next turning on the/their right
6 not to eat his crisps

Exercise 6

2 big round brown eyes
3 a horrible old cheese sandwich
4 an expensive new American car
5 smart black leather shoes
6 a mysterious little metal key

Grammar

Reported requests and commands			
Subject	Verb	Object	Infinitive
He	asked	someone	**to write** a number.
He	told	him	**not to show** anyone.
He	told	her	**to throw** it back.

Note

Be careful about changes to pronouns in reported speech, e.g. 'Throw it back to me.'

*He told her to throw it back to **him**.*

Practice

4 Report the requests and commands. Use *asked* or *told*.

1 The teacher to Class Six: Don't talk!
  The teacher told Class Six not to talk.
2 Harry to Joe: Can you carry a bag for me, please?
3 A police officer to us: Get off your bikes!
4 Julie to Tom: Please help me with the washing-up.
5 Ben to Sam: Please don't tell anyone.
6 The dentist to his patient: Relax!

5 (7/02) Listen and complete the requests and commands.

1 He told them *not to move*.
2 She asked me ___.
3 The teacher asked everyone ___.
4 She told us ___.
5 He told the tourists ___.
6 Jack asked his friends ___.

Vocabulary: Adjective word order

We often put two or three adjectives together before a noun. They usually go in this order:

opinion	size	age	shape	colour	origin	material	noun
amazing					Scottish		festival
	huge	old					theatre
	big		square				area
	little			red		rubber	ball

6 Put the words in the correct order.

1 blue beautiful dress cotton a
  a beautiful blue cotton dress
2 eyes big round brown
3 a sandwich cheese old horrible
4 new American expensive car an
5 black smart shoes leather
6 little key a metal mysterious

7 Describe each picture with three adjectives from the box.

- delicious • glass • modern
- old • pink • round • square
- tall • thin • comfortable
- woollen • little

1 a *tall* ___ ___ man   2 a pair of ___ ___ ___ socks

3 a ___ ___ ___ building   4 a ___ ___ ___ cake

Pronunciation: Compression /ˈevri/ every

8 (7/03) **Go to page 117.**

Listen

9 (7/04) **Ray is showing his friend Sandy some photos he took while he was in Edinburgh. Listen and complete the summary.**

Ray was walking along [1]*the street* when he saw [2]___. There was a sign that said '[3]___'. People stopped, sat down and [4]___. Then a girl came along. Her [5]___ told her to play something. She played really [6]___. People asked her [7]___, but she was embarrassed and she [8]___.

Extra practice

For more practice, go to page 108.

Put the Ss into teams. Ask a player from the first team to add an adjective to the first item, e.g. *a green scarf*. The next team adds a new adjective in the correct order e.g. *a green silk scarf*. The next team adds one more, *e.g. a beautiful green silk scarf* until they have used between three and five adjectives. If a member of a team chooses an unsuitable adjective, places an adjective in the wrong order or cannot add a further adjective to the description, the next team takes over.

Give scores if you wish: add one point for each adjective correctly placed; deduct one point for an unsuitable or incorrectly placed adjective.

Continue the game with the other items.

Extra practice
Page 128

eText
📀 **Video and Animation**

Pronunciation: Compression /ˈevri/ *every*

Use your

English: Speak on the phone

MOTIVATOR 7a

Exercise 7

1 a tall thin old man
2 a pair of comfortable pink woollen socks
3 a modern square glass building
4 a delicious little round cake

Exercise 8a

everywhere (3) favourite (2) comfortable (3)

Exercise 9

2 a piano 3 Play me 4 played 5 friend 6 well
7 to play their favourite songs 8 walked off/left

Extension ◼

Adjective word order

Bring in some items, or photos of items, for Ss to describe. These could be simple things from home, e.g. a box, a scarf, a hat, or kitchen items such as a mug. Show one item to the class and check they know what it is.

Look back <<<

Adjective word order

Tell the class that you're thinking of something in the classroom and say, for example: *It's a small brown leather thing.* Ask the Ss if they can guess what the 'thing' is, e.g. a wallet or a handbag.

In pairs Ss should think of five more things in the classroom (or that other Ss have with them) and write three or four adjectives to describe each one. Ss then read their adjectives to another pair to guess.

Background note

The London Eye:
See Background notes for Lesson 6a.

Exercise 1
Australia

Exercise 2
The staff recognised their <u>accents</u> because they were customers. The cashier <u>wasn't</u> very frightened when she saw the robbers. They stole $132,000 and <u>planned</u> <u>to escape</u> to Mexico. They were arrested and went to prison in the <u>USA</u>.

Grammar
Tell

7b He said he was writing a book.

Grammar Reported statements
Vocabulary Appearance

One of the least successful bank robberies in history took place in Colorado, USA, in 2005. The police officer who arrested the robbers said they were the 'dumbest criminals ever'.

Anthony Prince and Luke Carroll had disguised their faces with ski masks and goggles, but the bank staff recognised them anyway. They told police that the men were regular customers and that they had recognised them straightaway from their Australian accents. They were able to describe two fair-skinned young men of medium build, both with short dark curly hair and one with a small moustache and beard. To remove any possible doubt, they also told police that the men worked in a nearby sports shop and had forgotten to remove their name tags!

One of the cashiers told the police that she had given them a lot of single dollar notes. 'I told them the bags would be very heavy, but they ignored me. I laughed because they didn't seem very bright,' she said.

The men stole $132,000 and later posed for photographs with the money in their hands. They planned to escape to Mexico, but not surprisingly they were arrested before they left the country.

After about four years in prison, they returned to Australia. Prince told reporters he was very sorry. He said that he couldn't explain his behaviour and that he'd learnt from his mistakes. He also said he was writing a book about the robbery.

Read

1 Listen and read the story. Where were the robbers from?

Comprehension

2 Rewrite the summary, correcting the mistakes.

Two <u>Americans</u> robbed a bank in Colorado. The staff recognised their faces because they were customers. The cashier was very frightened when she saw the robbers. They stole $132,000 and escaped to Mexico. They were arrested and went to prison in Australia.

1 Two Australians robbed a bank …

74

Grammar

Reported statements	
Direct statement	**Reported statement**
	He **said** (that) … He **told** me (that) …
'I**'m** very sorry.'	… he **was** very sorry.
'I**'m writing** a book.'	… he **was writing** a book.
'I **recognised** them from their accents.'	… he **had recognised** them from their accents.
'I**'ve learnt** from my mistakes.'	… he **had ('d) learnt** from his mistakes.
'We**'ve forgotten** to remove our name tags.'	… they**'d forgotten** to remove their name tags.
'The bags **will** be very heavy.'	… the bags **would be** very heavy.
'I **can't** explain my behaviour.'	… he **couldn't** explain his behaviour.

Choose the correct option to complete the rule.

Tell / Say is always followed by a direct object.

Exercise 3
2 'I didn't enjoy the film.' 3 we would wash up later 4 'He lives in Birmingham.' 5 David had gone home 6 'I didn't get your message.' 7 Jack couldn't go out 8 'We're not going on holiday.'

Exercise 4
. . . they had done a lot. Yuko said (that) in their first week they went/had gone to London and she'd had a ride on the London Eye. Yuko said (that) then they had travelled to Scotland, where they were staying with some friends. Yuko said (that) they spoke fast and she couldn't always understand the accent! Yuko said (that) it didn't matter, she loved it. Yuko said (that) she hadn't sent any postcards, but she would be back on Saturday and she'd have lots of photos!

Practice

3 **Complete the sentences.**

'I'm helping John with his homework.'	She said *she was helping John with his homework.*
'___.'	He told me that he hadn't enjoyed the film.
'We'll wash up later.'	I said ___.
'___.'	They told us he lived in Birmingham.
'David's gone home.'	He said that ___.
'___.'	She told me she hadn't got my message.
'Jack can't go out.'	They said ___.
'___.'	He told me they weren't going on holiday.

4 **Read the speech bubble, then report what Yuko said.**

¹We've been in the UK for two weeks and ²we've done a lot. ³In our first week we went to London and ⁴I had a ride on the London Eye. Then ⁵we travelled to Scotland, where ⁶we're staying with some friends. ⁷They speak fast and ⁸I can't always understand the accent! ⁹It doesn't matter, ¹⁰I love it. ¹¹I haven't sent any postcards, but ¹²I'll be back on Saturday and ¹³I'll have lots of photos!

Yuko said they'd been in the UK for two weeks and …

Vocabulary: Appearance

5a **Recall Look at the Word bank on page 112. Put the words in the correct lists. Which words go in more than one list?**

- Head/Hair: … • Face: *beard* • Body: …
- Age: … • Other: …

---

b 🔊 **Extension Listen and repeat. Then add the words to the correct lists.**

- attractive • bald • eyebrow
- fair/olive/dark-skinned • fat • fringe
- handsome • in his/her teens/twenties
- (of) medium-build • overweight • parting
- pretty • round • slim • spiky • square
- tattoo • teenage *(adj)* • thin • ugly
- well-built

6 **Look at the picture in Exercise 1 again. Read the description of the cashier and choose the correct options.**

She's an ¹attractive young / ugly old woman in her ²seventies / twenties, with ³medium-length / spiky ⁴dark / blond hair and a ⁵fringe / parting, a ⁶thin / round face and ⁷glasses / a walking stick. She's ⁸light-skinned / dark-skinned and ⁹well-built / slim.

Write

7a **Choose one of the people in the picture and make notes, using the headings from Exercise 5a.**

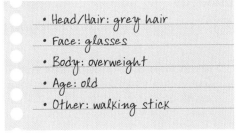

- Head/Hair: grey hair
- Face: glasses
- Body: overweight
- Age: old
- Other: walking stick

b **Now write a description, using your notes from Exercise 7a.**

Speak

8 **Work in pairs. Take turns to imagine you are one of the customers in the picture. Tell your partner what happened, using the ideas below.**

- Where were you? What were you doing?
- Who else was there? What happened?
- How did you feel?

I was standing …

Extra practice

➡ **For more practice, go to page 108.**

75

Exercise 5a

Head/Hair: blond, curly, dark, dark brown, fair, grey, light-brown, long, medium-length, short, straight, wavy

Face: beard, glasses, long, moustache

Body: large, medium-height, short, tall

Age: middle-aged, old, young

Other: beautiful, good-looking

Exercise 5b

Head/Hair: bald, fringe, parting, spiky

Face: eyebrow, round, square

Body: fat, (of) medium-build, overweight, slim, thin, well-built

Age: in his/her teens/twenties, teenage *(adj)*

Other: attractive, fair/olive/dark-skinned, handsome, pretty, tattoo, ugly

---

Exercise 6

2 twenties
3 medium-length
4 blond hair 5 fringe
6 thin 7 glasses
8 light-skinned
9 slim

Extension ■

Appearance

Bring in some photos of people with different features and display them somewhere prominent for the class to study. One S chooses a person for the others to guess: you could give the S a copy of one of the photos, making sure that no-one else can see, or they can pick one themselves from the display. Other Ss then ask questions, e.g.

S1: *Was the person you saw a man or a woman?*
S2: *The person I saw was a man.*
S3: *How old do you think he was?*
S2: *He was in his twenties.*
S4: *Was he wearing glasses?* etc.

When Ss have correctly guessed the identity of the person, a new S can take over.

Extra practice

Page 128

MOTIVATOR 7b

95

Appearance
Bring in some
photos of people
with differing
appearances.
Get the Ss to
describe them
using appropriate
appearance
vocabulary, e.g. *He
is a middle-aged
man in his fifties.
He has short, dark
hair …*

7c She asked if I could come …

Grammar	Reported questions
Function	Speak on the phone

Dialogue

1 🎧 Listen and read. Where is Jodie going on Saturday?

Mrs Hill: Hello, could I speak to Jodie Carter, please?
Luke: Sure, I'll get her. Who's calling, please?
Mrs Hill: This is Mary Hill, from Radio Talk London.
Luke: Right, just a minute … Jodie … JODIE!
…
Jodie: Hello, Jodie speaking. Go away, Luke.
…
Luke: So, have you won the competition?
Jodie: Well, I'm through to the final!
Luke: That's amazing. Well done. What did she ask you?
Jodie: I can't think … I'm so excited! Umm, she asked
how long it had taken to write the story and then
she asked which school I went to. And guess
what … she asked me if I could come to the
studio on Saturday.
Luke: That's brilliant. When will you know the winner?
Jodie: They'll tell us then. Live on air!
Luke: Wow! Who are you taking? Did she ask if you
wanted to bring a friend … or a brother?!
Jodie: No, hard luck, Luke, she didn't.

76

Phrases
• just a minute • I can't think
• (I'm) so (excited/lucky … !) • hard luck

Comprehension

2 **Choose the correct options.**
1 Mrs Hill phoned Luke / Jodie.
2 Jodie has **entered** / won a
competition.
3 Mrs Hill **knew** / asked about Jodie's
school.
4 She invited **a friend** / Jodie to the
studio.
5 Luke **wants to** / will go with her.

SOLVE IT!
3 What kind of competition was it?

Exercise 1
She's going to a radio studio.

Exercise 2
2 entered 3 asked 4 Jodie 5 wants to

Exercise 3
A (story) writing competition

Grammar

Reported questions

Wh- questions

Direct questions	Reported questions
'Who's calling?'	Luke asked (her) **who was calling**.
'How long did it take?'	She asked (me) **how long it had taken**.
'When will you know?'	He asked (her) **when she would (she'd) know**.

Yes/No questions

Direct questions	Reported questions
'Do you want to bring a friend with you?'	She asked (me) **if I wanted to bring** a friend with me.
'Have you won the competition?'	He asked (her) **if she had (she'd) won** the competition.
'Can you come to the studio?'	She asked (me) **if I could come** to the studio.

Practice

4 **Report the questions.**

1 Mrs Hill to Jodie: When can you visit us?
Mrs Hill asked *Jodie when she could visit them*.

2 Emma to Jodie: Have you met any of the other finalists?
Emma asked ___.

3 Luke: Who's in the final?
Luke asked ___.

4 Emma: What's the prize?
Emma asked ___.

5 Martin to Jodie: What's the story about?
Martin asked ___.

6 Luke to Jodie: When will they announce the winner?
Luke asked ___.

7 Mrs Hill to Jodie: Do you want to be a writer?
Mrs Hill asked ___.

8 Martin to Luke: Did you enter the competition, too?
Martin asked ___.

5 (7.08) **Listen and then report the questions.**

1 He asked (me) if he could ask me some questions.
2 She asked (me) how old I was.

Use your English: Speak on the phone

6 (7.09) **Listen and repeat. Then practise the conversation in pairs.**

A: Hello?
B: Hi. It's Mel here. Can I speak to Jo, please?
A: I'm afraid she's out. Can I take a message?
B: Yes, please. Can you ask her to call me?
A: OK, I'll tell her as soon as she gets back.

Answer the phone
Hello?
Hello. Luke speaking.
Hello, Jodie's phone.
Say who you are
Hello. This is Mary Hill.
Hi. It's Luke here.
Ask for somebody
Is Jodie there?
Can/Could/May I speak to Jodie, please?
Respond
Speaking.
Who's calling, please?
Just a minute/Hang on, I'll get him/her.
I'm sorry/I'm afraid he's/she's out.
Can I take a message?

7 **Practise similar conversations in pairs.**

Listen and write

8 (7.10) **Listen and complete the message.**

Amy – Anna called and left a message:
• She said …
• She asked you …
• The number is …
• She said …

Extra practice

For more practice, go to page 108.

Exercise 4

2 Emma asked Jodie if she had met any of the other finalists.
3 Luke asked who was in the final.
4 Emma asked what the prize was.
5 Martin asked Jodie what the story was about.
6 Luke asked Jodie when they would announce the winner.
7 Mrs Hill asked Jodie if she wanted to be a writer.
8 Martin asked Luke if he had entered the competition, too.

Exercise 5

3 He asked (me) what my address was.
4 She asked (me) what school I went to.
5 He asked (me) if English was my favourite subject.
6 She asked (me) when I had started learning English.
7 He asked (me) if I had ever been to the UK.
8 She asked (me) if I could speak any other languages.
9 He asked (me) what I was planning for the summer holidays.
10 She asked (me) if I would go to university in the future or if I would get a job.

Exercise 8

• She said (that) she had lost her mobile.
• She asked you to call her.
• The number is: 01783 593223.
• She said she'd be (would be) at home all afternoon.

Extension ▪▪

Speak on the phone/reported questions

In pairs Ss improvise a conversation using the prompts from Exercise 6. The S who 'answers the phone' takes a message. Ss then move on to another pair and ask and answer questions about the phone message, e.g.:
S1: *Hi (Gina), (Ryan) called this morning.*
S2: *What did he say?*
S1: *He asked if you could call him.*
S2: *Did he give you his number?*
S1: *Yes, it's …*

Extra practice
Page 128

eText
📀 **Video and Animation**

Use your
English: Reported statements, requests, commands and questions

MOTIVATOR 7c

Exercise 1

New Zealand, Canada, Australia

Exercise 2

1 Canada – Inuits; Australia – Aboriginal Australians

2 5,000 years – number of years the Inuits have lived in Canada

1970 – year of the first Arctic Games

1,500 years old – age of the didgeridoo

1–3 metres – length of didgeridoo

Exercise 3

2 T 3 DS 4 F 5 T

SKILLS FOCUS: **READING**

ACROSS **CULTURES**

Get started

1 Look at the photos. Can you guess the countries?

Read

> **READING TIP:** HOW TO READ A TEXT FOR SPECIFIC INFORMATION
>
> When you look for specific information, for example countries, names or dates, scan the text quickly to find the information you need. Look for capital letters and numbers. You don't need to read the rest of the text in detail.
> Now do Exercise 2.

2 🎧 Read the article quickly and answer the questions.

1 Which countries and indigenous cultures are mentioned in the article?
New Zealand – Maori ...

2 How many numbers are there in the article? What do they refer to?

Comprehension

3 Read the article. Answer true (T), false (F) or doesn't say (DS).

1 People wear traditional clothes for the Maori dance. *T*
2 'Kapa Haka' dancers dance, sing and shout.
3 Inuit games are only played in the winter.
4 The didgeridoo looks like a guitar.
5 Today you can hear the didgeridoo mixed with more modern music.

Sandy Blaire:
Reporting on World Culture

Welcome to my latest report to find out about indigenous cultures in the modern world!

I began in New Zealand. Last week I spoke to Maaka, a Maori from Auckland. He told me about a typical Maori dance called 'Kapa Haka'. It's a mixture of song, war cries and dance. The dancing has a lot of combat movements and the dancers wear traditional Maori costume. You can see a haka at every New Zealand rugby game. The New Zealand players perform it in front of the other team before the match. I looked it up on YouTube – they look like real warriors. It's awesome!!

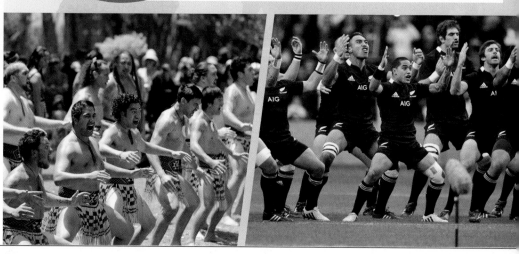

78

Listen

4 🎧 7/12 **Listen to a Skype conversation between Sandy and Karima. Answer the questions.**

1 What does 'Inuit' mean? *It means 'people'.*
2 Where do the Inuit people traditionally live?
3 Why did they invent games?
4 How many types of games are there?
5 Why does Karima often lose the voice games?
6 What is Karima going to send Sandy?

Next stop: Canada! The Inuits have lived in Canada for over 5,000 years and are famous for their traditional games. I asked Karima, an Inuit from northern Canada, to tell me about them. She said that life in the Arctic could be hard and it was important for people to have strong minds and strong bodies. So the Inuits invented games to help them survive during their long hunting trips. My favourite game is the 'kneel jump'. You start on your knees and jump forward. The person who jumps the furthest wins. Karima told me all about the Arctic Games. It seems the competition began in 1970 and it has both traditional games and modern sports, like ice hockey.

Finally I spoke to Kylie, an Aboriginal Australian from Sydney and I asked her about Aboriginal music. She told me about the didgeridoo. The didgeridoo's an Aboriginal musical instrument over 1,500 years old. It's a pipe that's 1–3 metres long and yes, you blow into it! Today you can still listen to traditional didgeridoo music or fusions with hip-hop or rock! Kylie told me that her uncle was the didgeridoo player in a group. Check out her photo!

Speak

5a **In pairs, discuss the questions.**

1 Before you visit a new country, which of these things do you think are important to find out about? Decide with your partner: 1 = most important, 6 = least important.
   ☐ the famous sights
   ☐ the landscape
   ☐ the music
   ☐ the people
   ☐ interesting facts about the culture
   ☐ the language
2 Which country in the magazine article would you like to visit? Why?

b **Imagine you are going to visit the country you talked about in Exercise 5a. Think of five questions to ask when you get there.**

Project

6 **Do a project to find the answers to the five questions you talked about in Exercise 5b.**

   • Write a title for your text.
   • Use your questions from Exercise 5a as paragraph headings.
   • Write the information you have discovered under each heading.
   • Download two or three images to go with your text.

NEW WORDS
• indigenous • Maori • war cry • combat
• costume • warrior • the Inuits
• the Arctic • mind • survive
• Aboriginal Australian • didgeridoo • pipe

79

Exercise 4

2 In the Arctic regions, for example northern Canada.
3 To keep people healthy and happy.
4 Five types (ball games, jumping games, wrestling games, bone games and voice games)
5 Because she often laughs.
6 She's going to send a video link of a voice game.

Extension ▰▰▰

When the Ss have completed their project in Exercise 6, get them to work with a partner to compare what they found out about their chosen country. What was the most interesting thing they discovered: was it on the music, the people, the famous sights, etc.?

Monitor Ss as they talk, giving help where needed. More confident Ss could present their most interesting discovery to the class, either individually or with their partner.

Exercise 1

2 Thank you very much 3 kind of you 4 I'm very sorry 5 but 6 for 7 With best wishes 8 PS 9 with

Exercise 2

1 Hemmingford High 2 10 3 his trip to Alaska 4 Arctic winter 5 they were on half-term holiday

7e Thank you

SKILLS FOCUS: WRITING A THANK YOU LETTER

Get ready to write

1 Read the letter and complete it with the words and phrases from the box.

- With best wishes • but • Dear • for • kind of you
- I'm very sorry • PS • Thank you very much • with

Hemmingford High School
Hilton
JKI2 5DR
I2th May

¹*Dear* Mr Bennett,
² ___ for coming to our school last month. It was very ³ ___ to give us so much of your time. We all loved hearing about your trip to Alaska and learning about the Inuit people. My favourite part of your talk was when you told us about the Arctic winter. It was also interesting to hear about how the Inuit go hunting and fishing.
⁴ ___ this letter is a little late, ⁵ ___ your visit was the day before our half-term holiday. We're back at school now and starting work on our project about the North Pole!
Thank you again ⁶ ___ a great afternoon.
⁷ ___
Matthew Davis and Year I0
⁸ ___

Good luck ⁹ ___ your next expedition. I hope you will come back and tell us about it one day!

2 In pairs, complete the summary of the letter.

Mr Bennett visited ¹ ___ School and talked to Year ² ___ about ³ ___. Matthew's favourite part was hearing about the ⁴ ___. The letter is late because ⁵ ___.

WRITING TIP: A THANK YOU LETTER

Always start a letter with *Dear…* . It's OK to use first names but to be polite, use *Mr/Mrs/Ms* + surnames.
End the letter with phrases like these:
Love from, With love, Yours (if you know the person well)
With best wishes (if you want to be more polite)
Yours sincerely (if you don't know the person at all)
Some useful expressions:
Thank you (very much) for + noun / -*ing*
I'm (really/very) sorry … but …

Write

3a Read the poster about an event at your school.

King Edward School, Westminster Road, WR12 1PQ

Thurs 7th April at 7 p.m. Explorer Timothy Shanklin talks about his recent trip to the Amazon jungle. Learn about the Peruvian tribes he stayed with and see some of his wonderful photos.

---

b You attended the talk with some friends. Now write a thank you letter to Mr Shanklin.

1 Thank him for coming and say what you enjoyed about the talk.
2 Apologise for writing late (you have just done exams).
3 End the main part of the letter in a polite and friendly way.
4 Add a PS (optional).

7 Language Revision

Grammar (20 marks)

1 Report the requests and commands. Use *told* or *asked*.

0 Mrs Jones to the class: 'Stop talking and listen to me!'
Mrs Jones told the class to stop talking and listen to her.

1 Anna to Claire: 'Could you help me, please?'

2 Police officer to John: 'Don't cycle without lights at night.'

3 Josh to his mum: 'Can you give me a lift to school, please?'

4 The magician to Jenny: 'Write the number on the card.'

.../4

2 Write sentences using reported speech and the words in brackets.

0 'We're going on holiday on Monday.' (They said …)
They said that they were going on holiday on Monday.

1 'I don't want to go home.' (Elsa said …)

2 'Ben had a great time on his birthday.' (Tom said …)

3 'I'll do the washing-up.' (Rob …)

4 'Jack's been to the USA twice.' (Mary told us …)

.../8

3 Put the words in the correct order. Then write the direct question.

0 to I school asked The reporter went me where
The reporter asked me where I went to school.
'Where do you go to school?'

1 asked drink wanted if we a My mum

2 her what could time She asked I meet

3 He going I was to asked who me invite

4 asked doing officer were The police we us what

.../8

Vocabulary (12 marks)

4 Put the adjectives in the correct order.

0 It's a(n) Japanese old interesting comic.
It's an interesting old Japanese comic.

1 They're black expensive leather shoes.

2 It's a(n) American exciting new film.

3 They're metal round small glasses.

4 He's a(n) young Italian popular actor.

5 Complete the words.

0 He hasn't got any hair. He's b<u>ald</u>.

1 They're good-looking. They're a___.

2 He's too heavy. He's o___.

3 She's very thin. She's s___.

4 Her hair almost covers her eyes. She's got a f___.

5 Bart and Lisa Simpson have got s___ hair.

6 I've got a picture on my arm. It's a t___.

7 Babies usually have r___ faces.

8 She's a teenager. She's in her t___.

.../8

Phrases/Use your English (8 marks)

6 Complete with phrases from the box.

> • hard luck, • Could I speak to • I can't think,
> • I'm so excited! • Just a minute,

A: Hello. ⁰ *Could I speak to* Justin Smith, please?
B: ¹___ I'll get him for you. Who's calling?
A: *The Quiz* magazine.
C: Hello. It's Justin Smith here.
A: Hello, Justin. You've won some money in a competition.
C: Er … , ²___ ³___ Have I won the hundred pound prize?
A: No,⁴___ Justin. You've only won ten pounds I'm afraid.

.../4

7 Look at the jumbled conversation. Number the lines in the correct order.

☐ a) Who's calling, please?
☐ b) Hang on. I'll get her… . Kelly.
☑ c) Hi, could I speak to Kelly, please?
☐ d) It's Eddie.
☐ e) Hello. It's Kelly here.

.../4

🔊 7 13 LISTEN AND CHECK YOUR SCORE	
Grammar	…/20
Vocabulary	…/12
Phrases/Use your English	…/8
Total	…/40

81

Exercise 3

1 My mum asked if we wanted a drink. 'Do you want a drink?'

2 She asked what time I could meet her. 'What time can you meet me?'

3 He asked me who I was going to invite. 'Who are you going to invite?'

4 The police officer asked us what we were doing. 'What are you doing?'

Exercise 4

1 expensive black leather 2 exciting new American 3 small round metal 4 popular young Italian

Exercise 5

1 attractive
2 overweight 3 slim
4 fringe 5 spiky
6 tattoo 7 round
8 teens

Exercise 6

1 Just a minute,
2 I can't think,
3 I'm so excited!
4 hard luck,

Exercise 7

2 a) 3 d) 4 b) 5 e)

eText
🎮 **Games**

Boat Game
Hangman
Pelmanism

Exercise 1

1 Anna asked Claire to help her.

2 The police officer told John not to cycle without lights at night.

3 Josh asked his mum to give him a lift to school.

4 The magician told Jenny to write the number on the card.

Exercise 2

1 Elsa said (that) she didn't want to go home.

2 Tom said (that) Ben had had a great time on his birthday.

3 Rob said (that) he would do the washing-up.

4 Mary told us (that) Jack had been to the USA twice.

ROUND-UP 1

ROUND-UP 2

Tell the Ss to look at the webpage headline and the photo on page 82 of the Students' Book. In pairs or small groups, ask them to discuss what the headline *Too much, too young?* might mean. Why do they think the headline ends with a question mark? What might be the pros and cons of success at a young age?

After discussion pairs/groups share their views with the class.

8 FEELINGS

8a How would you feel?

Grammar Second conditional
Vocabulary -ed and -ing adjectives

Get started

1 Do you ever watch reality TV shows? Tell the class.

Read

2 🔊 Listen and read the webpage. Why is Gary lonely?

Comprehension

3 Tick (✓) the true sentences. Correct the false ones.
1 Gary won a swimming competition.
  Gary won a singing competition.
2 He moved house.
3 He misses his old life.
4 *Jackson17* doesn't like Gary.
5 *dustyrose* and *mayab* would like to change places with Gary.
6 *twinkle* doesn't understand Gary's problem.

Grammar

Second conditional
Statements
If I **had** his opportunities, I **wouldn't look** back.
I**'d** probably **feel** the same **if** I **was/were** Gary.
If I **could change** places with Gary, I**'d do** it straightaway.
Questions and short answers
How **would** you **feel if** you **were** in Gary's situation?
Would you **miss** anything?
Yes, I **would**./No, I **wouldn't**.

> **Note**
> After *I*, *he*, *she* or *it*, we can use *was* or *were*.
> *Were* is more formal than *was*.
> *I'd feel the same if I was/were Gary.*
> BUT to give advice, we say: *If I were you, I'd …*

Too much too young?

Many people dream of fame and fortune, but teen singer Gary Williams, who recently won the TV talent show *The Wow Factor!*, has found it a disappointing experience.

Practice

4 Read the situations. Then write sentences with the second conditional form of the verbs.
1 I want to buy a new mobile, but I haven't got enough money.
  If I *had* (have) enough money, I *'d buy* (buy) a new mobile.
2 Jack usually goes out on Saturdays, but this week he's ill.
  If he ___ (not be) ill, he ___ (go) out.
3 I'd like to help you with your Maths, but I don't understand it!
  If I ___ (understand) it, I ___ (help) you!
4 You really don't need to worry.
  I ___ (not worry) if I ___ (be) you.
5 Joe wants to text Katie, but he doesn't know her number.
  Joe ___ (text) Katie if he ___ (know) her number.
6 We want to watch TV but we have lots of homework.
  We ___ (watch) TV if we ___ (not have) lots of homework.

82

Exercise 2
Because he doesn't often see his friends.

Exercise 3
2 ✓ 3 ✓ 4 ✗ *Jackson17* thinks he's amazing.
5 ✗ *dustyrose* and *mayab* wouldn't like to change places with Gary. 6 ✓

Exercise 4
2 wasn't/weren't, would 3 understood, would/'d help 4 wouldn't worry, was/were 5 would text, knew 6 would/'d watch, didn't have

Exercise 5
2 were, would you enter 3 would you say, didn't like 4 could, would you go 5 was/were, could, would it be

Since seventeen-year-old Gary won the competition, he has moved with his family to a large country house with a big swimming pool. He has left school to concentrate on his career in show business and has a personal tutor to help him with his exams. However, Gary is bored with his new life.

'I've got lots of money now, but I miss school,' he told us. 'It was exciting at first, but it isn't now. I don't often see my friends and I don't like all the travelling. I think maybe I'll go back to school.'

How would YOU feel if you were in Gary's situation? Would you miss anything? We'd love to hear your views.

If I had his opportunities, I wouldn't look back. Chances like that don't come along very often. So, if I were you, Gary, I'd stay there! PS I voted for him. He's amazing!
Jackson17, Cardiff

I think I can understand. If you were rich and famous, like Gary, how would you know your real friends? Some people would only like you for your money. I'd hate it.
dustyrose, Leeds

I'd probably feel the same if I was Gary. I think I would be quite lonely if I didn't see my school friends any more. I think I would miss them and regret moving away.
mayab, Malvern

If I could change places with Gary, I'd do it straightaway. He's incredibly lucky. It's the chance of a lifetime.
twinkle, Swansea

5 Complete the questions with the second conditional form of the verbs.
1 What *would you do* (you/do) if you *found* (find) a wallet on the bus?
2 If you ___ (be) a talented singer, ___ (you/enter) a talent show?
3 What ___ (you/say) if you ___ (not like) your friend's new hairstyle?
4 If you ___ (can) choose a holiday, where ___ (you/go)?
5 If your house ___ (be) on fire and you ___ (can) only save one thing, what ___ (it/be)?

Speak

6 Work in pairs. Ask and answer the questions from Exercise 5.
A: *What would you do if you found a wallet on the bus?*
B: *I'd look for a name and address inside it.*

Vocabulary: *-ed* and *-ing* adjectives

7 🔊 Listen and repeat. Then complete the sentences with words from the box.

- amazed/amazing • amused/amusing
- annoyed/annoying • bored/boring
- disappointed/disappointing
- embarrassed/embarrassing
- excited/exciting • frightened/frightening
- interested/interesting
- shocked/shocking • surprised/surprising
- tired/tiring

1 When I went to see the film I was excit*ed*, but I'm afraid it was disappoint*ing*.
2 We were very surpris___ when the lights went out, but nobody was frighten___.
3 At first the book was quite interest___, but I quickly became bor___.
4 Joe dropped his dinner. He was embarrass___, but we thought it was amus___.
5 Please turn that music down – it's very annoy___ and I am very tir___.
6 The concert was amaz___, but the price of the tickets was shock___.

Pronunciation: Elision /dj/
(*would_you, did_you*)

8 🔊 Go to page 117.

Listen

9 🔊 Tom and Amy are talking about being famous. Listen, then answer in pairs.

Give three reasons why …
1 Amy would like to be rich and famous.
She'd go shopping, …
2 Tom thinks it would be awful.

Write

10 Write a short paragraph. Begin like this:
I would/wouldn't like to be rich and famous because …

Extra practice

For more practice, go to page 109.

83

In their pairs, the Ss imagine that one of them has just won (or lost) a talent show; the other S is a friend/interviewer who asks them how they feel. Each partner should use the three adjectives at least once, e.g.:
A: *(Katie), you've just won Dance for Your Life. How do you feel?*
B: *I'm very surprised! But happy, too.*
A: *Was it frightening, performing in front of so many people?* etc.
More confident Ss can act out their conversation for the rest of the class. Ss can vote on which pair makes the best use of their adjectives.

Extra practice
Page 129

eText
Video and Animation
Grammar: Second conditional
Pronunciation: Elision /dj/
Use your English: Make suggestions

MOTIVATOR 8a

Exercise 7
2 surprised, frightened 3 interesting, bored
4 embarrassed, amusing 5 annoying, tired
6 amazing, shocking

Exercise 9
1 She'd have her photograph in magazines. She'd travel the world.
2 You'd get bored. People would follow you everywhere. People would say unkind things about you.

Extension

-ed and -ing adjectives
Write a selection of -ed and -ing adjectives on cards and turn the cards face down. Now ask Ss, in pairs, to pick up three adjectives at random from the pile.

103

Ask one S to go out of the room. The rest of the class chooses one *-ed* or *-ing* adjective from the list in Exercise 7 in Lesson 8a.

The S comes back and asks individual Ss to do certain actions. They have to act in the way suggested by the adjective, e.g. as though they are *bored* or they've just done something *tiring*.

After two or three Ss have performed, the S tries to guess the adjective. They should say both the *-ed* and the *-ing* form.

8b I wish we could stay longer.

Grammar *I wish* with past simple
Vocabulary Phrasal verbs with *out, up, on*

Get started

1 Look at the photo. What are the people doing? Have you ever done the same thing?

Read

2 Listen and read Maya's blog. Where are wishing trees traditional?

Maya in London

SUNDAY

Only three more days in London. I wish we could stay a bit longer – we certainly wouldn't run out of things to do! Never mind, we'll come again.

We went to a fair at our cousins' school on Saturday and saw this – it's a wishing tree. Children wrote their wishes on a piece of paper and then tied them to the branches.

We spent ages reading what other people had written. Here are some of my favourite ones.

1 I wish I was good at sport.

2 I wish we lived in a bigger house.

3 I wish my mum didn't work on Saturdays.

4 I wish my grandma wasn't ill.

5 I wish my dad had a job.

6 I wish I wasn't an only child.

7 I wish my brother and I got on better.

8 I wish I could speak Japanese.

9 I wish I could have a pet.

There were too many to read all of them. I had to give up! Of course we wrote our own wishes, too – but I'm not telling you what I wrote – it's a secret!

When I got home, I found out a bit more about wishing trees (I looked them up on dad's laptop). They're traditional in quite a few places. For example, in Japan they have them outside their temples. I think it's a beautiful idea.

84

Comprehension

3 Answer the questions in pairs.

1 Where did Maya see the tree?
at her cousins' school
2 What were people writing on the pieces of paper?
3 Did Maya read all the wishes on the tree?
4 What does she want to keep secret?
5 What did she do after the fair?

Exercise 1

They are tossing a coin into a fountain.

Exercise 2

in Japan

Exercise 3

2 their wishes 3 No, she didn't. 4 her wish 5 She read about wishing trees on her dad's laptop/the internet.

Vocabulary: Phrasal verbs with *out, up, on*

4 🔊 **8/06** Listen and repeat. Then match the phrasal verbs (1–10) to the correct meanings (a–j).

1 find out – e discover

> **out** • ¹find out • ²look out • ³run out (of)
> **on** • ⁴get on • ⁵go on • ⁶turn on
> **up** • ⁷cheer up • ⁸get up • ⁹give up
> • ¹⁰look up

a) be careful, keep watch b) be friends
c) become happy d) continue
e) discover f) get out of bed
g) have none left h) start (a machine)
i) stop (doing) something
j) find information (about)

5 Complete the sentences with words from Exercise 4. Then make sentences with the remaining phrasal verbs.

1 Don't worry. *Cheer* up.
2 There isn't any milk. We've ___ out.
3 This puzzle is impossible. I ___ up!
4 We shouldn't stop now. Let's go ___.
5 The roads are very icy tonight, so look ___.
6 'Who's that girl?' 'I don't know. Let's find ___.'

Grammar

> **I wish with past simple**
>
> **I wish** we **could** stay longer.
> **I wish** my mum **didn't work** on Saturdays.
> **I wish** I **wasn't/weren't** an only child.

Practice

6 Read the situations, then complete the sentences. Use the correct form of the verbs in the box.

> • be • not be • can • go • have • not live

1 I wish I *could* buy a new coat.
2 I'm too young to drive. I wish I ___ older.
3 I need a phone. I wish I ___ some money.
4 I wish my best friend ___ to my school.
5 It's noisy here. I wish we ___ on a main road.
6 I don't want to get up. I wish it ___ Monday morning.

7 Write two sentences about each picture. Use *I wish*, the prompts from the box and your own ideas.

> • be a celebrity • have a new bike
> • can draw and paint • live in a castle
> • not get homework • can play the piano

1 I wish I could play the piano.
I wish I was musical.

Listen

8 🔊 **8/07** Listen to Josh asking Anna some questions. Complete the sentences.

1 The question is: If you *could change three things in your life, what would they be*?
2 The rules are: You can't wish you ___ and you can't wish you ___.
3 Anna's first wish is: I wish ___.
4 Her second wish is: I wish ___ because ___.
5 Her third wish is: I wish ___. Then we could ___.

Speak and write

9a Look at Exercise 8 again. Read the question and the rules. What would your three wishes be? Why? Tell your partner.

b Write your wishes, and give reasons. Then tell the class.

I wish I could speak perfect English. I'd like to get a job in the USA.

Extra practice

▶ For more practice, go to page 109.

85

Exercise 8

2 were rich, had more wishes
3 I could play the saxophone
4 I was good at acting, I'd like to be a famous film star
5 we didn't have school in the morning, stay in bed until lunchtime

Extension ▰

Phrasal verbs with *out, up, on*
Ask the Ss to work in pairs to make up a conversation between two people. They should use three, or if possible four, of the phrasal verbs from Exercise 4 in Lesson 8b. They should try to make the conversation flow as naturally as possible. Monitor the pairs as they work, giving help where necessary. When Ss are happy with their conversation, they put it down on paper. More confident pairs could then act it out for the class. The rest of the class could vote on whose conversation is the best/sounds the most natural.

Extra practice
Page 129

MOTIVATOR 8b

Exercise 4
2 a) 3 g) 4 b) 5 d) 6 h) 7 c) 8 f) 9 i) 10 j)

Exercise 5
2 run 3 give 4 on 5 out 6 out
+ Students' own answers

Exercise 6
2 was/were 3 had 4 went 5 didn't live 6 wasn't

Exercise 7
2 I wish I lived in a castle. (I wish I was/were rich.)
3 I wish I didn't get any homework. (I wish my bag wasn't so heavy.)
4 I wish I could draw and paint. (I wish I was/were artistic.)
5 I wish I was/were a celebrity. (I wish I could sing.)
6 I wish I had a new bike. (I wish I had more money.)

Look back ‹‹‹

I wish with past simple

Ss work in small groups. Each S thinks of three things to tell the others in their group what they wish. Two of the statements should be true and one should be false. The Ss take it in turns to make their statements and guess which are true/untrue. The Ss who are guessing can ask questions to test the 'truth' of the wishes.

Exercise 1

The Wow Factor!

Exercise 2

1 *Jodie*, Emma
2 Luke 3 Stella, Emma 4 Jodie, Luke 5 Luke, Jodie

Exercise 3b

2 cartoon
3 the news
4 talent show
5 sitcom/comedy
6 chat show
7 wildlife programme
8 quiz show

Exercise 4

£2.50

Exercise 5

2 so 3 such an 4 so 5 such 6 such a

8c It was so boring I fell asleep.

Grammar	*so* + adjective … *(that)* …
	such (a/an) + adjective + noun *(that)* …
Vocabulary	Types of TV programme
Function	Make suggestions

Dialogue

1 🔊 **08** Listen and read. Which programme is starting?

Jodie: Great. It's *The Wow Factor!* after the news. It's my favourite show.
Luke: Oh please! It was so boring last week I nearly fell asleep.
Jodie: Boring? It wasn't. Remember Kevin? The judges made such nasty comments that he cried!
Luke: Oh come on, guys. Let's watch a comedy or a quiz show.
Jodie: No way! It's the final tonight. I'm pretty sure who'll win. Stella's such a fantastic singer everyone will vote for her.
Luke: You mean the others are so awful that there won't be any choice.
Emma: I think Stella's really talented. I voted for her five times.
Luke: What a waste of money!
Jodie: OK, Luke. If you don't want to watch it, why don't you get us some snacks?
Luke: Hmmm, maybe in a minute. Jodie, move your feet, I can't see the screen.
Jodie: But I thought …
Luke: Sssh! It's starting.

Phrases
• No way! • What a waste of (money)!
• in a minute

Comprehension

2 Complete the sentences with names from the box.

> Jodie   Emma   Luke   Stella

1 *Jodie* and ___ enjoy watching *The Wow Factor!*
2 ___ wants to watch a different programme.
3 ___ sings on the show and ___ voted for her.
4 ___ asks ___ to get some food.
5 ___ surprises ___.

86

Exercise 6

2 They had such good teachers (that) they passed their exams.
3 It was such a bad film (that) lots of people left.
4 They were such delicious cakes (that) I ate three.
5 We travelled such a long way (that) it took all day.

Extension

Types of TV programmes

Play 20 questions with TV programmes. Demonstrate first by choosing a well-known TV programme which Ss then have to guess. Explain that they should find out what type of programme it is first and they can only ask *yes/no* questions, e.g. *Is it a soap opera? Is it a sports programme? Is it on TV every week?* etc.

When Ss have guessed, put them into small groups to play the game.

Vocabulary: Types of TV programme

3a 🎧8/09 **Listen and repeat. Which types of programme do you like and which don't you like?**

- cartoon • chat show • comedy
- cookery programme • documentary • film
- the news • quiz show • reality TV show
- sitcom (situation comedy) • soap opera
- sports programme • talent show
- wildlife programme

b 🎧8/10 **Listen and say which type of programme it is. Which one has two possible answers?**

1 – sports programme

SOLVE IT!

4 🎧8/10 **Listen again. How much did Emma spend when she voted for Stella last week?**

Grammar

so + adjective … (that) …

It was **so boring (that)** I nearly fell asleep.

such (a/an) + adjective + noun (that) …

Stella's **such a fantastic singer (that)** everyone will vote for her.
The judges made **such nasty comments (that)** he cried.

5 **Complete the sentences with one or two words.**

1 That's *such a* great film I've seen it three times.
2 The show was ___ funny we couldn't stop laughing.
3 It was ___ old film that it was in black and white.
4 The audience were ___ pleased they laughed and clapped.
5 They were ___ terrible players that they lost 13–0.
6 She was ___ good singer she won the contest.

6 **Join the sentences with so or such (a/an) + adjective (that) …**

1 Jake was tall. He hit his head on the ceiling.
Jake was so tall (that) he hit his head on the ceiling.
2 They had good teachers. They passed their exams.
3 It was a bad film. Lots of people left.
4 They were delicious cakes. I ate three.
5 We travelled a long way. It took all day.

Use your English: Make suggestions

7 🎧8/11 **Listen and repeat. Then practise the conversation in pairs.**

A: How about watching the football?
B: No, thanks. I'd rather watch a film.
A: OK, do you fancy a James Bond film?
B: Yes, that sounds good.

Make suggestions
What/How about watching the news?
Let's watch a comedy.
We could watch a DVD.
Do you fancy watching the football?
Why don't we watch a cartoon?
Shall we watch a documentary?

Respond
Yes,/OK, that sounds good.
I'm not sure.
No, not really.
I don't really fancy that/watching a film.
I don't really like documentaries.

Express preferences
I'd rather (not) watch a cartoon.
I'd prefer (not) to watch that show.

8 **In pairs, practise similar conversations about next weekend. Use the ideas in the box or your own ideas.**

- phone for a pizza • go to town
- go swimming • do some revision
- listen to music • go to a rock concert

Extra practice
For more practice, go to page 109.

87

Extra practice
Page 129

MOTIVATOR 8c

eText
 Video and Animation

Grammar: *so* + adjective … (that) …; *such* (a/an) + adjective + noun (that)

Exercise 2

Because people were sending horrible messages to Andy online.

Exercise 3

1 Andy had won a prize and he had become the captain of the football team.
2 A teacher's pet is the teacher's favourite student.
3 He was very upset.
4 He didn't want to talk about it.
5 She tried to talk to the bullies.

Exercise 6

2 Andy should tell his parents.
3 They would tell the school and make the situation worse.
4 She offers to go with him to tell a teacher.
5 Yes.

Exercise 7

The teacher says 2, 3 and 5.

Exercise 8a

2 Mrs Williams to the students.
3 One of the bullies to the other bullies.
4 Andy to Anna.
5 Anna to Andy.

8d Online bullying

SKILLS FOCUS: LISTENING AND SPEAKING

REAL LIFE ISSUE

1 Andy had received the school prize for 'best student'. That wasn't all – the sports teacher had made him captain of the football team, too. When he read the message, he was very upset.

Hello, teacher's pet

2 HAVE YOU SEEN WHAT THEY'RE SAYING ABOUT YOU ONLINE? IT'S HORRIBLE.

DROP IT, ANNA. I DON'T CARE. I'M FINE.

Several people were posting nasty messages online. When his friend Anna tried to discuss it, he told her to leave him alone.

3 I WISH I COULD DO SOMETHING.

The messages continued. Sometimes Andy replied, but that made it worse. Anna was worried, but what could she do?

4 YOU WEREN'T ON FORM TODAY, ANDY. IS EVERYTHING OK?

EVERYTHING'S FINE, THANKS.

CAPTAIN

Andy couldn't concentrate on anything. He was so embarrassed and ashamed he didn't want to tell anyone.

5 STOP IT, IT'S SO MEAN.

WE AREN'T HURTING ANYONE.

Anna asked the bullies to stop, but they said it was just a bit of fun. They told her not to waste her time on Andy.

6 IF I TOLD THE TEACHERS, IT WOULD MAKE IT WORSE. AND NOW EVEN ANNA'S TALKING TO THEM AND NOT ME.

Andy felt terrible. He didn't know what to do.

NEW WORDS
- post (v) • nasty • on form
- concentrate • ashamed • bully (n)
- a bit of fun • waste time

88

Extension

In groups, Ss could act out Andy's story. Different Ss take the roles of Andy, Anna, the teacher and, depending on the size of your class, two of the bullies. Groups could adapt the story line, as they wish, as long as they keep the core theme of online bullying.

Before they begin, they need to decide who takes which role, the gist of the story and if they wish to add an ending to the story. If they add an ending, they will need to discuss what each of them wrote in Exercise 8b and agree on which ending they think works best.

Monitor Ss as they play their roles, giving help where needed. More confident groups could act out their story for the rest of the class.

Get started

1 Work in pairs. Say or find out what 'to bully' means. Why do people bully other people? Discuss your ideas, then tell the class.

Read

2 Listen and read the story. Why was Anna worried?

Comprehension

3 Discuss the questions in pairs, then tell the class.

1 What two things happened just before the messages started?
2 What do you think 'teacher's pet' means?
3 How did Andy react to the first message?
4 What happened when Anna talked to him about the messages?
5 What did Anna do next?

Speak your mind!

SPEAKING TIP: EXPLAIN YOUR IDEAS
Don't just give one word answers. Try to expand them and add a sentence or two to explain your ideas.
Now do Exercise 4.

4 Work in pairs. Read the advice for Andy and add your own ideas if you wish. Then number the advice from best to worst: 1 = the best.

☐ Do nothing. The bullies will soon get bored.
☐ Tell a teacher or your parents.
☐ Reply to the messages – be nasty back!
☐ It's simple. Don't go online or use your phone.
☐ Discuss what's happening with your friends.
☐ Your own ideas.

5 Discuss in pairs. What do you think Andy should (and shouldn't) do?

A: I think he should … because …
B: I don't agree. I don't think …

Listen

LISTENING TIP: BE PATIENT
If you don't understand everything, don't worry. Listen for key words, and wait for the next sentences.
Now do Exercise 6.

6 Listen to the conversation, then answer the questions.

1 What does Andy want to say to Anna?
He wants to say 'sorry'.
2 What is Anna's first suggestion?
3 Why doesn't he think it's a good idea?
4 What does Anna offer to do?
5 Does he accept the offer?

7 Listen to the conversation with Mrs Williams. Tick (✓) what she says.

1 ☐ It's best to do nothing.
2 ☐ The bullies will start bullying someone else.
3 ☐ They don't understand what they're doing.
4 ☐ Andy should try to make friends with them.
5 ☐ She's going to talk to everyone.
6 ☐ Andy should fight back.

Speak and write

8a Work in pairs. Read the speech bubbles. Who is speaking and who are they talking to?

1 I've heard stories about bullying from lots of different people.

Mrs Williams is talking at the meeting to all the students.

2 If it doesn't stop I will call a meeting for all your parents.

3 Do you think she'll tell our parents?

4 Ha ha, she really frightened them. You're a real friend.

5 No problem. I'm glad things are better now.

b How does the story end? Choose one of the ideas below, or use your own ideas. Add details to the idea and then write the end of the story.

- One of the bullies apologises and after some time he and Andy become friends.
- Andy and Anna start an anti-bullying campaign at their school.
- Some messages continue and as a result, Mrs Williams punishes some of the students.

89

Exercise 1

1 would you feel,
you won 2 you
saw, would you do
3 wouldn't worry,
I were/was you
4 Would Rachel be,
I brought

Exercise 2

1 I wish we didn't
have Maths
today.
2 I wish the bus
wasn't (always)
late.
3 I wish I didn't feel
tired.
4 I wish I could go
out tonight.

Exercise 3

1 so frightening
2 such an old
3 so bored
4 such an exciting

Exercise 4

1 disappointing
2 excited
3 annoying
4 shocked

Exercise 5

1 get 2 give 3 run
4 go

Exercise 6

1 opera 2 show
3 life 4 corn

Exercise 7

2 c) 3 b) 4 e) 5 d)
6 f)

Exercise 8

1 I don't 2 I'd prefer
3 What about
4 I'd rather
5 don't really
6 why don't
7 We could

---

8 Language Revision

Grammar (16 marks)

1 Complete the sentences using the second conditional.

0 What kind of TV show _would you be_ (you/be) in if _you could_ (you/can) choose?
1 How ___ (you/feel) if ___ (you/win) a talent show?
2 If ___ (you/see) an accident, what ___ (you/do)?
3 I ___ (not worry) if ___ (I/be/you).
4 ___ (Rachel/be) annoyed if ___ (I/bring) a friend to her party?

.../8

2 Write sentences starting with *I wish*.

0 It's Monday morning.
I wish it wasn't Monday morning.
1 We have Maths today.
2 The bus is always late.
3 I feel tired.
4 I can't go out tonight.

.../4

3 Complete the sentences with *so* or *such (a/an)* and the words in the box.

• old • bored • frightening • ~~bad~~ • exciting

0 He was _such a bad_ singer that everyone laughed.
1 The film was ___ that I hid behind the sofa.
2 It was ___ TV that it was black and white.
3 I was ___ that I fell asleep.
4 It was ___ show that everyone watched it.

.../4

Vocabulary (12 marks)

4 Choose the correct options.

0 I was [surprised] / surprising when I saw the birthday cake!
1 The documentary was very **disappointing / disappointed**.
2 I was very **exciting / excited** by the story. You'll love it.
3 It was very **annoyed / annoying** when the train was late.
4 I was **shocked / shocking** when my mobile rang.

.../4

5 Complete the sentences with verbs from the box.

• ~~find~~ • get • give • go • run

0 Look at a dictionary to _find_ out the answers.
1 We aren't friends. We don't ___ on.
2 This is too difficult. I ___ up.
3 There isn't much milk. We might ___ out.
4 I'm really tired. I can't ___ on much longer.

.../4

6 Complete the types of TV programmes.

1 soap ___   3 wild___ programme
2 chat ___   4 sit___

.../4

Phrases/Use your English (12 marks)

7 Look at the jumbled conversation. Number the lines in the correct order.

☐ 1 a) Fred: Hey guys. How about going to the cinema?
☐ b) Fred: No way! The screen is too small.
☐ c) Ben: What a waste of money! I've got loads of films on my computer.
☐ d) Alex: Come on guys. Let's watch TV. Fred you can get some crisps.
☐ e) Ben: No, it isn't.
☐ f) Fred: Hmm, maybe in a minute.

.../5

8 Complete with phrases from the box.

• What about • why don't • I'd prefer
• don't really • I'd rather • ~~Shall we~~ • I don't
• We could

A: ⁰ _Shall we_ watch a documentary?
B: ¹___ fancy that. ²___ to watch a film.
A: ³___ watching *Skyfall*?
B: ⁴___ not watch that. I ⁵___ like action films.
A: OK, ⁶___ you choose something?
B: ⁷___ watch The Simpsons.
A: OK, that sounds good.

.../7

 LISTEN AND CHECK YOUR SCORE

Grammar	.../16
Vocabulary	.../12
Phrases/Use your English	.../12
Total	**.../40**

90

ROUND-UP 1

ROUND-UP 2

eText

Games

Boat Game

Hangman

Pelmanism

110

Skills Revision

Skills Revision

Read

1 Read the article about Mark the teenage magician. Complete the factfile with the numbers in the box.

- 50,000 • ten • eleven • two • ~~seventeen~~ • five

Name: Mark
Age: [1]*seventeen*
Number of Twitter followers: [2]___
Number of magic awards won: [3]___
Age of his first performance in the theatre: [4]___
Age he performed his first magic trick: [5]___
Number of appearances on TV shows: [6]___

2 Read the article again and complete the notes.

1 Mark likes ___.
2 He would like to see ___ more.
3 Some people aren't nice about ___.
4 If he wasn't a(n) ___ he'd be a(n) ___.

Listen

3 🔊 8 16 Listen to the conversation. Answer true (T), false (F) or doesn't say (DS).

0 Fred wants his sister to do his homework. *T*
1 Alice's Maths homework is easier than Fred's.
2 Mr Philips told Fred to give him the homework on Tuesday.
3 Fred doesn't look up the answers online.
4 Alice is going to the concert with Belinda.
5 Alice's mum told her not to go out with Gina.

Write

4 Write a blog entry about your favourite TV programme. Use the notes to help you.

- name and type of programme
- where and when you can watch it
- the people in the programme
- what happens in the programme
- why you like it

My favourite TV programme is …

THAT'S MAGIC!

Mark Foster is a celebrity magician and he's only seventeen years old. He performed his first trick when he was five years old and was performing in the theatre by the age of eleven. He has appeared in ten TV shows and has performed all over the country. He's also won two magic awards. When I asked him what he liked doing in his spare time he said that he liked sleeping. 'I wish I had more time to see my friends, but I don't.' Foster regularly appears on TV in front of half a million viewers. I asked him if he was afraid of anything and he told me: 'I worry that I might run out of ideas or forget my tricks, but I love being on TV.' Mark has over 50,000 followers on Twitter. He says 'I love my tweets, but some people can be quite rude about my card tricks.' What would Mark be if he wasn't a magician? 'I'd be an artist of some kind. I'm into design and painting.' And after that, he disappeared … !

NOW I CAN		
Read	find information in an article.	☐
Listen	identify the key details in a conversation.	☐
Write	write a blog about a TV programme.	☐

91

Exercise 1

2 50,000 3 two 4 eleven 5 five 6 ten

Exercise 2

1 sleeping 2 his friends 3 his card tricks
4 a magician, an artist

Exercise 3

1 F 2 DS 3 T 4 F 5 T

eText

📀 **Additional video lesson**

To watch a vlog *Who's got talent*, go to Students' eText, page 71.

For the worksheets and teaching notes go to the Teacher's Resource Materials folder.

111

Look forward ⟫⟫

Tell the Ss to look at the photo on pages 92–93 of the Students' Book. Focus on the title of this lesson, *You can't afford to buy it*. Ask some lead-in questions (you can write them on the board):

1 *Where do you think Tom and Emma are?*
(in a computer/ electronics shop)

2 *What items can you see on display in the shop? What other things do you think the shop might sell?*
(monitor/screen, games console, games; other things such as laptops, tablets, smartphones, computer accessories)

3 *What do you think Tom and Emma are saying?*

Exercise 1

Tom would like to buy a games console, a tablet computer and some new apps.

Exercise 2

2 DS 3 DS 4 T 5 F 6 F

Exercise 3

£150

9a You can't afford to buy it.

Grammar Verb with infinitive or gerund
Vocabulary Computer language

Dialogue

1 🎧 Listen and read. Which things would Tom like to buy?

Comprehension

2 Answer true (T), false (F) or doesn't say (DS).

1 Emma prefers laptops to tablets. *T*
2 Tom likes computer games.
3 Emma doesn't like computer shops.
4 Emma likes the games console.
5 Tom's got enough money to buy the games console.
6 Emma says she'll buy the console with Tom.

Phrases

- I know what you mean, - I'd so like …
- , that's all. - for a bit - go halves
- Nice try,

SOLVE IT!

3 How much is the games console?

Vocabulary: Computer language

4 Recall Complete the words. Then check the Word bank on page 112.

1 *send* an email.
2 o___ an attachment
3 d___e old files
4 ___n__t to the i__t__t
5 protect your PC from v___es
6 d___wn___d s___f___w___e

92

Tom: Look at all this cool stuff. What do you think? Which is better, a tablet or a laptop?

Emma: A laptop. I don't really like using touchscreens. I prefer to have a keyboard.

Tom: I know what you mean, but I'd so like a tablet. Come on, let's go in.

Emma: Oh no. Knowing you, you'll decide to test every game in the shop.

Tom: No, I promise not to be long. I fancy trying out some new apps, that's all.

Emma: Well, OK. I don't mind going in for a bit.

…

Emma: Why do you keep staring at that games console, Tom?

Tom: Well, it's so cool. Do you like it?

Emma: Umm, what do you want me to say? Yes, it's great, but look at the price. You can't afford to buy it.

Tom: I could save my pocket money.

Emma: Tom, you get £5 a week. It'll take you thirty weeks.

Tom: We could go halves.

Emma: Nice try, Tom, nice try.

5 🎧 Extension Listen and repeat. Then match the sentences (1–6) to words from the box. There are four extra words.

- app (application) - charge - games console
- MP3 player - reboot - smartphone - tablet
- touchscreen - upload - wi-fi

1 You can connect to the internet with this phone. *smartphone*
2 You don't need a mouse – just touch this.
3 This is a small, flat, rectangular computer.
4 This is broadband without wires.
5 If the computer crashes, do this.
6 Do this when your phone needs more power.

Speak

6 Discuss in pairs or groups. If you could buy one thing from a computer shop, what would you choose? Why?

I'd buy a smartphone. Then I'd have everything I need, all in one place!
I wouldn't. I'd go for a …

Exercise 4

2 open 3 delete 4 connect, internet 5 viruses 6 download software

Exercise 5

2 touchscreen 3 tablet 4 wi-fi 5 reboot 6 charge

Exercise 7

2 doing, to notice 3 riding, damaging 4 seeing, to visit 5 to call, to hear 6 getting, to go out

Exercise 8

2 switching 3 to look 4 to solve 5 trying 6 to take 7 to give 8 charging 9 to work

Grammar

Verb with infinitive

You**'ll decide to test** every game in the shop.

I **promise not to be** long.

(can) afford, agree, decide, expect, hope, manage, offer, promise, refuse, seem, want

Note

We can also use a direct object after *want*:

*What do **you want me to** say?*

Verb with gerund

I **fancy trying out** some new apps.

I **don't mind going** in for a bit.

admit, avoid, can't stand, deny, enjoy, fancy, finish, give up, keep, look forward to, not mind, miss, practise, stop, suggest

Note

The verbs *hate, like, love, prefer* and *start* can be followed by either an infinitive or a gerund.

Practice

7 **Complete the sentences with the correct form of the verbs in brackets.**

1 Sam can't stand *playing* (play) football, but he enjoys *watching* (watch) it on TV.

2 Tom always avoids ___ (do) the washing-up and Mum never seems ___ (notice).

3 Dan admitted ___ (ride) the bike without permission, but he denied ___ (damage) it.

4 Jack's friends miss ___ (see) him and they want him ___ (visit) them soon.

5 John promised ___ (call) so I expect ___ (hear) from him soon.

6 I don't mind ___ (get) wet, but Jane refuses ___ (go out) in the rain.

8 **Complete with the correct form of verbs from the box.**

> • charge • download • give • look • solve
> • switch • take • try • work

My sister wanted [1]*to download* some apps on to her new smartphone, but the phone kept [2]___ off. I offered [3]___ at it, but I didn't manage [4]___ the problem. After about an hour we gave up [5]___ and my sister decided [6]___ the phone back to the shop. She wanted them [7]___ her money back, but the shop assistant suggested [8]___ the phone for 24 hours. That seemed [9]___ because it's OK now.

Speak and write

9a **Work in pairs. Complete the sentences with infinitives or gerunds. Then tell your partner.**

1 I can't stand *getting up*.

2 I don't mind ___.

3 I've given up ___.

4 I enjoy ___ .

5 I'm looking forward to ___.

6 I hope ___.

7 I expect ___.

8 I miss ___.

b **Write about your partner.**

Rosa can't stand doing the washing-up. She doesn't mind …

Extra practice

For more practice, go to page 110.

---

eText

🖥 **Video and Animation**

Grammar: Verb with infinitive or gerund

MOTIVATOR 9a

Extension

Computer language

Write the heading *Computer language* on the board. Give Ss, in pairs, one minute to list all the computer language vocabulary they now know in English. After one minute, ask how many words they have written down. They then swap their lists with another pair who check and correct any spelling mistakes. Record all the words on the board.

Ss should give two points for a correctly spelt word, and one point for a correct word, but with a spelling mistake.

Extra practice

Page 130

Verb with infinitive or gerund

Ss write *infinitive* and *gerund* on separate cards/ slips of paper. Call out different verbs from the Grammar boxes in Lesson 9a, e.g. *refuse*, *suggest*. Ss hold up the appropriate card to indicate whether the verb is followed by an infinitive or a gerund. If the verb can be followed by either an infinitive or gerund, Ss should hold up both their cards. Individual Ss could take turns to do the calling out.

Exercise 2

It's like a triathlon (race of running, swimming and cycling) but the athlete juggles at the same time.

Exercise 3

2 don't have
3 all 4 continued
5 the fastest ever 'juggathlete'

Exercise 5b

1 goal, spectators, pitch, referee
2 coach, team, score, points, win
3 beat, racket, net, umpire

9b He had to swim on his back.

Grammar Rules and obligation: *must* and *have to*
Vocabulary Sport (equipment, people and actions)

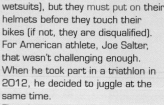

SUPERMAN!

Have you ever watched (or competed in) a triathlon? If so, you already know that it isn't easy. Competitors have to run, swim and cycle long distances – but that's not all. They mustn't stop between each section and they even have to change their clothes fast (it's part of the race!). They don't have to wear special clothes when they are cycling (some cycle in their wetsuits), but they must put on their helmets before they touch their bikes (if not, they are disqualified). For American athlete, Joe Salter, that wasn't challenging enough. When he took part in a triathlon in 2012, he decided to juggle at the same time.

First, he swam nearly half a kilometre (he had to swim on his back, of course!). While he was swimming (in the sea, not a pool!), he managed to juggle three balls. Next, he cycled 26 kilometres. He could only use one hand because he had to hold the handlebar with the other, but he juggled two balls the whole way.

Finally, he ran nearly six and a half kilometres and juggled three balls at the same time.

He only dropped a ball three times. Luckily it happened while he was swimming, so he didn't have to go back for it – it was floating next to him!

Joe crossed the line in just under two hours. Spectators lined the track and cheered. He hadn't won the race, but he'd set a world record for the juggling triathlon (the 'juggathlon'!).

Get started

1 What is the hardest sport you've ever tried? Did you enjoy it? Why?/Why not?

Read

2 (9 03) Read the article. What is a 'juggathlon'?

Comprehension

3 Choose the correct options.
1 A triathlon is **three separate races /** one continuous race .
2 The athletes **have / don't have** a rest after each section.
3 Joe Salter juggled for **all / part** of the triathlon.
4 When he dropped a ball, he went **back / continued**.
5 Joe was **the first across the line / the fastest ever** 'juggathlete'.

94

Exercise 6

2 don't, to 3 have 4 must, mustn't 5 had 6 have

Exercise 7

3 When traffic lights turn red, you must/have to stop.
4 You mustn't text your friends in class. 5 ✓
6 Teachers don't have to wear uniforms.

Exercise 8

2 table tennis 3 keep moving 4 keep hitting the ball
5 drop their bats 6 10 points 7 table skating

Extension ▮

Sport/Rules and obligation: *must* and *have to*

In pairs, Ss choose a sport and write down the rules. They then explain the rules to the class (without naming the sport), using *must/have to* as appropriate. Can anyone guess the sport?

Extra practice

Page 130

Vocabulary: Sport (equipment, people and actions)

4 Recall Think of sports and say where you play them. Then check the Word bank on page 112.

A: You play basketball on a court.

5a 🎧(9/04) Extension Listen and repeat.

Equipment:	• ball • basket • bat • glove • goal • helmet • net • racket • (shin) pads • wetsuit
People:	• athlete • coach • cyclist • goalkeeper • player • referee • spectator • team • umpire
Actions:	• beat (your opponent/a team) • hit/kick/throw/pass (the ball) • play/win/lose/draw (a match) • score (a goal/point)

b Choose the correct options.

1 Yesterday I went to a football match. When United **scored** / won a brilliant **point / goal**, some **spectators / players** ran on to the **track / pitch** and the **referee / goalkeeper** stopped the game.

2 Anna loves basketball. She was happy when the **umpire / coach** chose her for the **team / court**. She didn't **score / beat** any **points / matches**, but she helped to **win / beat** the match.

3 When the tennis player **beat / won** his opponent, he threw his **bat / racket** on the ground and jumped over the **net / basket**. Then he shook hands with the other player and the **spectator / umpire**.

Grammar

Rules and obligation: *must/have to*

Obligation	
Present	**Past**
Competitors **have to run, swim** and **cycle** long distances. They **must put** on their helmets.	He **had to swim** on his back.
They **mustn't stop** between each section.	
No obligation	
Present	**Past**
They **don't have to wear** special clothes.	He **didn't have to go** back.

Note
We often use *must / mustn't* for written rules.

Practice

6 Complete each gap with one word.

1 Football referees *mustn't* kick the ball.
2 You ___ have ___ wear goggles at the swimming pool.
3 Basketball players don't ___ to be tall, but they often are.
4 Tennis players ___ use rackets. They ___ throw or kick the ball.
5 In 2012, a Polish football match ___ to stop because of a cow on the pitch.
6 Before 2003, cyclists in the Tour de France didn't ___ to wear helmets.

7 Tick (✓) the sentences that are true and correct the ones that are false. Sometimes there are two correct answers.

1 ☒ Train passengers mustn't buy a ticket.
Train passengers must/have to buy tickets.
2 ☑ Before mobile phones, people had to use landlines.
3 ☐ When traffic lights turn red, you don't have to stop.
4 ☐ You have to text your friends in class.
5 ☐ A hundred years ago, drivers didn't have to take a test.
6 ☐ Teachers have to wear uniforms.

Listen

8 🎧(9/05) Listen to Harry and Cathy. Complete the description of Harry's new game.

The game is ¹*ice-skating* and ² ___ together. Players have to ³ ___ round the table and they have to ⁴ ___ over the net at the same time. They mustn't ⁵ ___. They have to score ⁶ ___ to win. The game is called ⁷ ___.

Write

9 Now invent your own sport. Put two sports or activities together and write a description of it. Then give it a name.

My new sport is called … It's …

Extra practice

➤ For more practice, go to page 110.

95

eText
📺 Video and Animation

Grammar: Rules and obligations: *must* and *have to*

`MOTIVATOR 9b`

Sport

Play 20 questions with different sports and/or people in sport (such as *referee*). Demonstrate first by choosing a sport which Ss then have to guess. Explain that they can only ask *yes/ no* or *sometimes* questions, e.g. *Do you play in a team? Do you play outside?*

When Ss have guessed, put them into small groups to play the game.

Exercise 2

Luke might visit Martin.

9c It's so different from London.

Grammar and vocabulary Adjectives with prepositions
Function Say goodbye

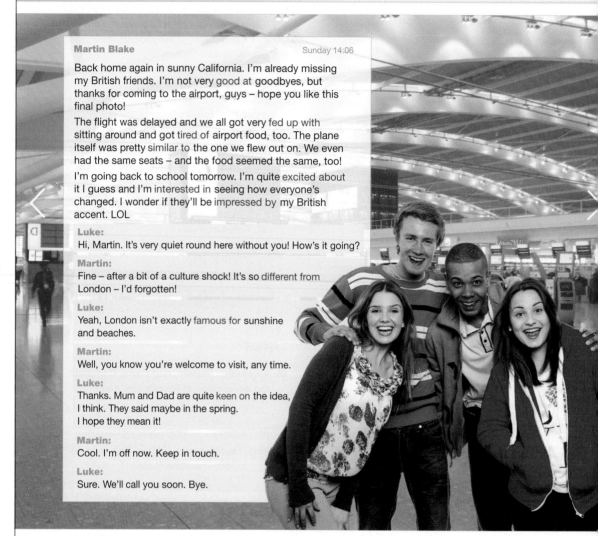

Martin Blake   Sunday 14:06

Back home again in sunny California. I'm already missing my British friends. I'm not very good at goodbyes, but thanks for coming to the airport, guys – hope you like this final photo!

The flight was delayed and we all got very fed up with sitting around and got tired of airport food, too. The plane itself was pretty similar to the one we flew out on. We even had the same seats – and the food seemed the same, too!

I'm going back to school tomorrow. I'm quite excited about it I guess and I'm interested in seeing how everyone's changed. I wonder if they'll be impressed by my British accent. LOL

Luke:
Hi, Martin. It's very quiet round here without you! How's it going?

Martin:
Fine – after a bit of a culture shock! It's so different from London – I'd forgotten!

Luke:
Yeah, London isn't exactly famous for sunshine and beaches.

Martin:
Well, you know you're welcome to visit, any time.

Luke:
Thanks. Mum and Dad are quite keen on the idea, I think. They said maybe in the spring. I hope they mean it!

Martin:
Cool. I'm off now. Keep in touch.

Luke:
Sure. We'll call you soon. Bye.

Get started

1 Which do you prefer, going away on holiday or coming home again? Why? Tell your partner.

Read

2 Listen and read Martin's webpage. What might happen next spring?

96

Comprehension

3 Discuss the questions in pairs.
1 Who said goodbye to Martin at the airport? How do you know?
2 How did Martin and his family feel at the airport? Why?
3 What is Martin looking forward to? What does he think his friends will notice?
4 What does Martin say about the place where he lives? What does Luke know about it?
5 Does Luke want to visit Martin? How do you know?

Exercise 3

1 Luke, Jodie and Emma said goodbye to Martin. They are all in the photo that was taken at the airport.
2 They felt bored, because the plane was late.
3 Martin's looking forward to going back to school. He thinks his friends will notice his British accent.

4 It's very different from London. Luke knows that it's very sunny there and it's got lots of beaches.
5 Yes, he does. Because he hopes his parents are serious about the idea.

Exercise 4

2 with 3 of 4 to 5 about 6 in 7 by 8 from 9 for 10 on

Grammar and vocabulary

Adjectives with prepositions

I'm not very **good at** goodbyes.
We all got very **fed up with** sitting around.
It's so **different from** London.

> **Note**
> The preposition is followed by a noun or pronoun or the
> -ing form of the verb.

Practice

4 Complete the table with the correct prepositions. Use the webpage in Exercise 2 to help you.

¹good/bad/surprised		*at*
²fed up/bored/angry/annoyed		
³tired/scared/frightened/proud		
⁴similar		
⁵excited/upset/worried	+	
⁶interested		
⁷impressed		
⁸different		
⁹famous/responsible		
¹⁰keen		

5 Complete the sentences with the words from the box and the correct preposition.

> • bored • different • interested
> • responsible • scared • similar • surprised
> • upset

1 Kate's phone is *similar to* mine – they're almost the same.
2 I have to do some housework. I'm ___ the washing-up.
3 Ella isn't very happy. She's just had her exam results and she's ___ failing them.
4 We weren't expecting to win. We were ___ the result.
5 Jack isn't like his brother at all. He's completely ___ him.
6 Help! There's a spider! I'm really ___ them!
7 John's got lots of books about planes. He's very ___ flying.
8 Let's watch a different programme. I'm getting a bit ___ this one.

Speak

6 Talk about you. Choose five words from the box and make true sentences about you. Then tell your partner.

> • bad • bored • fascinated • fed up
> • good • interested • keen • proud • tired
> • worried

I'm interested in old films.

Pronunciation: Linking sounds

quite excited about it

7 🎧 9/07 Go to page 117.

Use your English: Say goodbye

8 🎧 9/08 Listen and repeat. Then practise the conversation in pairs.

A: Have a good trip. We'll miss you.
B: Thanks. I'll miss you, too.
A: Let us know when you get there.
B: Sure. Thanks again for everything.
A: See you again soon, I hope. Take care.
B: You too. Bye, then. See you soon.

Say goodbye	
Parting remarks	**Responses**
Have a good/safe trip!	Thank you./Thanks.
Have a great time!	
Take care./Look after yourself.	I will. You, too.
Let us know when you get there.	Sure./I will.
Don't forget to call/ text/keep in touch.	No, I won't.
See you soon!	Yes, I hope so./See you.

9 Now practise similar conversations in pairs.

Extra practice

➤ For more practice, go to page 110.

Extra practice
Page 130

eText
📀 **Video and Animation**

Pronunciation: Linking sounds

Use your English: Say goodbye

MOTIVATOR 9c

Exercise 5

2 responsible for 3 upset about 4 surprised at
5 different from 6 scared of 7 interested in
8 bored with

Extension ▬▬

Adjectives with prepositions

Write -ed and -ing adjectives that express feelings on cards. Cut these up, then put Ss into small groups and give each group a set of cards, which they put face down. Ss should take turns to turn over a card, read it and then mime the adjective. The others should guess which feeling is being mimed. To further extend this game, get Ss to write sentences, including a context for the adjective and then mime it. The others should guess the context.

Example: *You're fed up with waiting for the bus.*

Exercise 2
Sentence 2

Exercise 3
2 C 3 H 4 L 5 H 6 C

Exercise 5
2 c) 3 b) 4 c) 5 c)
6 a)

9d Sporting passions

SKILLS FOCUS: READING

ACROSS **CULTURES**

Learn about some different sports!

We all know something about football, the big teams, the famous players, but there are other sports! In different parts of the world people get excited about watching games that you might not know.

Ireland

Did you know that hurling is the national game in Ireland and is the fastest game on grass? It's over 3,000 years old so it must be good. And it's dangerous, too! You have to wear a helmet unless you want a nasty knock on the head. You play it with a wooden stick called a 'hurley' and in a team of fifteen incredibly fast players. You can hit the ball with your hand or the stick, but you mustn't hold the ball in your hand for more than four steps. The women's version is called 'camogie'.

West Indies

The West Indies cricket team has players from fifteen Caribbean nations and they are all crazy about the game. Cricket is a bat and ball game played by two teams of eleven players. One team bats the ball and tries to score as many runs as possible. The other team bowls and fields, trying to get the batsmen out. Some bowlers can bowl the ball at a speed of 100 miles per hour. You need a lot of spare time to watch cricket because it's a slow game and can take five days to play!

Get started

1 What sports are popular in your country? Do you have a national sport?

Read

READING TIP: HOW TO UNDERSTAND WRITER PURPOSE
Texts can have different purposes. The writer uses a text to do one of three things:
1 to explain facts
2 to tell a story
3 to give opinions about something
When you read a text decide which one of these three purposes is the writer's main aim.
Now do Exercise 2.

98

2 Read the article and decide which sentence (1–3) describes the writer's purpose.

1 To express an opinion about sports using words such as 'love, like, can't stand'.
2 To give information using lots of facts and figures.
3 To tell a story using past tenses, descriptions and dramatic expressions.

Extension

When the Ss have completed their fact sheet in the Exercise 6 project, they could work with a partner to interview each other about their chosen team sports.
Ss may find it helpful to listen again to Josh asking Hailey about her project in Exercise 5.
Monitor Ss as they talk, giving help where needed. More confident pairs could present their Q&As to the rest of the class.

Canada

The national Canadian summer sport is lacrosse which is similar to hockey. But it's different from hockey because the stick has a net at the end to hold the ball and it's a much more dangerous game! In the men's game you must wear a lot of protective gear: gloves, shoulder pads, helmets and a rib guard. 200 years ago it was a Native American warrior game played in teams of hundreds of players – today it's played in teams of ten, but it's still a game for warriors!

NEW WORDS

- grass • knock • stick • step • bat
- bowl • field • get someone out • batsman
- bowler • spare time • protective (sports) gear
- rib guard

Comprehension

3 Read the article again. Complete the sentences with hurling (H), lacrosse (L) or cricket (C) .

1 _L_ is similar to hockey.
2 _L_ is played with teams of eleven people.
3 _H_ is thousands of years old.
4 _C_ was first played by Native Americans.
5 _H_ is the quickest moving outdoor field sport.
6 _L_ isn't a fast game and can take a few days to play.

Speak

4 Answer the questions.

1 Would you like to play any of the sports in the article? Which ones would you prefer to watch?
2 In general, which sports:
a) are the most dangerous?
b) are the most difficult to learn?
c) are the most boring?
d) have the fittest athletes?
e) have the most expensive kit?
f) have the highest paid players?

Listen

5 🎧 (9/10) Listen to Hailey and Josh talking about a school project. Choose the correct options.

1 Cricket was first played in England in the ___.
a) twentieth century (b) sixteenth century
c) fifteenth century
2 Today cricket is played in ___ countries.
a) 6 b) 150 c) 100
3 The 'Ashes' is ___.
a) a type of cricket b) a famous competition
c) the first cricket game in 1882
4 The batsman tries to ___.
a) hit the wickets b) jump over the wickets
c) run between the wickets
5 Hailey ___ gets fed up with watching cricket.
a) never b) usually c) sometimes
6 Hailey's going to see England against ___.
a) the West Indies b) New Zealand c) India

Project

6 Write a fact sheet about a team sport you don't know much about (e.g. beach volleyball or ice hockey). Answer the questions. Download useful images and links to videos from the internet.

- What is the history of the sport?
- Where in the world is this sport popular?
- What is the objective of the game?
- How is the game played?
- Do you need any special equipment?

Beach volleyball was first played in California …

99

Exercise 1

Her favourite part was the class trip to the British Museum. Her least favourite part was exam time.

Exercise 2

2 F 3 DS 4 DS 5 T

Exercise 3a

2 However
3 However
4 Although
5 Although

Exercise 3b

2 Although I didn't get a part in the school play, I helped behind the scenes.

3 Although Tomas isn't very good at sport, he loves playing basketball.

4 We usually walk to school. However, we caught the bus today.

5 Although my favourite subject is Art, I like History, too./My favourite subject is Art. However, I like History, too.

9e Looking back

SKILLS FOCUS: WRITING A DISCURSIVE TEXT

Get ready to write

1 Read the essay. What was Jackie's favourite part of the school year? What was her least favourite part?

2 Answer true (T), false (F) or doesn't say (DS).

1 Jackie liked the British Museum. *T*
2 She visited lots of different rooms there.
3 She loves all sport.
4 She passed her exams.
5 They're going to have a party.

WRITING TIP: CONTRAST LINKERS
although and *however*

Although and *however* have the same meaning as *but*. Notice the punctuation.
Although links two clauses to make one sentence.
Although *we've had a lot of work this year, I've enjoyed being in Year 10.*
Although *I'm not very good at it, it's now my favourite sport.*
However, followed by a comma, introduces the new idea in a second sentence.
However, *it was such a nice feeling when they were over that it was almost worth it!*
Now do Exercise 3.

3a Complete the sentences with *although* or *however*.

1 *Although* I enjoy school, I don't like doing exams.
2 I didn't get a part in the school play. ___, I helped behind the scenes.
3 Tomas isn't very good at sport. ___, he loves playing basketball.
4 ___ we usually walk to school, we caught the bus today.
5 ___ I like History, my favourite subject is Art.

b Work in pairs. Say the sentences in Exercise 3a in different ways, using *although* or *however*.

I enjoy school. However, I don't like doing exams.

My school year
by Jackie Roberts

Although we've had a lot of work this year, I've enjoyed being in Year 10. The highlight for me was our class trip to the British Museum. I'd never been there before and I thought it was amazing. I only saw the Ancient Egypt part but I definitely want to go back soon and explore some more.

I started playing hockey this year. Although I'm not very good at it, it's now my favourite sport. I'm going to carry on with it next year, I hope.

Of course not everything has been great. The worst part was exam time. This year the exams were really hard. However, it was such a nice feeling when they were over that it was almost worth it.

It's been a good year, but I'm looking forward to the last day of term. We're planning a party. Everyone will bring something to eat and we'll play music, dance and play some games, too. It'll be fun and then we'll be on holiday!

4a Think back over your school year. Make notes about the things that you enjoyed and didn't enjoy. Use the ideas in the box or your own ideas.

- exams • trips • subjects • friends
- illness • holidays • parties • sport
- concerts, plays, etc

b Read the essay in Exercise 1 again, then write your own essay: *My school year.* Use *although* and *however* where possible.

- Say what you've enjoyed the most.
- Say what you've enjoyed the least.
- Say what you're looking forward to in the future.

100

Grammar (20 marks)

1 Choose the correct options.

0 I fancy trying / to try out a new computer game.
1 She can't stand listening / to listen to rock music.
2 Dan refused to do / doing his homework.
3 We managed arriving / to arrive on time.
4 He denied stealing / to steal the money.
5 I suggested to go / going to the cinema.
6 You promised not to tell / not telling my mum.
7 I can't afford to buy / buying a new bike.
8 Jane enjoyed to eat / eating the pizza.

.../8

2 Complete the sentences with *mustn't* or the correct form of *have to*.

0 You *mustn't* take food into a swimming pool.
1 You ___ pay for the ticket. It's free!
2 Police officers usually ___ wear uniforms.
3 John ___ get up early on Saturdays to go to work.
4 You ___ ride your bike at night without lights.
5 We can buy lunch at school so we ___ take sandwiches.
6 Jack's finished his exams so he ___ do any homework.

.../6

3 Rewrite the sentences. Use the adjectives in brackets and the correct preposition.

0 Prices in the USA and in the UK are not the same. (different)
Prices in the USA are different from prices in the UK.
1 We were not happy, because of the rain. (fed up)
2 I don't want to listen to this music. (tired)
3 David thinks he might fail his Maths exam. (worried)
4 Kyle is the person who does the cooking. (responsible)
5 Your laptop is like mine. (similar)
6 I think snakes are scary. (scared)

.../6

Vocabulary (9 marks)

4 Match the verbs (0–4) to the phrases (a–e).

0 – d

0 download
1 connect
2 delete
3 protect
4 send

a) files you don't want
b) your computer from viruses
c) an email
d) software
e) to the internet

.../4

5 Circle the word that is different.

0 basket   ball   referee   goal
1 draw   cyclist   goalkeeper   player
2 helmet   glove   racket   spectator
3 athlete   pass   umpire   team
4 win   lose   score   coach
5 (shin)pads   bat   hit   net

.../5

Phrases/Use your English (11 marks)

6 Complete with phrases from the box.

- I know what you mean.   • Nice try,
- I'd so like   • that's all.   • go halves.

A: ⁰I'd so like to go to the match, but the tickets are really expensive!
B: ¹___ But, I know how to get some cheap tickets.
A: Knowing you, that doesn't surprise me!
B: I just have to make a few calls, ²___ We can ³___
A: ⁴___ but I'd rather watch it on TV!

.../4

7 Complete with words from the box.

- trip   • will   • forget   • too   • yourself
- touch   • won't   • soon

A: Look after ⁰*yourself.*
B: I ¹___. You, ²___.
C: I wish I was going on holiday. Have a safe ³___.
D: Thanks. See you ⁴___.
E: Don't ⁵___ to keep in ⁶___.
F: I ⁷___.

.../7

 LISTEN AND CHECK YOUR SCORE

Grammar	.../20
Vocabulary	.../9
Phrases/Use your English	.../11
Total	**.../40**

101

Exercise 5
1 draw 2 spectator
3 pass 4 coach
5 hit

Exercise 6
1 I know what you mean. 2 that's all.
3 go halves.
4 Nice try,

Exercise 7
1 will 2 too 3 trip
4 soon 5 forget
6 touch 7 won't

ROUND-UP

eText
🎮 **Games**

Boat Game

Hangman

Pelmanism

Exercise 1
1 listening 2 to do 3 to arrive 4 stealing 5 going
6 not to tell 7 to buy 8 eating

Exercise 2
1 don't have to 2 have to 3 has to 4 mustn't
5 don't have to 6 doesn't have to

Exercise 3
1 We're fed up with the rain.
2 I'm tired of listening to this music.
3 David is worried about failing his Maths exam.
4 Kyle is responsible for the cooking.
5 Your laptop is similar to mine.
6 I'm scared of snakes.

Exercise 4
1 e) 2 a) 3 b) 4 c)

Unit 1 Performance

1a I'm going to apply.

Students' Book, page 102

Exercise 1

wind: clarinet, flute, saxophone, trumpet

string: violin

keyboard: keyboard, piano

percussion: drums

Exercise 2

2 's going to

3 Are you going to

4 'll

5 're going to see

6 'll

1b I'm going out.

Students' Book, page 102

Exercise 1

3 I'll probably fail

4 ✓ 5 You'll have 6 ✓

7 You'll feel 8 ✓

Exercise 2

2 is playing

3 'll be good

4 on 3rd November

5 the youth club

6 at eight o'clock

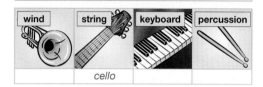

Extra practice

Unit 1

Lesson 1a

1 Put the instruments in the correct lists.

• ~~cello~~ • clarinet • drums • flute • keyboard
• piano • saxophone • trumpet • violin

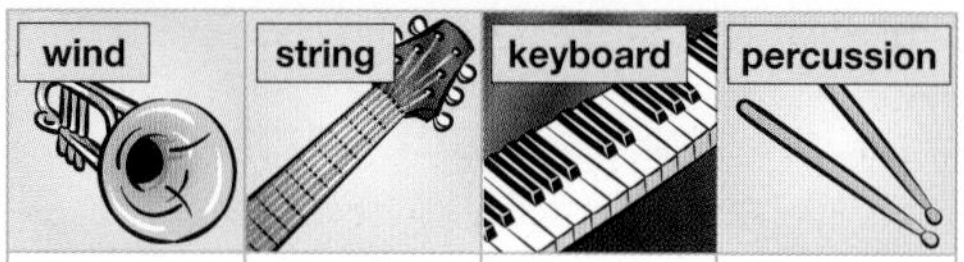

wind	string	keyboard	percussion
	cello		

2 Choose the correct options.

1 A: What are you planning for the summer?
B: We'll / **'re going to** go camping.
2 A: The sky is very dark.
B: Yes, it**'ll / 's going to** rain.
3 A: I like that T-shirt.
B: **Will you / Are you going to** buy it?
4 A: Let's have lunch.
B: OK, I**'ll / 'm going to** see what's in the fridge.
5 A: Where are they going?
B: The cinema. They**'ll see / 're going to see** *Mr Bean*.
6 A: I need some help with my homework.
B: Why don't you ask Tim? I'm sure he**'ll / 's going to** help you.

Lesson 1b

1 Tick (✓) the correct sentences. Correct the wrong ones. Use *going to* or *will*.

1 Have a look in my diary. What time **is Sarah arriving**? ✓
2 You need a warm coat. ~~It's snowing~~ later.
It's going to snow.
3 Maths is so hard! I**'m probably failing** the exam next week.
4 I don't like that kind of film. **I'm not going** to the cinema.
5 Don't run across the road. **You're having** an accident.
6 I like John. **Is he coming** to your party?
7 Go to bed early. **You're feeling** better tomorrow.
8 Sheena is training hard. She**'s cycling** in a competition next week.

2 Complete with phrases from the box.

• is playing • at eight o'clock • 'll be good
• ~~fancy going~~ • on 3rd November
• the youth club

Hi!

Do you [1]*fancy going* to a concert? My brother's band [2]____ and I think it [3]____. It's [4]____ – that's next Friday. It's at [5]____ and it starts [6]____.

I hope you can come.

See you soon.

Joe

Lesson 1c

1a Write sentences to compare these things. Use the adjectives in brackets and your opinions.

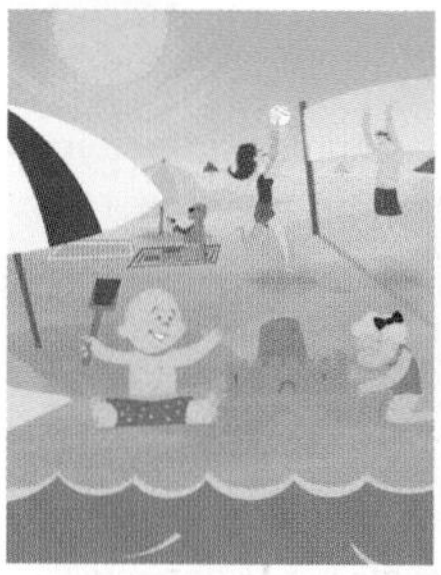

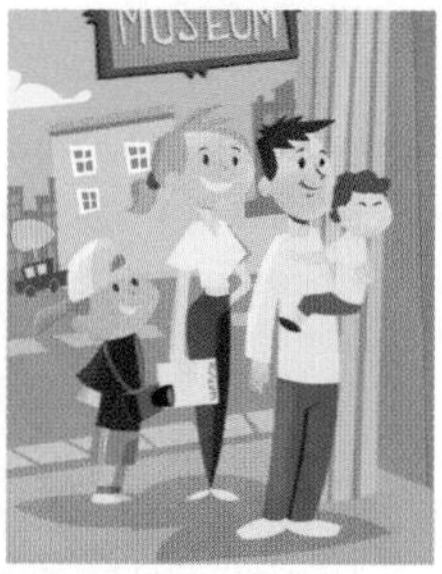

1 a day at the beach/a day in a city (relaxing, exciting)
A day at the beach is much more relaxing than a day in a city, but it isn't as exciting.
2 a pizza/a salad (expensive, healthy)
3 a bicycle/a car (cheap, comfortable)
4 English/my language (difficult, beautiful)

b Write your opinions with the superlative form of the adjectives in brackets.

1 school subject (easy, interesting)
Maths is the easiest subject and Geography is the most interesting.
2 animal (intelligent, friendly)
3 day of the week (good, bad)
4 food (delicious, cheap)

102

1c They're the best films ever!.

Students' Book, page 102

Exercise 1a

2 A pizza is much more expensive than a salad, but it isn't as healthy.

3 A bicycle is much cheaper than a car, but it isn't as comfortable.

4 English is much more difficult than my language and it isn't as beautiful.

Exercise 1b

Student's answers will vary. Check for accuracy.

Unit 2

Lesson 2a

1 Read the situations and write sentences. Use the present perfect simple and *just, yet, already* or *never*.

1 Jack's nervous about his trip to London. (go/to the UK before)
  He's never been to the UK before.
2 John's room looks great. (tidy/it)
3 Emma isn't going to the cinema with her friends. (see/the film twice)
4 Rosie is going to be late for school. (not wake up)
5 My parents are relaxing in the sitting room. (get/home from work)
6 I'm very hungry. (not have/breakfast)
7 John doesn't need to borrow that book. (read/it)
8 The children on the beach are very excited. (see/the sea before)

Lesson 2b

1 Complete the sentences with relationship words and phrases.

1 Steve is my friend. I *get on* well with him.
2 My brother is going ____ ____ a really nice girl.
3 They don't look happy. I think they're having an ____.
4 Ben isn't her boyfriend now. They ____ ____ last week.
5 Jane is very happy these days. I think she has fallen ____ ____ ____ somebody!
6 They were married for ten years, but then they got ____.

2 Complete the conversations. Use the past simple or present perfect simple form of the verbs, or short answers.

meet
A: ¹*Have you ever met* (you/ever) a famous person?
B: Yes, I ²____. About ten years ago, I ³____ Paul McCartney!
A: Where ⁴____ (you) him?
B: In a music shop.

break
A: ⁵____ (you/ever) a bone?
B: Yes, I ⁶____. I ⁷____ my toe last year.
A: How ⁸____ (you) it?
B: I was playing football, in the wrong shoes.

Lesson 2c

1a Complete the sentences with *who, which, where* or *whose*.

1 Luke is a man *who* doesn't often get angry.
2 I've just seen the film ____ you told me about.
3 I don't believe the stories ____ my brother tells.
4 I'd like to live in a place ____ it never rains.
5 She's the girl ____ father was on TV last night.
6 Where's the CD ____ we were listening to?
7 I'm going to invite the people ____ I like.
8 Here's somebody ____ wants to speak to you.
9 They are the boys ____ I met at the youth club.
10 This is the house ____ my grandmother lives.

b Which sentences don't need a relative pronoun? Write the new sentences.

2 I've just seen the film you told me about.

Unit 3

Lesson 3a

1 Look at the information. Then complete the conversation with the words from the box.

• deep • depth • height • high • length
• long • ~~old~~ • wide • width

1,149 m
49 m
12 m 134 m 12 m

Sydney Harbour Bridge: opened 1932

A: How ¹*old* is the Sydney Harbour Bridge?
B: No idea! Let's look on the internet. ... Well, it opened in 1932.
A: OK, and how ²____ is it?
B: Its ³____ is 1,149 metres.
A: Right. What about its ⁴____ ?
B: It says here the bridge is 134 metres ⁵____.
A: Great. And how ⁶____ is it?
B: Its ⁷____ is 49 metres.
A: I need to know the ⁸____ of the water, too.
B: It's twelve metres ⁹____ at both ends of the bridge.

103

Unit 2 That's life

2a I've just told you.
Students' Book, page 103

Exercise 1

2 John's just tidied it.
3 Emma's already seen the film twice.
4 Rosie hasn't woken up yet.
5 My parents have just got home from work.
6 I haven't had breakfast yet.
7 John's already read it.
8 The children have never seen the sea before.

2b He asked me out.
Students' Book, page 103

Exercise 1

2 out with 3 argument 4 broke up 5 in love with
6 divorced

Exercise 2

2 have 3 met 4 did you meet 5 Have you ever broken
6 have 7 broke 8 did you break

2c He asked me out.
Students' Book, page 103

Exercise 1a

2 which 3 which
4 where 5 whose
6 which 7 who
8 who 9 who
10 where

Exercise 1b

3 I don't believe the stories my brother tells.
6 Where's the CD we were listening to?
7 I'm going to invite the people I like.
9 They are the boys I met at the youth club.

Unit 3
City life

3a Too big to see it all on foot.
Students' Book, page 103

Exercise 1

2 long 3 length
4 height 5 high
6 wide 7 width
8 depth
9 deep

Exercise 2

2 It's too cold to go out without a coat.

3 I don't get up early enough to catch the bus.

4 We were too late to get tickets.

5 He is clever enough to understand the problem.

6 He isn't old enough to go to school.

3b You can't miss it.

Students' Book, page 104

Exercise 1

2 Go left out of the library to the end of the road. Turn right and take the first right. The park is on the left.

3 Go right out of the cinema. Go straight on and take the first left. The sports centre is on the right, opposite the police station and the newsagent/ next to the petrol station.

4 Go left out of the pharmacy. Go along Joyner Street and take the second turning on the left into York Road. The art gallery is on the left, opposite the square.
OR: Go left out of the pharmacy. Go along Joyner Street and take the first turning on the left into Princess Street. The art gallery is on the right, opposite the petrol station.

2 Read the situations and write sentences with *too ... to* or *(not) ... enough to.*

1 I'm tired. I can't stay awake for the film.
I'm too tired to stay awake for the film.

2 It's cold. Don't go out without a coat.

3 I don't get up early. I never catch the bus.

4 We were late. We didn't get tickets.

5 He is clever. He understands the problem.

6 He isn't very old. He doesn't go to school.

Lesson 3b

1 Look at the map on page 34 and write directions.

1 Go left out of the tourist information centre and go along Princess Street. The supermarket is on the left, it's opposite the music shop.

from	to
1 the tourist information centre	the supermarket
2 the library	the park
3 the cinema	the sports centre
4 the pharmacy	the art gallery

Lesson 3c

1 Read the situations and write sentences with *there is/are* and *too many/much* or *not enough.*

1 This party is awful. (noisy people)
There are too many noisy people.

2 I'm going to the shops. (food)

3 This road is always very busy. (cars)

4 I don't understand. (information)

5 We can't sit down. (chairs)

6 The streets are dirty. (rubbish)

2 Complete the sentences with *some/any/no/ every* and *one/thing/body/where.*

1 I don't know *anybody* who lives in London.

2 Oh no! I've dropped my glass. There's milk ____.

3 Listen! ____ is calling your name!

4 Tom is very popular, ____ likes him.

5 I can't find my mobile ____.

6 They've all gone out. There's ____ at home.

7 Let's find ____ peaceful for our picnic.

8 Ouch! There's ____ in my eye!

104

Unit 4

Lesson 4a

1 Complete the sentences so that they mean the same.

1 I haven't seen Jim since 10 a.m. It's 12 p.m. now.
I *haven't seen Jim for* two hours.

2 We moved here in 2009 and we still live here.
We ____ 2009.

3 The last time we saw them was in July.
We ____ July.

4 They first met when they were at primary school.
They have known each other ____.

5 They got married in 1990 and they are still married.
They ____ years.

6 He went to sleep ten hours ago. He's still asleep.
He ____ ten hours.

2 Complete the sentences with *make* or *do.* Then match the statements (1–5) to the replies (a–e).

1 – d

1 You need to be smart. A good haircut will *make* a difference.

2 I'm really nervous! I don't want to ____ a mistake.

3 Dad has asked me to ____ some work for him. I'm going to paint the door.

4 When are you going to ____ the shopping?

5 Which subjects are you going to ____ next year?

a) You'll be fine. Just ____ your best.
b) Later. I have to ____ my homework now.
c) I'm not sure. I can't ____ a decision!
d) You're right. I'll ____ an appointment at the hairdresser.
e) OK, but please don't ____ a mess.

3c We throw away too many things.

Students' Book, page 104

Exercise 1

2 There isn't enough food.

3 There are too many cars.

4 There isn't enough information.

5 There aren't enough chairs.

6 There's too much rubbish.

Exercise 2

2 everywhere 3 Somebody/Someone 4 everyone/ everybody 5 anywhere 6 nobody/no one
7 somewhere 8 something

Lesson 4b

1 Look at the picture and information. Then write sentences about Gina. Use the present perfect continuous form of the verbs in the box and *for* or *since*.

• support • ~~learn~~ • go • wear • play

1 Gina has been learning Italian for a year.

1 first Italian lesson: a year ago
2 started playing the guitar: age fourteen
3 started wearing glasses: three years ago
4 first day at Manor School: age eleven
5 became Manchester United supporter: five years ago

Lesson 4c

1 Ryan is talking to his grandfather. Complete the conversation with the correct form of *used to* or short answers.

Ryan: Where ¹*did you use to go* (you/go) to school?
Grandfather: In London. I ² ____ (travel) to school by bus. We ³ ____ (not have) a car. We ⁴ ____ (go) by bus or Tube, or we ⁵ ____ (walk).
Ryan: I suppose you ⁶ ____ (not use) computers at work, either.
Grandfather: You're right. I saw my first computer when I was about thirty!
Ryan: ⁷ ____ (you/have) a TV?
Grandfather: Yes, we ⁸ ____. I'm not 100, you know!

2 Look at the responses and complete the conversations with the correct form of the verbs.

1 A: *I didn't go out* (not go out) last weekend.
   B: Didn't you? How boring!
2 A: ____ (win) £2,000 in a competition.
   B: Has she? How exciting!
3 A: ____ (break up).
   B: Have they? How sad!
4 A: ____ (not go) to school tomorrow.
   B: Aren't you? How nice!
5 A: ____ (not tell) us his name.
   B: Hasn't he? How strange!
6 A: ____ (not be) a very good match.
   B: Wasn't it? How annoying!

Unit 5

Lesson 5a

1 Complete the text with the present simple passive form of the verbs in the box.

• dry • grow • ~~make~~ • mix • put (x 2)
• remove • roast • send

HOW FAIRTRADE CHOCOLATE IS MADE

Chocolate ¹*is made* from cocoa beans. The beans ² ____ in parts of Africa, Asia and Central and South America. They ³ ____ in the sun and then they ⁴ ____ in bags and ⁵ ____ to factories across the world. In the factories, the beans ⁶ ____ in big ovens. Then they ⁷ ____ in machines and a liquid ⁸ ____ from the beans. This liquid ⁹ ____ with different ingredients to make chocolate.

4 She has been going to Manor School since she was eleven.
5 She has been supporting Manchester United for five years.

4c She used to be a Goth.
Students' Book, page 105

Exercise 1
2 used to travel
3 didn't use to have
4 used to go
5 used to walk
6 didn't use to use
7 Did you use to have
8 did

Exercise 2
2 She's won
3 They've broken up 4 I'm not going
5 He hasn't told
6 It wasn't

Unit 5
Around the world
5a They were made in Thailand.
Students' Book, page 105

Exercise 1
2 are grown 3 are dried 4 are put
5 are sent
6 are roasted
7 are put
8 is removed
9 is mixed

Unit 4 Time passes
4a I haven't seen the sun for weeks.
Students' Book, page 104

Exercise 1
2 We've lived here since 2009.
3 We haven't seen them since July.
4 They have known each other since primary school.
5 They've been married for years.
6 He's been asleep for ten hours.

Exercise 2
1 d) make 2 make a) do 3 do e) make 4 do b) do
5 do c) make

4b You've been talking for ages.
Students' Book, page 105

Exercise 1
2 She has been playing the guitar since she was fourteen.
3 She has been wearing glasses for three years.

Exercise 2

2 weren't invented
by 3 was designed
by 4 was made
5 was the first
computer built
6 was built

5b I couldn't sleep.

Students' Book, page 106

Exercise 1

2 could/was able to
3 couldn't 4 wasn't
able to 5 was
able to

5c Plato, who was born in Athens, ...

Students' Book, page 106

Exercise 1

2 e) 3 c) 4 b) 5 a)

Exercise 2

2 mean 3 right
4 agree 5 true
6 opinion 7 right

---

2 Complete the magazine interview with the past passive form of the verbs.

Ask the expert

COMPUTERS

Q Who ¹*were computers invented by* (computers/ invent by)?
A Computers ²____ (not invent by) one person. One early invention was a machine that could count.

Mechanical Babbage computer

It ³____ (design by) Charles Babbage, in 1830. Another important invention was the typewriter. The first one ⁴____ (make) in 1867, by three Americans.
Q When ⁵____ (the first computer/build)?
A The first 'general' computer ⁶____ (build) in the USA in 1943. It was enormous. In fact, it filled a whole room!

Lesson 5b

1 Complete the text about Albert Einstein with the correct form of *could* or *was able to*. (Sometimes there is more than one correct answer.)

When Albert Einstein was a child, his family did not think he was extra clever. In fact, they were worried because the young Albert ¹*couldn't/ wasn't able to* (not) speak until he was about three.

At school, Albert didn't get very good marks, but he taught himself Maths and Physics at home. The young Einstein ²____ speak two languages (German and English), but he ³____ (not) write very well. His spelling was terrible!

Einstein ⁴____ (not) go to university because he failed the entrance exams. However, he wrote some brilliant articles about Physics. In 1905, a magazine published the articles and the university of Zurich offered him a job. At last he ⁵____ go to university!

106

Lesson 5c

1 Complete the text with the clauses in the box.

a) whose first language is Portuguese
b) where millions of tourists go every year
c) which means 'January River'
d) ~~who were Portuguese~~
e) where they were able to leave their ships safely

Rio de Janeiro

In January 1502, some ships arrived on the coast of Brazil, and the sailors, ¹*d* , saw an amazing sight. There was an enormous harbour, ²__. They called the harbour 'Rio de Janeiro', ³__, because they thought it was the end of a river.

After that, many Europeans followed and a city grew up around the harbour. These days it is a beautiful place, ⁴__. Many of the citizens, ⁵__, are descended from those early explorers.

2 Complete the conversation.

A: Are you watching TV again? I ¹*think* we spend too much time in front of the TV.
B: I know what you ²____, but some programmes are really good.
A: Yes, you're ³____, but most of them are awful.
B: I ⁴____, there's a lot of bad stuff on TV, but it is a good way to relax.
A: Yes, that's ⁵____. But in my ⁶____, it's usually a waste of time.
B: You're ⁷____, but I'll still watch it!

Unit 6

Lesson 6a

1 Look at the weather map. Then write sentences. Say what you will/won't take and say why, using *will*, *won't*, *may* or *might*. (50% = *may/might*, 100% = *will/won't*)

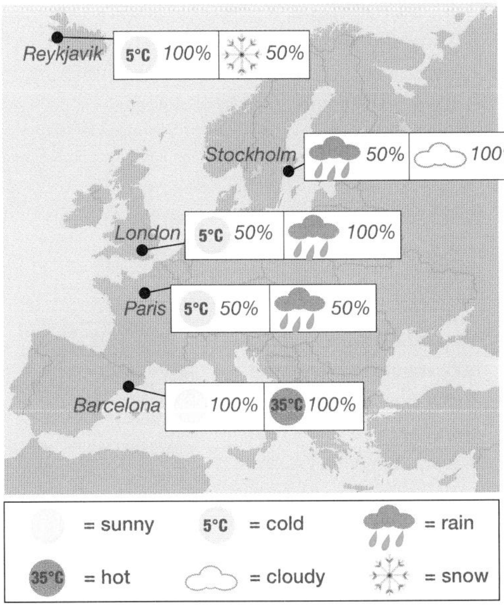
Reykjavik 5°C 100% 50%
Stockholm 50% 100%
London 5°C 50% 100%
Paris 5°C 50% 50%
Barcelona 100% 35°C 100%
= sunny
5°C = cold
= rain
35°C = hot
= cloudy
= snow

1 I'm going to Stockholm. (raincoat, sun hat)
I'll take a raincoat because it might rain. I won't take a sun hat because it'll be cloudy.
2 She's going to Barcelona. (sunglasses, jumper)
3 They're going to London. (jumpers, sandals)
4 We're going to Paris. (jumpers, umbrellas)
5 He's going to Reykjavik. (warm coat, skis)

2 Complete the conversations.

A: I'm sorry, I've forgotten your book. [1]*Shall* I go home and get it?
B: [2]____ worry, it's OK. I don't need it today.
A: OK, thanks. I promise I [3]____ forget it tomorrow.

A: I'm worried about the Science exam.
B: You'll [4]____ fine.
A: But I can't remember anything.
B: [5]____ you like [6]____ to come and revise with you tonight?
A: No, thanks, there's [7]____ need. My sister's going to help me.

Lesson 6b

1 Complete the sentences with the opposite of the adjectives in the box. Use *un-*, *in-* or *im-*.

• interesting	• experienced	• formal	• usual
• ~~dependent~~	• necessary	• patient	• possible

1 When Jack left home and got a job, he became *independent*.
2 Don't read this book, it's really ____.
3 Nobody can do this puzzle, I think it's ____.
4 Katie is sometimes ____ with the children and shouts at them.
5 It's very ____ to have snow in May.
6 Don't bring any money. It's ____.
7 She started her new job last week so she's still really ____.
8 He always wears ____ clothes, like T-shirts.

2 Jim is going to do a parachute jump at an air show. Make sentences. Then number them in the correct order.

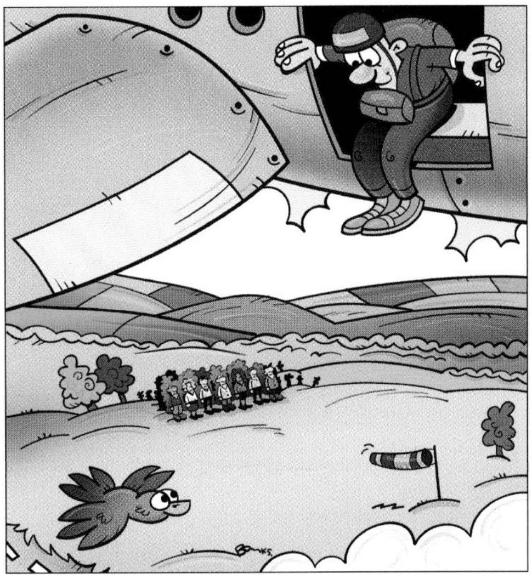

1 – c When he's ready, he'll jump out of the plane.

a) as soon as | he | jump | he | start | counting to ten
b) if | the first parachute | not work | he | open | the second parachute
c) when | he | be | ready | he | jump | out of the plane
d) as soon as | he | land | the crowd | cheer
e) when | he | get | to ten | he | open | his parachute
f) he | land | in a field | unless | he | be | unlucky

107

6b If she's here, we'll invite her.

Students' Book, page 107

Exercise 1

2 uninteresting
3 impossible
4 impatient
5 unusual
6 unnecessary
7 inexperienced
8 informal

Exercise 2

2 a) As soon as he jumps, he'll start counting to ten.
3 e) When he gets to ten, he'll open his parachute.
4 b) If the first parachute doesn't work, he'll open the second parachute.
5 f) Unless he's unlucky, he'll land in a field.
6 d) As soon as he lands, the crowd will cheer.

Unit 6 Things to remember

6a It might snow.

Students' Book, page 107

Exercise 1

2 She'll take sunglasses because it'll be sunny. She won't take a jumper because it won't be cold.
3 They'll take jumpers because it may/might be cold. They won't take sandals because it'll rain.
4 We'll take jumpers because it may/might be cold. We'll take umbrellas because it may/might rain.
5 He'll take a warm coat because it'll be cold. He'll take skis because it may/might snow.

Exercise 2

2 Don't 3 won't 4 be 5 Would 6 me 7 no

6c The two men hadn't met before.

Students' Book, page 108

Exercise 1

2 were 3 hadn't arrived 4 had phoned 5 wondered 6 thought 7 looked 8 found 9 hadn't posted

Unit 7

Reporting speech

7a He told her to throw it.

Students' Book, page 108

Exercise 1

2 He asked her not to be late.

3 He told her to wear something warm.

4 He asked her to bring some lunch.

5 He told her not to forget her camera.

6 He asked her to tell him Jack's email address.

Exercise 2

2 It's a large oval gold mirror.

3 They're dangerous long white teeth.

4 It's a small old wooden house.

5 They're delicious pink French cakes.

6 It's a scary big black insect.

7b He said he was writing a book.

Students' Book, page 108

Lesson 6c

1 Complete the story with the past simple or past perfect form of the verbs.

Jamie and Ella were ready for their party. They ¹*had prepared* (prepare) everything and now they were waiting for their guests. They ²____ (be) very excited. An hour later, they were not so happy. Their guests ³____ (not arrive) and nobody ⁴____ (phone). 'What has happened?' they ⁵____ (wonder). Then they ⁶____ (think) of something awful. They ⁷____ (look) in Jamie's backpack and ⁸____ (find) the invitations. They ⁹____ (not post) them!

Unit 7

Lesson 7a

1 Find six requests or commands in the email. Then report them using *tell* or *ask*.

1 Don told Katie to meet them outside the post office at eight.

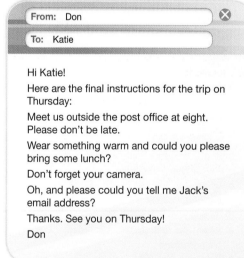

From: Don
To: Katie

Hi Katie!
Here are the final instructions for the trip on Thursday:
Meet us outside the post office at eight. Please don't be late.
Wear something warm and could you please bring some lunch?
Don't forget your camera.
Oh, and please could you tell me Jack's email address?
Thanks. See you on Thursday!
Don

108

2 Put the adjectives in the correct order to make one sentence.

1 It's a beautiful bag. It's blue and it's little.
   It's a beautiful little blue bag.

2 It's an oval mirror. It's large and it's gold.

3 They are white teeth. They are long and dangerous.

4 It's a small house. It's wooden and it's very old.

5 They are French cakes. They are pink and delicious.

6 It's a black insect. It's big and scary.

Lesson 7b

1 Write what the girl says in reported speech.

1 She said they'd had a terrible journey.

¹We had a terrible journey, and ²we arrived very late. ³Since then, everything has been fine. ⁴Everyone's really friendly. ⁵We've met some cool people. ⁶It's a fantastic place. ⁷I can see the sea from my room. ⁸I'll send you some photos. ⁹I don't want to come home!

Lesson 7c

1 Look at Mrs Hill's notes from the interview with Jodie. Report the questions that she asked.

1 She asked how old she was.

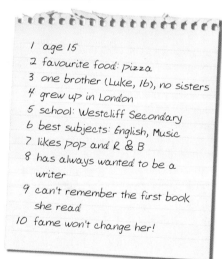

1 age 15
2 favourite food: pizza
3 one brother (Luke, 16), no sisters
4 grew up in London
5 school: Westcliff Secondary
6 best subjects: English, Music
7 likes pop and R & B
8 has always wanted to be a writer
9 can't remember the first book she read
10 fame won't change her!

Exercise 1

2 She said (that) they had arrived very late.

3 She said (that) everything had been fine since then.

4 She said (that) everyone was really friendly.

5 She said (that) they'd met some cool people.

6 She said (that) it was a fantastic place.

7 She said (that) she could see the sea from her room.

8 She said (that) she'd send me/us some photos.

9 She said (that) she didn't want to come home.

7c She asked if I could come ...

Students' Book, page 108

Exercise 1

2 She asked what her favourite food was.

3 She asked if she had brothers and/or sisters.

4 She asked where she had grown up.

5 She asked where she went to school.

6 She asked what her best school subjects were.

7 She asked what music she liked.

8 She asked if she had always wanted to be a writer.

Unit 8

Lesson 8a

1 Write sentences using the prompts and your own ideas. Use the second conditional.

1 If I/can/choose a present, I/ask/for …
If I could choose a present, I'd ask for a computer.

2 If I/can't/find my key, I …

3 If I/find/a lost dog, I …

4 If my friend/be/fed up, I …

5 If I/win/£50, I/buy …

2 Complete the sentences with the correct form (*-ed* or *-ing*) of the words in the box. There is one extra word.

- annoy • disappoint • ~~embarrass~~ • frighten
- surprise • tire

1 If I didn't have enough money at the supermarket checkout, I'd be *embarrassed*.

2 If an earthquake woke me up in the night, it would be very ____.

3 If someone borrowed my bike and didn't give it back, it would be really ____.

4 If I was ready to go on holiday, but then I couldn't go, I'd be very ____.

5 If my favourite celebrity knocked on my door, I'd be really ____.

Lesson 8b

1 Look at the pictures and write sentences with *I wish*.

1 *I wish I had long hair.*

My dream …

¹ have/long hair
²be/rich
³not live/in a city

⁴speak/Spanish
⁵can/play/the guitar
⁶know/all the words to this song

Lesson 8c

1 Write the programme types.

1 A summary of what's happening around the world.
the news

2 Diver Jo Ruskin explores the Great Barrier Reef.

3 Who can answer the question first? Fun for all the family.

4 Will Charley finally ask Jane to marry him? Watch tonight's dramatic episode.

5 Mike Parks talks to the singer Danii Minogue, sister of Kylie.

6 The family goes on holiday and Eric practises his Spanish. Quite funny.

2 Make sentences with *so* or *such … (that)*.

1 Lady Blecksdale was rich. She owned a lot of jewellery.
Lady Blecksdale was so rich (that) she owned a lot of jewellery.

2 The jewellery was valuable. It was kept in a bank.

3 When it was stolen, she was upset. She offered a reward.

4 It was a big story. It was in all the newspapers.

5 The robbers had been careful. They hadn't left any clues.

6 However, it was a big reward. One of the robbers called the police.

7 He was stupid. He thought he would get the reward money.

8b I wish we could stay longer.

Students' Book, page 109

Exercise 1

2 I wish I was rich.

3 I wish I didn't live in a city.

4 I wish I could speak Spanish.

5 I wish I could play the guitar.

6 I wish I knew all the words to this song.

8c It was so boring I fell asleep.

Students' Book, page 109

Exercise 1

2 documentary
3 quiz show 4 soap opera 5 chat show
6 sitcom

Exercise 2

2 The jewellery was so valuable/ It was such valuable jewellery (that) it was kept in a bank.

3 When it was stolen she was so upset (that) she offered a reward.

4 It was such a big story (that) it was in all the newspapers.

5 The robbers had been so careful (that) they hadn't left any clues.

6 However, it was such a big reward (that) one of the robbers called the police.

7 He was so stupid (that) he thought he would get the reward money.

9 She asked if she could remember the first book she had read.

10 She asked if fame would change her.

Unit 8 Feelings

8a How would you feel.

Students' Book, page 109

Exercise 1

Possible answers:

2 If I couldn't find my key, I'd go to my neighbour's house.

3 If I found a lost dog, I'd take it to the police station.

4 If my friend was/were fed up, I'd take her out for the day.

5 If I won £50, I'd buy a new top.

Exercise 2

2 frightening 3 annoying 4 disappointed 5 surprised

Unit 9
Moving on

9a You can't afford to buy it.
Students' Book, page 110

Exercise 1
2 save, stick
3 attachments, virus 4 keyboard, mouse 5 connect, broadband 6 search, download

Exercise 2
2 I denied eating the last biscuit.
3 We managed to solve the problem.
4 We offered to help.
5 He promised to be early.
6 I admitted telling a lie.
7 They refused to do it.

9b He had to swim on his back.
Students' Book, page 110

Exercise 1
2 beat 3 lost 4 won
5 scored 6 drew

Exercise 2
2 has 3 have 4 have
5 don't 6 have
7 have 8 have

9c It's so different from London.
Students' Book, page 110

Exercise 1
2 with 3 at 4 on 5 in

Unit 9

Lesson 9a

1 Complete the sentences with words from the box.

> • attachments • broadband • connect
> • ~~delete~~ • download • keyboard • mouse
> • save • search • stick • virus

1 I don't want this email, so I'll _delete_ it.
2 I'm going to ____ my work onto a memory ____.
3 Don't open ____ from people you don't know. You might get a ____.
4 A laptop doesn't need a separate ____ or ____.
5 The fastest way to ____ to the internet is with ____.
6 I'll ____ for the information and then ____ it onto my computer.

2 Rewrite the sentences. Use the verbs in brackets.

1 You shouldn't eat chocolate for breakfast. (stop)
   You should stop eating chocolate for breakfast.
2 I didn't eat the last biscuit. (deny)
3 We were able to solve the problem. (manage)
4 We asked if we could help. (offer)
5 He said he would be early. (promise)
6 I'm afraid I told a lie. (admit)
7 They said they wouldn't do it. (refuse)

Lesson 9b

1 Look at the football scores and complete the text with words from the box. There are two extra words.

> • beat • drew • hit • lost • passed
> • ~~played~~ • scored • won

MANCHESTER UNITED	ARSENAL

Manchester United ¹_played_ Arsenal and Arsenal ²____ them. Manchester United ³____ the match and Arsenal ⁴____ it.

ENGLAND	FRANCE

England ⁵____ one goal and so did France. England ⁶____ 1–1 with France.

---

2 Complete the text with words from the box.

> • don't • has • have (x 5)

Tough life for gymnast

Ann Jones meets fourteen-year-old gymnast, **Jane Macy**.

How often do you practise, Jane?
I ¹_have_ to get up early three times a week to practise before school. I hate getting up – my mum ²____ to shout very loudly! I don't usually practise in the evenings because I ³____ to do my homework.

Do you wish you had more free time?
Not really, because I love gymnastics. But I wish I didn't ⁴____ to get up early and I wish I could do the things my friends do – they ⁵____ have to worry about their food and they don't ⁶____ to go to bed early every night.

How old do you ⁷____ to be to go to the Olympic Games?
The rules say girls ⁸____ to be fifteen for gymnastics so I'm nearly old enough!

Lesson 9c

1 Complete the email with prepositions.

> From: Pete
> To: Claire
>
> Hi Claire
>
> It was great to hear from you and thanks for calling from the airport. I'm sorry ¹_about_ missing your party. I was really annoyed ²____ myself!
>
> I guess you're back home now. Have you seen all your old friends yet? Were they surprised ³____ your British accent?
>
> I'd love to visit you in the States and Julie and Dan are keen ⁴____ the idea, too.
>
> Anyway, I'm going to watch the football now. I know you're interested ⁵____ the scores so I'll let you know later.
>
> Bye for now.
>
> Pete

Welcome

Welcome a

Personality adjectives
- annoying • bad-tempered • big-headed
- bossy • clever • cute • easy-going
- friendly • funny • generous • hard-working
- helpful • honest • kind • lazy • loyal
- mean • polite • quiet • rude • shy • tidy
- unfriendly • untidy

Welcome b

House and furniture
Rooms • bathroom • bedroom
- dining room • hall • kitchen • living room
- study

Parts of a house • balcony • basement
- ceiling • chimney • door • downstairs
- floor • garage • garden • gate • landing
- loft • roof • stairs • steps • upstairs
- wall • window

Fittings • bath • cooker • dishwasher
- fridge • shower • sink • toilet
- washbasin • washing machine

Furniture • armchair • bed • bookcase
- carpet • CD player • chair
- chest of drawers • clock • computer
- cupboard • curtains • desk
- DVD player • lamp • mirror • plant • shelf
- sofa • table • television (TV) • wardrobe
- wastepaper bin

Welcome c

Jobs
- actor • artist • beautician • builder
- carpenter • cashier • chef • dentist
- detective • director • doctor • electrician
- engineer • farmer • firefighter • hairdresser
- housewife • journalist • mechanic • model
- musician • nurse • pilot • plumber
- police officer • politician • receptionist
- reporter • secretary • shop assistant
- ski instructor • sound engineer • taxi driver
- teacher • TV presenter • vet
- waiter/waitress

Welcome d

Clothes
- baseball cap • boots • cardigan • coat
- dress • hat • hoodie • jacket • jeans
- leggings • sandals • shirt • shoes
- shorts • skirt • socks • sweater
- sweatshirt • tights • top • trainers
- trousers • T-shirt

Accessories
- belt • gloves • pocket • scarf • tie • zip

Styles
- baggy • casual • sleeveless • smart
- tight

Patterns
- checked • flowery • patterned • plain
- spotted • striped

Unit 1

Lesson 1a

Types of music
- classical • country and western • folk
- heavy metal • hip-hop • jazz • Latin
- pop • R & B • rap • reggae • rock • soul
- techno

Unit 2

Lesson 2a

Household jobs
- do the cleaning • do the cooking
- do the ironing • do the shopping
- do the washing • do the washing-up
- do the vacuuming • empty the dishwasher
- lay the table • make breakfast/lunch/dinner
- make the bed • take the rubbish out
- tidy your room • wash the car

Lesson 2c

Family
- grandmother • grandfather • grandparents
- mother (mum) • father (dad) • parents
- brother • sister • son • daughter
- husband • wife • aunt • uncle • nephew
- niece • cousin • an only child

111

Unit 3

Lesson 3a

Transport
- bike • boat • bus • car • caravan
- coach • ferry • helicopter • lorry
- minibus • moped • motorbike • plane
- scooter • ship • taxi • train • tram
- underground (Tube) • van

Lesson 3b

Places in town
- art gallery • bank • bookshop
- bus stop • café • car park • cashpoint
- cinema • computer shop • factory
- hospital • hotel • library • market
- museum • music shop • newsagent
- office • park • petrol station • pharmacy
- police station • post office • restaurant
- school • shop • shopping centre • sports centre • square • station • supermarket
- swimming pool • theatre
- tourist information centre • town hall
- travel agent • zoo

Unit 5

Lesson 5c

Landscape and environment
- coast • forest • island • lake • mountain
- ocean • river • sea • tree

Unit 6

Lesson 6a

Holiday activities
- go camping • go climbing/climb
- go mountain biking • go shopping/shop
- go sightseeing/sightsee • go skiing/ski
- go sunbathing/sunbathe
- go swimming/swim • go to a museum
- go to a beach • go windsurfing/windsurf
- play beach volleyball

Unit 7

Lesson 7b

Appearance
- beard • beautiful • blond • curly
- dark • dark brown • fair • glasses
- good-looking • grey • large
- light brown • long
- medium-height • medium-length
- middle-aged • moustache • old • short
- straight • tall • wavy • young

Unit 9

Lesson 9a

Computers and computer language
Nouns: • attachment • broadband • charger
- connection • email • file • internet (net)
- keyboard • laptop • memory stick • mouse
- password • PC (desktop computer)
- printer • scanner • screen • software
- virus • website

Verbs: • attach • burn • charge • connect (to) • crash • delete • download • open
- print • receive • save • search (for) • send
- surf

Lesson 9b

Sports and activities
- (do) athletics • (play) basketball
- (play) beach volleyball • (do) boxing
- (play) cricket • (go) cycling • (play) football
- (play) golf • (do) gymnastics
- (go) ice-skating • (do) judo
- (do) karate • (go) karting
- (go) motor racing • (go) mountain biking
- (play) rugby • (go) skateboarding
- (go) skiing • (go) snowboarding
- (go) swimming • (play) tennis
- (play) volleyball • (go) windsurfing

112

Pronunciation

Unit 1 Lesson 1b

🎧 Exercise 5 /eɪ/ gr<u>ea</u>t, /aɪ/ l<u>i</u>ke

a **Listen and repeat.**

/eɪ/ great /aɪ/ like

b **Listen. Is the sound /eɪ/ (1) or /aɪ/ (2)? Listen again and repeat.**

great 1 like 2 afraid ages arrange baby birthday decide diary fine five OK I'd invite late make my place stay why

c **Listen and repeat. Then practise saying the sentences.**

1 What time did you write in your diary?
2 I'm afraid five o'clock is too late in the day.
3 I'd like to invite you to stay on my birthday.

Unit 2 Lesson 2c

🎧 Exercise 7 /æ/ f<u>a</u>mily, /ɑː/ f<u>a</u>ther

a **Listen and repeat.**

/æ/ family   /ɑː/ father

b **Put the words in the correct lists. Then listen and check.**

adult anxious are argument aunt exam family father hand have last married matter natural part party start

/æ/	/ɑː/
adult	are

c **Listen and repeat. Then practise saying the sentences.**

1 Dad had an argument with my aunt.
2 Let's relax and have a party.
3 I can't do the exam but my father can.

Unit 3 Lesson 3b

🎧 Exercise 6 Sentence stress and rhythm

a **Listen and underline the words that are stressed. Then listen and repeat.**

1 Can you <u>tell</u> me the <u>way</u> to the <u>hospital, please</u>?
2 How do I get to the park?
3 Turn left and go straight on.

b **Practise saying the sentences. Replace the words in bold with the words in brackets.**

1 Can you tell me the way to the **hospital**, please? (post office/music shop/library)
2 How do I get to the **park**? (bank/zoo/square)
3 Turn left and **go straight on**. (then turn right/ it's on the right)

Unit 4 Lesson 4b

🎧 Exercise 5 /ɪə/ w<u>e're</u>, /eə/ wh<u>ere</u>

a **Listen and repeat.**

/ɪə/	/eə/
we're	where
here	hair
fear	fair
dear	dare
really	rarely
ear	air

b **Underline the /ɪə/ sounds and circle the /eə/ sounds. Then listen and check.**

A: Are we <u>nearly</u> th(e)re?
B: No, we're nowhere near.

A: Look! Her hair isn't really fair!
B: Ssh, dear. Don't stare!

A: Come and sit here, Claire.
B: Where? On that chair?

c **Practise the conversations in Exercise 5b in pairs.**

Unit 4 Lesson 4c

🎧 Exercise 6 Rising intonation (to show interest)

a **Listen to the six exchanges. Which responses show interest?**

1 A: I don't feel very well.
   B: Don't you?
2 A: It was brilliant.
   B: Was it?
3 A: John's got a new bike.
   B: Has he?
4 A: I can speak German.
   B: Can you?
5 A: I didn't go to school yesterday.
   B: Didn't you?
6 A: Kate hasn't arrived yet.
   B: Hasn't she?

b **Listen and repeat the responses. Sound interested each time.**

113

Unit 5 Lesson 5a

🎧 5 03 Exercise 5 /kl/ clothes, /pl/ player

a **Listen and repeat.**

clothes necklace clean clear clever clock climb class

place player plastic plate please plenty pleasant apply

b **Listen and repeat. Then practise saying the sentences.**

1 Can I have a plastic plate, please?
2 Take plenty of clean clothes.
3 This is a pleasant place to play.
4 It's clear that this class is clever.

Unit 6 Lesson 6a

🎧 6 03 Exercise 5 /ʒ/ leisure, /ʃ/ shoes

a **Listen and repeat.**

/ʒ/ leisure usually television
/ʃ/ shoes sure prediction

b **Listen. Is the sound /ʒ/ (1) or /ʃ/ (2)? Listen again and repeat.**

sure 2 usually 1 English casual measure mushroom special station cash machine unusual

c **Listen and repeat. Then practise saying the sentences.**

1 I'm sure Josh sells mushrooms for cash.
2 We usually watch television in our leisure time.
3 Let's get some cash from the machine at the station.

Unit 7 Lesson 7a

🎧 7 03 Exercise 8 Compression /ˈevri/ every

a **Listen and write down the number of syllables you hear. Then listen, check and repeat.**

extraordinary 4 everywhere favourite comfortable

b **Listen and repeat.**

interesting chocolate dictionary business restaurant secretary temporary factory

c **Listen and repeat. Then practise saying the phrases.**

a temporary secretary
a comfortable restaurant
a chocolate factory
an interesting dictionary

Unit 8 Lesson 8a

🎧 8 03 Exercise 8 Elision /dj/ would‿you, did‿you

a **Listen and repeat.**

Would you? What would you do?
Did you? Did you think it was interesting?

b **Listen and repeat. Then practise the conversation in pairs.**

A: What would you do if you saw a spider?
B: I'd run away.
A: Would you? I saw a spider last night.
B: Oh, did you? And what did you do?
A: I said 'hello'.

Unit 9 Lesson 9c

🎧 9 07 Exercise 7 Linking sounds quite‿excited‿about‿it

a **When a consonant sound is followed by a vowel, we link the sounds together. Listen and repeat.**

quite‿excited‿about‿it
I'm‿interested‿in
talked‿it‿over

b **Listen and repeat. Then practise saying the sentences.**

1 Jack is keen on airports.
2 He's interested in everything.
3 He's awfully good at art.
4 He isn't bad at anything.

114

Unit 1

Lesson 1a

Types of music and musical instruments

cello
clarinet
double bass
drums
flute
guitar
keyboard
piano
saxophone
trumpet
violin
voice

portfolio
record of achievements

Lesson 1b

babysitting
(He) can/can't make it.
Hang on.
What's up?

Lesson 1c

Adjectives of opinion

amazing
awesome
awful
boring
complicated
confusing
disappointing
dull
enjoyable
excellent
exciting
frightening
funny
interesting
sad
scary
violent

absolute favourite
special effects
superhero
without a doubt

Lesson 1d

backstage
be into (something)
cash
choir
choral
compete
fort
fusion
gear
marquee
perform

rehearse
semi-finals (of a
    competition)
take place
tough

Unit 2

Lesson 2a

calculator
charity shop
good for you!
Ha ha, very funny
How do you know?
sort out
you do that

Lesson 2b

Relationship words and phrases

argue/have an
    argument (with)
ask somebody out
be friends (with)
be/get annoyed (with)
break up (with)
fall in love (with)
fall out (with)
get divorced (from)
get engaged/married
    (to)
get on well (with)
go out (with)
make up

it's driving me mad
shocked

Lesson 2c

Family

daughter/son-in-law
fiancée/fiancé
married
mother/father-in-law
single (person)
sister/brother-in-law
stepmother/father
stepsister/brother

affect
anxious
attention
freedom
leader
(an) only child
peacemaker
share
trust
unimportant

Lesson 2d

a couple of
blast

drop out
guess what
hero-worship (v)
spare
taste (in music, etc.)
mean (= unkind)
look forward to
It's up to (you).
That's just it.

Unit 3

Lesson 3a

Adjectives and nouns of measurement

age
big
cost
deep
depth
distance
expensive
far
fast
height
high
length
long
old
size
speed
wide
width

avoid
cable car
crowded
double-decker
on foot
rickshaw
sights

Lesson 3b

cross over
I mean, …
I'm a bit lost.
straight on
the (first) turning
what now?

Lesson 3c

Countable and uncountable nouns

air
city
glass
hole

litter
luggage
news
plastic
problem
pollution
rubbish
traffic

average
global warming
greenhouse gas
ground
hole
increase
land (n)
landfill site
methane
one third
overseas
poison
recycle
refuse collector
waste (v)

Lesson 3d

appreciate
commentary
cruise
fit
harbour
hero
home-made
illuminated
pirates
skyline
skyscraper
tales
underground
waterways

Unit 4

Lesson 4a

Collocations with *make* and *do*

do a subject
do nothing/something
do some exercise
do some/the shopping
do your best
do your homework/
    some work/the
    housework
make a decision
make a difference
make a drink/a cake/a
    sandwich/a meal
make a mess
make a mistake

115

make a noise
make an appointment
  (with)
make friends (with)
make (some) money

Californian
mostly
pretty much
settle in
surfboard
to be honest
welcome (v)

Lesson 4b

Phrasal verbs with
  look
look after
look at
look for
look forward to
look up

at last!
Don't tell me ...
for ages
I'm in!
It's about …
Let's just say ...
We're on it!

Lesson 4c
guess
no idea
make-up
take off (clothes, etc.)

Lesson 4d
abandon
as you say
basically
cheat
copy (v)
in (big) trouble
in a fix
instead of
nobody else
obviously
stuff (n)
talk something through
tell on somebody
the thing is, …
What's the point?

Unit 5

Lesson 5a

Materials
cardboard
cotton
denim
fur
glass
gold

leather
metal
paper
plastic
rubber
silk
silver
suede
wood (*adj* wooden)
wool (*adj* woollen)

junk
last (v)
record player
run (= organise)
Thailand
the sixties

Lesson 5b

Verbs of action
carry
drop
fall
float
jump
land
lift
pull
push
sink
slip
take off
trip

basket
bright
bump
calm
clear
field
hot-air balloon
roar
you bet

Lesson 5c

Landscape and
  environment
bush
cliff
coastline
desert
harbour
hill
path
rock
stream
valley
waterfall
wood(s)

affect
area
cause
cover

disappearance
discovery
evidence
fountain
hurricane
mysterious
palace
philosopher
tsunami
tunnel

Lesson 5d
cave
chain
creatures
end up
endangered species
glow worm
hand in hand
luminous
on your own
overlook
regret
slippy
stalactite
stalagmite
torch

Unit 6

Lesson 6a

Holidays
B & B (bed and
  breakfast)
campsite
caravan
cottage
(self-catering) flat
hostel
hotel
motor home
tent
villa

cabbage
duck
fried
marmalade
prepared
probably
toast

Lesson 6b

Adjectives with
  prefixes: *un-*, *in-* **and**
  im-
impatient
impossible
impractical
inconvenient
independent
inexperienced
informal

unattractive
uncomfortable
unfit
unfriendly
unhappy
unhealthy
uninteresting
unkind
unlikely
unnecessary
unpleasant
unpopular
untidy
unusual

break up (e.g. a school)
Come on up!
hide
How are you doing?
knowing (him)
Quick
That's (him)!
Who else

Lesson 6c

Collocations with *lose*
lose a match
lose interest
lose sight (of
  something)
lose touch (with
  someone)
lose weight
lose your memory
lose your temper
lose your way

adopt
amazingly
apart
behave
coincidence
communicate
fiction
genes
identical
manage
separate
twins

Lesson 6d
(You're) a natural.
ache
corner shop
exhausted
forever
lean (leant)
Now what?
(I'm) off to bed
spoil

116

136

Unit 7

Lesson 7a
approach
card
colourful
fix (n)
marvellous
possibly
report
spooky
unicycle

Lesson 7b
Appearance
attractive
bald
eyebrow
fair/olive/dark-skinned
fat
fringe
handsome
in his/her teens/
  twenties
(of) medium-build
overweight
parting
pretty
round
slim
spiky
square
tattoo
teenage (adj)
thin
ugly
well-built

accent
arrest
behaviour
bright (= intelligent)
disguise
dollar
dumb
ignore
name tag
nearby
note (= paper money)
pose
prison
regular
remove
robbery
single
straightaway
successful
surprisingly

Lesson 7c
(I'm) so (excited/lucky
  ...!)
hard luck
I can't think
just a minute
live
on air

Lesson 7d
Aboriginal Australian
the Arctic
combat
costume
didgeridoo
indigenous
the Inuits
Maori
mind
pipe
survive
war cry
warrior

Unit 8

Lesson 8a
**-ed and -ing
  adjectives**
amazed
amazing
amused
amusing
annoyed
annoying
bored
boring
disappointed
disappointing
embarrassed
embarrassing
excited
exciting
frightened
frightening
interested
interesting
shocked
shocking
surprised
surprising
tired
tiring

career
chance
competition
concentrate
fame
incredibly
lifetime

lonely
lucky
opportunity
personal
show business
situation
tutor
view (= opinion)
vote

Lesson 8b
**Phrasal verbs with
  out, up, on**
cheer up
find out
get on
get up
give up
go on
look out
look up
run out (of)
turn on

branch
fair (n)
secret
tie (v)

Lesson 8c
**Types of TV
  programme**
cartoon
chat show
comedy
cookery programme
documentary
film
the news
quiz show
reality TV show
sitcom (situation
  comedy)
soap opera
sports programme
talent show
wildlife programme

final (n)
nasty

Lesson 8d
a bit of fun
ashamed
bully (n)
concentrate
embarrassed
nasty
on form
waste time

Unit 9

Lesson 9a
Computer language
app (application)
charge
games console
MP3 player
reboot
smartphone
tablet
touchscreen
upload
wi-fi

that's all.
fancy
for a bit
go halves
I know what you mean.
I'd so like . . .
Nice try.
pocket money
save
stare

Lesson 9b
**Sport (equipment,
  people and actions)**
Equipment
ball
basket
bat
glove
goal
helmet
net
racket
(shin) pads
wetsuit

People
athlete
coach
cyclist
goalkeeper
player
referee
spectator
team
umpire

Actions
beat (your opponent/a
  team)
hit/kick/throw/pass (the
  ball)
play/win/lose/draw (a
  match)
score (a goal/point)

challenging
cheer
disqualified

117

handlebar
juggle
line (v)
section
set
triathlon
world record

Lesson 9c

**Adjectives with
  prepositions**
angry with
annoyed with
bad at
bored with
different from
excited about
famous for
fed up with
frightened of
good at
impressed by
interested in
keen on
proud of
responsible for
scared of
similar to
surprised at
tired of
upset about
worried about

culture shock
delay (v)
final (adj)
keep in touch
LOL
sunshine
yawn

Lesson 9d

bat
batsman
bowl
bowler
get someone out
grass
field
knock
protective (sports) gear
rib guard
spare time
step
stick

118

Infinitive	Past	Past participle	Infinitive	Past	Past participle
be	was/were	been/gone	light	lit	lit
beat	beat	beaten	lose	lost	lost
become	became	become	make	made	made
begin	began	begun	mean	meant	meant
bend	bent	bent	meet	met	met
break	broke	broken	pay	paid	paid
bring	brought	brought	put	put	put
build	built	built	read	read /red/	read /red/
burn	burnt	burnt	ride	rode	ridden
buy	bought	bought	ring	rang	rung
catch	caught	caught	run	ran	run
choose	chose	chosen	say	said	said
come	came	come	see	saw	seen
cost	cost	cost	sell	sold	sold
cut	cut	cut	send	sent	sent
do	did	done	shake	shook	shaken
draw	drew	drawn	shine	shone	shone
dream	dreamt	dreamt	show	showed	shown
drink	drank	drunk	shut	shut	shut
drive	drove	driven	sing	sang	sung
eat	ate	eaten	sink	sank	sunk
fall	fell	fallen	sit	sat	sat
feel	felt	felt	sleep	slept	slept
fight	fought	fought	smell	smelt	smelt
find	found	found	speak	spoke	spoken
fly	flew	flown	spend	spent	spent
forget	forgot	forgotten	spread	spread	spread
get	got	got	stand	stood	stood
give	gave	given	steal	stole	stolen
go	went	gone/been	sting	stung	stung
grow	grew	grown	swim	swam	swum
hang	hung/hanged	hung/hanged	take	took	taken
have	had	had	teach	taught	taught
hear	heard	heard	tear	tore	torn
hide	hid	hidden	tell	told	told
hit	hit	hit	think	thought	thought
hold	held	held	throw	threw	thrown
hurt	hurt	hurt	understand	understood	understood
keep	kept	kept	wake	woke	woken
know	knew	known	wear	wore	worn
learn	learnt	learnt	win	won	won
leave	left	left	write	wrote	written
lend	lent	lent			

119

139

Class audio script

Welcome
d What is it?

 Audio script

1

A: Hello, my name is [*crackle*].

B: Sorry, *what's* your name?

2

A: Hi, I want to speak to [*crackle*], please.

B: Sorry, *who* do you want to speak to?

3

A: Yesterday we went to [*crackle*].

B: Sorry, *where* did you go yesterday?

4

A: Sorry, I can't come because [*crackle*].

B: Sorry, *why* can't you come?

5

A: It was very expensive. It cost [*crackle*].

B: Sorry, *how much* did it cost?

6

A: My number is [*crackle*].

B: Sorry, *what's* your number?

Unit 1 Performance
1a I'm going to apply

 Audio script

Toby: So, how did it go?

Jess: Oh, it was horrible. I was so nervous.

Toby: What did they ask you?

Jess: Oh, you know, they asked about my favourite music and that kind of thing.

Toby: That sounds OK.

Jess: Yes, I suppose so. But I didn't say anything very interesting.

Toby: So, when will you hear?

Jess: Hear what?

Toby: The result? When are they going to tell you?

Jess: They told me then. At the end of the interview.

Toby: Oh, Jess, I … I'm sorry, …

Jess: I got in!!!!

Toby: What? But I thought … oh, wow, that's amazing.

Jess: I know. I can't believe it.

Toby: How are you going to celebrate?

Jess: I'm not sure. I expect my mum will cook a special meal tonight. And I'm going to tell my grandparents this afternoon, they'll be really pleased.

Toby: Right. So, you're going to start a new school. I hope you won't forget all your old friends.

Jess: Of course I won't. I'll miss you a lot. But we'll hang out at weekends, like we do now, that won't change.

Toby: Hey, Jess, can I have your autograph? You'll be famous one day and it'll be worth a lot of money.

Jess: Oh, ha ha.

1d Music festivals.

 Audio script

Conversation 1

Len: Did you know that there are over 150 music festivals in the UK every year?

Janet: Wow, that's a lot!

Len: And for all kinds of music. There are rock festivals, jazz festivals and even dance and electronic music festivals.

Janet: I suppose Glastonbury is the best.

Len: It's certainly one of the biggest, but I don't think it is the best. I'm going to the Big Chill Multi-media music festival. It's much better than Glastonbury.

Janet: When are you going?

Len: In August. Do you fancy coming along?

Janet: I'll have to ask my dad.

Conversation 2

Eliot: What are you doing this weekend, Robert?

Robert: I'm playing in a concert on Saturday night.

Eliot: Oh. Do you play in a band?

Robert: No, I play in the National Youth Orchestra. It's much bigger than a band.

Eliot: Wow. That sounds great. Where's the concert?

Robert: At the Royal Albert Hall. It's a bit scary.

Eliot: What instrument do you play?

Robert: The trumpet.

Eliot: Best of luck!

Unit 2 That's life
2c People who you can trust

 Audio script

Girl: Hi, Harry, you look happy.

Boy: Yeah, guess what? I'm an uncle!

Girl: Wow! You're only fifteen. That's a bit young, isn't it?

Boy: Yes, well, my sister Jackie is ten years older than me. I'm the youngest and she's the oldest.

Girl: Oh, right, she's married, isn't she?

Boy: Yeah, that's right. She got married two years ago.

Girl: I remember now. I've seen the photos at your house.

Boy: That's right! She's just had a baby.

Girl: Girl or boy?

Boy: A girl. My niece! Her name's Alice.

Girl: So you're Uncle Harry. Has she got any aunts?

Boy: Yes, she's got three. There's my other sister Lucy and then Andy's got two sisters.

Girl: Who's Andy?

Boy: My brother-in-law of course. Jackie's husband.

Girl: Oh, right.

2d The Rock Roses.

🎧 2 11 **Audio script**

Ian: James, hi, listen, I've got some bad news.

James: Oh, what's that? Is everything alright?

Ian: Yes, well, it's just that I can't use that ticket, after all.

James: Oh no, why?

Ian: The kid who lives next door to us is having a birthday party. I forgot all about it.

James: Surely you can get out of it?

Ian: I'd like to, but I don't think I can.

James: Why don't you explain about the concert? It's a special one-off. I'm sure he'll understand.

Ian: Hmm, I'm not sure. I've already said I'll go. And, well, there aren't many people going.

James: OK, I get it. No problem, I can easily find someone else to take the ticket.

Ian: Yes, I'm sure you can. I feel really sick about it.

James: Well it's not all bad, Ian. I'm sure my dad will get some more tickets for something soon. So you can come next time.

Ian: Thanks, James. Do you think The Rock Roses will come back here again and play?

James: No, not here, but they're on tour. Maybe we can go and see them in another town. I'll ask my dad.

Skills Revision (page 31)

🎧 2 13 **Audio script**

Danny: Hi, Erica. Do you fancy going to a music workshop?

Erica: I'd love to, but what is it exactly?

Danny: It's great. It's a big musical event which is educational and fun. They tell you about different musical instruments and teach you how to play them. Well, you can try to play them! At the end we all play together.

Erica: It sounds a bit boring.

Danny: It's not. I've been twice and it's really exciting. Tom Sutherland, the guy who plays for The Rock Roses, gives some of the classes.

Erica: Tom Sutherland the drummer? Oh I love him!

Danny: Yes and it's this Saturday.

Erica: Oh no! I can't make it. I'm going shopping with my aunt and she wants to buy me a present. She's the aunt who has just got married to a millionaire!

Danny: Oh, I see. But the workshop's in the morning. Can't you meet her in the afternoon – the shops are still open then?

Erica: You're right. I'll meet her after lunch.

Danny: I'm sure you'll really enjoy it. It's much better than shopping.

Erica: Hang on, I'm going shopping, too, remember!

Unit 3 City life

3a Too big to see it all on foot.

🎧 3 03 **Audio script**

Man: Well, as you know DLR stands for the Docklands Light Railway. It opened in 1987 and is unusual because there are no drivers. The whole system is automatic.

Boy 1: How does it work, then? Is it safe enough to have no driver?

Man: Yes, it's perfectly safe. There's a big control centre with lots of computers. The staff can see every part of the line and every train.

Girl 1: How many stations are there?

Man: Good question. When it first opened there were only 15 stations and the line was only 13 kilometres long. They soon realised, though, that wasn't long enough.

Boy 2: Why not?

Man: Well, it was very popular, not just with ordinary Londoners, but with tourists, too.

Girl 2: You mean it was too successful?

Man: Well, yes, in a way. Anyway, it's grown! It's certainly big enough now to carry everyone. There are 45 stations and it's 34 kilometres long altogether. And about 200,000 passengers use it every day.

Boy 2: Wow! Is it like the Tube?

Man: No, the Tube is underground, but this railway is above ground – well, most of the time. You get really good views of London because it's quite high up, above street level. And it's pretty fast, too.

Girl 1: How fast is it?

Man: About 80 kilometres an hour.

Boy 3: How does it cross the river? Is there a bridge?

Man: Ah – well done. No, there isn't. That's where it does go underground! Under the river, in fact, through a tunnel. Yes, look, you can see where, on the map here …

3b You can't miss it.

🎧 3 04 **Audio script**

1

Reader: Find number 6, the library.

Boy: Hi, sorry, I'm a bit lost. Can you give me directions, please?

Girl: Sure. So, where are you now?

Boy: I'm outside the library.

Girl:	OK, go left, then turn right at the end of the road. Go straight on, then take the third turning on the right. Go past the cinema and it's on the right, on the corner of the square. I'm standing outside, you'll see me.
Boy:	OK, thanks.

2

Reader:	Find number 4, the art gallery.
Woman:	Hello? Listen, I'm sorry, but we're lost. How do we get there?
Man:	Oh, right, where are you now?
Woman:	Oh, we're standing in front of the art gallery, opposite the square.
Man:	Right, well, it's easy. Go across the square, then turn left into York Road. You'll see the park opposite you.
Woman:	OK, and then?
Man:	Walk down the road with the park on your left. You'll see it on the other side of the road. The entrance is round the corner, opposite the car park.
Woman:	Great. Thanks a lot.

3c We throw away too many things.

 Audio script

Man:	Hello and welcome to *Out and About*. This week we're in Banchester and we're asking people in the street how they feel about their town … OK, here goes … Excuse me, I'm from Radio Banchester, can I ask you a few questions?
Della:	Oh, yes, I suppose so. What sort of questions?
Man:	Well, first up, what's your name?
Della:	Della.
Man:	Right, Della. Do you live in Banchester, or are you just visiting?
Della:	I live here.
Man:	I see. And how do you feel about it? Is it a good place to live?
Della:	Well, it's OK. There aren't enough places for young people, though. I mean, there's the park and a bowling alley and that's about it.
Man:	There's a cinema, isn't there?
Della:	Yes, true. We go there sometimes. There isn't anywhere else, though. That's it.
Man:	Oh, well, what about sport? Is there anywhere you can go for some exercise?
Della:	Yeah, there's a sports club, but it costs too much money. I don't know anybody who goes there.
Man:	What about the shops?

Della:	Yeah, some of them are OK, but there are too many mobile phone shops, you know, and expensive clothes shops. I haven't got enough money for that kind of thing. I'd like more little cafés, I mean, somewhere to meet my friends and have a laugh. Oh, and there's litter everywhere around the shopping centre. Somebody should clear it up every day. It's disgusting.
Man:	Right, well, thank you very much, Della. Let's hope somebody from the council is listening …

3d Sightseeing – by land, sea or air!

🎧 **Audio script**

A:	Excuse me. Could you tell me what the best way to see the city is?
B:	Don't take the local city buses. They are too crowded to find a seat and there are too many different routes. The best way to see the sights is to take the hop-on hop-off tour bus. It stops everywhere.
A:	What is it exactly?
B:	It's an open-air double-decker bus that takes you around the main sights in Sydney and Bondi. It doesn't go too fast so you can take lots of photos. And you can get on and off as many times as you like.
A:	How long does the tour take?
B:	About 90 minutes, it's long enough to see everything.
A:	And how does the ticket work?
B:	You can buy a 24- or a 48-hour ticket and use the buses at any time.
A:	How often is there a bus?
B:	Every 15 minutes. The tour includes the Sydney Opera House and Bondi Beach. And there's a recorded commentary in English.
B:	Great. Just one more thing. Where does the tour start?
A:	It starts at the Central Station bus stop. But there are 34 bus stops along the route. Would you like to buy a ticket?
B:	Yes, please. I'd like two 24-hour …

Unit 4 Time passes
4b You've been talking for ages.

🎧 **Audio script**

Martin:	Hi, Emma. How's the badminton going?
Emma:	Oh, hi, Martin. Yes, it's going fine, thanks. Do you play badminton, too?
Martin:	No, I've never tried it. How long have you been playing?
Emma:	Oh, since I was about eight. I went to a kids' activity week one summer and learnt it there. What sports are you into?
Martin:	Well, I play basketball. I started that … oooh about ten years ago I guess, when I was about six.

Emma: Are you in a team?

Martin: Yes, back home I play in the school team. I'm not that good, but I'm keen.

Emma: So, what do you think of this sports centre? Do you like it?

Martin: Yes, it's OK. How long have you been coming here?

Emma: Oh, only for about six months. It's the best place round here for badminton. We don't do it at school.

Martin: Oh, right. What sports do you play at school?

Emma: Well, I've just started playing hockey. I quite like it. I only started last May, though, so I'm not very good. What about you? What do you do at school?

Martin: Well, since I arrived in the UK I've been playing soccer, I mean football. I've never played it before. I've watched it on TV quite a lot, but I only played my first game about three weeks ago! I'm pretty terrible. Luke and I kick around in the park sometimes, so I can practise.

Emma: Well, I'd better go and find my badminton partner. Nice to see you, Martin.

Martin: Sure, see you.

4c She used to be a Goth.

4 07 Audio script

1

A: Congratulations. You've won!

B: Have I?

2

A: Sorry, we're going to be late.

B: Are we?

3

A: That isn't my coat.

B: Isn't it?

4

A: Oh no, it's snowing.

B: Is it?

5

A: She won't remember.

B: Won't she?

6

A: I can't do this exercise.

B: Can't you?

7

A: She's going to a new school.

B: Is she?

8

A: They didn't enjoy the film.

B: Didn't they?

4d Right or wrong?

4 11 Audio script

Ned: Excuse me, Mr Benson, have you got a minute?

Mr Benson: Yes, sure, what is it, Ned?

Ned: Um, well, there's something I've got to tell you.

Mr Benson: Is there? That sounds interesting. What is it?

Ned: Well, er, it's about that last piece of homework I did. You know, the History project, about the Romans.

Mr Benson: Oh yes, of course. That was excellent, Ned. I was very impressed. You put a lot of work into it.

Ned: Well, that's it, umm, you see …

Mr Benson: Yes?

Ned: Well actually Chrissy and I did it together, and, er …

Mr Benson: Chrissy? Do you mean Christine Hunt?

Ned: Yes, we're friends, you see and we quite often do our homework together.

Mr Benson: Do you? But Chrissy just copied from the internet. It was quite obvious. Are you saying …?

Ned: Yes, I did the same thing. I suppose I changed more words round, I'm not sure. You didn't notice.

Mr Benson: Oh! No, you're right, I didn't.

Ned: I feel bad now, 'cos she's in trouble and I got an A.

Mr Benson: Yes, hmmm, I see. But Ned, the question is, did you understand it?

Ned: Yes, I think so.

Mr Benson: And did Christine, er, Chrissy, understand it, too?

Ned: I think so, yes.

Mr Benson: Well, I'll tell you what we'll do …

Audio script

Chrissy: Did you really go and tell Mr Benson? Thanks, Ned. But you're crazy. I suppose you're in big trouble now, as well as me.

Ned: Well, sort of. Actually we've both got a second chance.

Chrissy: What do you mean?

Ned: We have to stay after school tomorrow and do it again.

Chrissy: Are you joking?

Ned: No. We've got to do the work again, in the classroom. Without any books. Or computers. The thing is, I told him we understood it.

Chrissy: Did you? Ummm …

Ned: … and he said this way, we can prove it.

Chrissy: Oh, er, I see … And what about our marks? You got an A!

Ned: Yes, well, I'm going to try to keep it.

Chrissy: Really? How?

Ned: I'm going to go and find out all about the Romans. Right now.

Chrissy: Good thinking. Me, too. And fast!

Skills Revision (page 51)

Audio script

Reader: This is the Strand … the Strand is one of London's oldest roads near the River Thames. In fact 'Strand' means 'river bank' in old English. Some of London's finest institutions and houses are by the river. On your left here, you can see Somerset House. It looks like a royal palace, doesn't it? This house has been many different British institutions in the past, but today it is an arts and cultural centre.

Now on your left is Waterloo Bridge and the River Thames.

Coming up now we have the Savoy Hotel – London's most famous luxury hotel. Millionaires and stars have been staying here for over 100 years.

Now on the left we have the Adelphi Theatre. There are over forty traditional theatres here in the West End and about 13 million people come to shows, theatres and musicals every year. Before we finish …

Unit 5 Around the world
5b I couldn't sleep.

Audio script

Last summer, teenager Thomas Clark went to a summer fair in his village in the north of England. One of the stalls had a big sign saying 'Grand balloon race'. Thomas went to have a look. There were lots of balloons with pieces of paper attached to them. You could buy a balloon for £2.00, write your name and address on the paper, and then send it up into the sky. There was a prize for the person whose balloon went the furthest.

Thomas decided to buy a balloon. He paid his money, chose a blue balloon and wrote his name and address on the paper. He threw the balloon up into the air and it floated away. Thomas watched it for a few minutes and then, when he wasn't able to see it any more, he walked away and forgot all about it.

Two weeks later, Thomas went on holiday with his parents. They went camping in the south of France. One morning, Thomas was walking along a beach when he saw something on the sand. When he picked it up and looked at it, he couldn't believe his eyes. It was his balloon!

When he got home, Thomas contacted the people who organised the race and told them about his balloon. That's when he had his second surprise – his balloon was the winner – and he won £100!

Unit 6 Things to remember
6c The two men hadn't met before.

Audio script

1 A few years ago a twenty-two-year-old man called Rob Jones took part in the London Marathon. He'd never run a marathon before, but he had trained hard and he was well prepared. He was very excited as he joined hundreds of other athletes at the start line.

A huge crowd was lining the streets. Rob looked for his family, but he couldn't see them. He knew they were there somewhere – his mum, his dad and his eight-year-old sister Jenny. But it was impossible to find them in the crowd.

'Oh well,' he thought, 'I'd like a picture of this crowd, anyway. It's amazing.'

He took a little camera from his pocket, held it up to the crowd, and took a photo.

2 While Rob was preparing to start his race, his family were trying to get to the front of the crowd. It was no good – there were far too many people.

'Oh well,' said Mr Jones, 'let's get a picture anyway, it's amazing.'

He lifted Jenny up on to his shoulders and she took a photo with her father's camera.

3 About five hours later, Rob crossed the finishing line. He'd done it! He posed for photos and then went home to recover and to celebrate with his proud family.

A few days after that, Rob remembered the photos he'd taken. He looked on his camera and found them. Imagine his surprise when he saw a photo of his sister, Jenny. She was sitting on their dad's shoulders and holding a camera. He'd taken a photo of her, completely by chance.

4 That isn't the end of the story. You've probably guessed the rest. When Rob's family checked the photos that Jenny had taken, there was Rob. He was right in the middle of the picture, holding up his camera!

6d The ski trip.

6 12 Audio script

Sarah: Harry, what's going on? Is everything OK? I saw you talking to Don just now, you looked very serious.

Harry: We were talking about the fire.

Sarah: I thought so, Harry. I've been feeling so bad about that.

Harry: No need. It wasn't your fault. It just happened. Anyway, it's sorted now.

Sarah: When did you tell him?

Harry: I didn't tell him.

Sarah: You didn't?

Harry: No.

Sarah: I don't get it. What happened, then?

Harry: I couldn't think what to do and in the end I phoned my parents. I needed some advice, you know, from people who know all the facts.

Sarah: Oh, good idea. They know Don's parents, don't they?

Harry: Yes, they do. Anyway my mum and dad knew about the fire of course. Don's parents decided not to tell him. They didn't want him to worry.

Sarah: That's what you guessed, right?

Harry: Right. Anyway, Dad went round to Don's house and spoke to his parents. They decided to phone Don and tell him, so that's what they did. His mum phoned him about an hour ago.

Sarah: Oh, right. So, how's Don?

Harry: He was quite shocked, but he's fine now. He knows his family are all OK and they'll soon sort out the shop.

Sarah: So, he doesn't want to go home?

Harry: No, he doesn't. He's going to stay here. We're going home in three days' time anyway. Everything's cool, we can all stop worrying and have some fun.

Sarah: Good idea! Come on, let's get ready for some more skiing!

Skills Revision (page 71)

6 14 Audio script

1 It was small inside and we weren't able to do anything there, only sleep and cook. It had a small door and four windows. We parked the car outside. There was more space in the car! Mum said that we're going to stay in a hotel next year.

2 It was OK. We were right in the middle of the countryside. We were able to go rock climbing and walking in the mountains which was good. But because of the rain, which was really heavy, we couldn't leave the tent for a few days. Don't forget to pack a raincoat if you decide to go there.

3 We were able to visit all the sights, the museum and the cathedral, because we were in the city centre. The place we stayed at was good, but the restaurant was expensive. My friend Barbara had been there the year before so we decided to do the same.

4 As soon as we arrived we loved the place. It was beautiful, old, made of stone and in the middle of the countryside. Park House was built in the eighteenth century for a very rich family. Today there are sixty guest rooms and it's run by a travel company.

5 We wanted an adventure so Mum and Dad decided that a holiday by car was best. That way we could drive to a different place every day. We stayed in a different B & B every night. Because they are run by families they don't have restaurants, but we had some delicious cooked breakfasts. Some of the families were unfriendly and some of the houses untidy! It was a real adventure.

Unit 7 Reporting speech
7a He told her to throw it.

7 02 Audio script

1 Don't move!
2 Could you pass the sugar, please?
3 Look at the whiteboard, please.
4 Listen to me!
5 Take the next turning on your right.
6 Please don't eat my crisps.

7 04 Audio script

Girl: These are great pictures, Ray. Are you going to post them online?

Ray: Yes, I guess so. I'll sort out the best ones. Ha ha, look at this.

Girl: Oh, what's going on there, with the piano? An open-air concert or something?

Ray: No. Not at all. That piano was just there, in the street. Nobody was looking after it or anything. There was a big cardboard sign. It said 'PLAY ME' and people just stopped, sat down and played. It was so cool.

Girl: Really? Could they actually play?

Ray: Yes, I mean they weren't all great musicians or anything. But loads of people managed to play something. Some people just played funny little tunes, or a few notes, but some played properly, I mean really, really well. It was amazing.

Girl: So who's this girl, the one who's playing the piano?

Ray: She was walking past with a friend – he's there, look, the man in the bright blue shirt. He told her to play something. She didn't want to, in fact they nearly had an argument, then she suddenly said, 'Oh. OK then' and she sat down and started playing. I think it was Beethoven.

Girl: And?

Ray: She was fantastic. People stopped and listened and at the end they clapped like crazy. Then they started asking her to play their favourite songs.

Girl: Did she do it?

Ray: No, she didn't. She looked really embarrassed, stood up and walked off with her friend. But it was great, so cool.

7c She asked if I could come …

🎧 7 08 Audio script

1 Can I ask you some questions?
2 How old are you?
3 What's your address?
4 What school do you go to?
5 Is English your favourite subject?
6 When did you start learning English?
7 Have you ever been to the UK?
8 Can you speak any other languages?
9 What are you planning for the summer holidays?
10 Will you go to university in the future, or will you get a job?

🎧 7 10 Audio script

Girl: Hi, could I speak to Amy, please?

Boy: Sorry, she isn't here right now. Can I take a message?

Girl: Yes, thanks. Tell her Anna called.

Boy: OK …

Girl: … tell her I've lost my mobile.

Boy: Oh, that's bad. Hard luck.

Girl: Thanks. Anyway, can you ask her to call me on this number? It's 01783 593223.

Boy: OK, hang on … did you say 233?

Girl: No, 223.

Boy: Right. 01783 593223.

Girl: Yes. It's my home number. I'll be at home all afternoon. OK?

Boy: Sure, I'll tell her. Hope you find your phone soon.

Girl: Me, too. Thanks then. Bye.

7d Traditions around the world

🎧 7 12 Audio script

Sandy: Hi, Karima. Thanks for coming online to speak to me.

Karima: Sure no problem, Sandy.

Sandy: I wanted to ask you about the Inuit people. What does 'Inuit' mean?

Karima: Oh that's really easy. It means 'people', the people that have lived in Arctic regions, like northern Canada, for thousands of years.

Sandy: I must say, when I think of the Arctic, I don't really think about sports – it's too cold! So I'm really interested in hearing more about your traditional games. How many are there?

Karima: Lots and lots! They're mainly games that make you stronger, but some of them are just for fun. They were invented to keep people healthy and happy!

Sandy: And what types of games are there?

Karima: Well, there are ball games, jumping games, wrestling games and games with bones.

Sandy: Bones?!

Karima: Well not real bones any more. These are games like dominoes or puzzles.

Sandy: What's your favourite type of Inuit game?

Karima: I like the voice games.

Sandy: Singing songs?

Karima: Not really, well not like Justin Bieber! These are games where you make different noises with your voice.

Sandy: Noises?

Karima: Yes, that's right – there are no words. You stand opposite the other person and the game begins. Some noises are harder than others and it can be very tiring!

Sandy: How do you win?

Karima: If you need to stop to breathe or to laugh, then you lose the game. I don't often win because you stand very close to the other person. I usually start laughing!

Sandy: Sounds cool!

Karima: I'll send you a video link. You'll love it!

Sandy: And do you play more modern games?

Karima: Of course! Hockey, tennis, football, baseball, you name it.

Unit 8 Feelings

8a How would you feel?

8 03 Audio script

Amy: Wouldn't it be fantastic to be rich and famous, Tom! I'd love it!

Tom: Really, Amy? I think it would be awful.

Amy: Why? It would be wonderful. If I had lots of money, I would go shopping every day – fantastic!

Tom: Amy, if you went shopping EVERY DAY, I'm sure you'd soon get really bored. It wouldn't be exciting at all. And there's another thing …

Amy: What's that?

Tom: Well, if you were a celebrity, people would follow you everywhere. You know, photographers would follow you wherever you went. You'd never get away from them.

Amy: I'd like that. I'd like to see my photograph in magazines.

Tom: Would you? Are you sure? Some people would say unkind things about you and laugh at you …

Amy: If they did, I wouldn't listen to them. It would be amazing – I'd travel the world and have expensive holidays in fantastic places.

Tom: OK, OK. So you want to be rich and famous. How are you going to do it?

Amy: Hmmm. If I could sing, I'd join a band.

Tom: But you can't sing.

Amy: No, but I can dream.

8b I wish we could stay longer.

8 07 Audio script

Josh: OK, here's a question. If you could change three things in your life, what would they be?

Anna: What, anything?

Josh: No, not quite. You can't wish you were rich and you can't wish you had more wishes. OK?

Anna: OK.

Josh: Right. What's your first wish?

Anna: Easy. I wish I could play the saxophone. I've always wanted to.

Josh: Well, it's not too late to start learning. Anyway, what's your next one?

Anna: I wish I was good at acting. I'd like to be a famous film star and live in Hollywood.

Josh: Dream on, Anna! OK, last one.

Anna: Ummm. I'm not sure what to say now. Errr, I wish we didn't have school in the morning. Then we could stay in bed until lunchtime!

Josh: Good idea. I like that one!

8c It was so boring I fell asleep.

8 10 Audio script

1 [sfx: football crowd roaring]

2 [sfx: soundtrack for Tom and Jerry type cartoon]

3 Good evening. The President of the USA flew to China today for talks about …

4 Yes, it's time for you to vote for your favourite *Wow Factor!* singers now, just text the numbers you can see on the screen. Don't forget, though, texts cost 50p each …

5 [sfx: canned laughter]

6 Good evening and welcome. Tonight's guest is 007 himself, Daniel Craig.

7 As we watch, we see the mother bird flying back to the nest. She calls out to her babies and … look, they're opening their beaks, ready for the food she's brought back for them …

8 Hello, yes it's Saturday night and time for another game of *Ask Me Another*. So, let's meet our first contestant …

8d Online bullying

8 13 Audio script

Andy: Hi, Anna, have you got a minute?

Anna: Yes, sure. What is it?

Andy: Nothing really, it's just that, well, I wanted to say sorry.

Anna: What for?

Andy: Well, look, I know I've been horrible to you … I told you to leave me alone. You were only trying to help. Sorry.

Anna: That's OK. I know you're having a rubbish time.

Andy: Yes, I sure am. I just wish it wasn't true, but it is. I don't know what to do.

Anna: What about your parents? Why don't you tell them?

Andy: They'd just worry. That's no help. And they'd tell the school – and I'd be teacher's pet again. I can't do anything.

Anna: Well I don't agree. Why don't you talk to Mrs Williams? You really like her. I'll come with you if you like.

Andy: Really?

Anna: Yes, of course. Come on, Andy, what do you say?

Andy: Oh, well, OK, I guess … thanks, Anna.

🎧 8 14 Audio script

Mrs Williams: Well, Andy, I'm glad you and Anna have told me about this. You've done the right thing, you know.

Andy: But if they find out I've told you, it'll make it worse.

Mrs Williams: Don't worry, I will make sure that doesn't happen. First, have you any idea who these bullies are? Do you know their names?

Andy: Well, yes, but I don't want to tell you. Can we just leave it?

Mrs Williams: If we do that, it's true they will probably get bored and stop, in the end. But then they'll move on to somebody else, and do the same again. Is that what you want?

Andy: Well, no, of course not. But …

Mrs Williams: Andy, these bullies don't understand what they're doing. They think they aren't hurting anyone, because they aren't hitting you or throwing things at you. They don't realise they're hurting you anyway.

Andy: Well, maybe, but they wouldn't care, anyway. They don't like me.

Mrs Williams: Do you like them?

Andy: No, of course not. I just want them to leave me alone.

Mrs Williams: Right, well, that's what they will do, I will make sure of that.

Anna: What are you going to do, Mrs Williams?

Mrs Williams: I'm going to call a special meeting for all of Year Ten and we're going to have a long talk. Don't worry, Andy I won't mention your name. Oh, and listen, I know it's difficult, but try and ignore the bullies. Don't respond to them in any way. Can you do that?

Andy: Yes, OK …

Skills Revision (page 91)

🎧 8 16 Audio script

Alice: What's up, Fred?

Fred: I wish I had more time to do my Maths homework. Can you do it for me?

Alice: Of course I can't. Mum said you had to finish it before dinner.

Fred: Would you do it if I gave you some of my pocket money?

Alice: I would … if you paid me all of it.

Fred: That's terrible. Anyway it's not as difficult as your homework.

Alice: Of course it isn't. I'm two years older than you and I'm doing A-levels.

…

Fred: I asked Mr Philips if I could give him my homework next week.

Alice: What did he say?

Fred: No.

Alice: Ha ha, nice try!

Fred: I wish I could look up the answers to these sums online. Could you turn on the computer?

Alice: Oh come on, Fred! It's not as bad as that. Listen. I'll help you, but only if you help me.

Fred: What do you want?

Alice: If I were you, I'd speak a bit more nicely to me.

Fred: OK. What would you like, Alice?

Alice: Well first of all I want all of your pocket money for this week and I want you to tell Mum that I'm going to a concert with Belinda on Friday night.

Fred: Why don't you tell her?

Alice: Because I'm not going with Belinda.

Fred: Oh. Who are you going with, then?

Alice: I'm going with Gina and it's a pop concert in Liverpool. I'm really excited about it, but Mum told me not to go out with Gina any more.

Fred: Ah ha! Now you've told me! I'll give you five pounds and you do all the homework.

Alice: You … bully!

Unit 9 Moving on
9b He had to swim on his back.

🎧 9 05 Audio script

Cathy: I like the idea of joggling, you know, juggling and running, but it sounds really hard.

Harry: Yes, it does. Hmmm … what other sports could go together? What about ice-skating and table tennis?

Cathy: That sounds awful. How would you play it? What would the rules be?

Harry: Oooh, I don't know … Players have to keep moving round the table – and they have to keep hitting the ball over the net at the same time.

Cathy: Genius. Ummm, what do they have to do with their bats?

Harry: Good question. They mustn't drop them.

Cathy: OK and how do you win? How many points do you have to score? Twenty?

Harry: Hmmm. No, that's too many. Let's say, ummm, ten.

Cathy: Fine. And what would you call this new game? Table skating?

Harry: Yes, that's it.

9d Sporting passions

9 10 Audio script

Josh: Hi, Hailey. How's the project going?

Hailey: Oh great. I'm writing about cricket.

Josh: I don't know much about cricket! What have you learned?

Hailey: Well. It was first played by the English in the sixteenth century.

Josh: Really!

Hailey: Then during the time of the British Empire it was introduced in places like the West Indies, India and Pakistan.

Josh: Yes, they love playing cricket in those countries.

Hailey: And it's also very popular in Australia, New Zealand and South Africa. In fact about 100 countries play cricket today.

Josh: They have competitions against each other, don't they?

Hailey: Yes, they do. The oldest competition is called the Ashes.

Josh: The what?

Hailey: The Ashes. A.S.H.E.S. It's between England and Australia and the first match was in 1882.

Josh: Cool. What are the rules of cricket then?

Hailey: OK. First of all the batsman has to hit the ball as far as possible. Then he can run in between the wickets.

Josh: What are wickets?

Hailey: They are three sticks in the ground, they're the goalposts if you like.

Josh: How does the batsman score points?

Hailey: When he runs between the wickets, he scores a 'run'.

Josh: Oh that sounds very complicated to me. And don't you get tired of watching this game?

Hailey: Sometimes I get fed up of watching it because it can last for hours and even days. The Ashes games last five days.

Josh: Gosh. That's a long time. Have you been to see a match? I mean a live match?

Hailey: Never. But I'm going with my dad to see England versus the West Indies. I'm really looking forward to it.

Workbook answer key

Welcome
a What are you doing here?

Exercise 1

2 e) 3 f) 4 a) 5 d) 6 b)

Exercise 2

2 bossy 3 easy-going 4 generous 5 lazy
6 rude 7 shy 8 untidy

Exercise 3

2 a) 3 e) 4 g) 5 c) 6 f) 7 b)

Exercise 4

2 What are you doing 3 I'm waiting
4 where are you going 5 I'm going
6 He plays 7 Do you like 8 I prefer
9 Are you going 10 The bus is coming

b I've got some photos.

Exercise 1

2 wastepaper bin 3 floor 4 wall 5 ceiling
6 balcony

Exercise 2

2 bookcase 3 wardrobe 4 carpet
5 dishwasher 6 mirror 7 upstairs,
downstairs 8 washbasin, sink 9 fridge
10 garage

Exercise 3

2 b) 3 b) 4 a) 5 c) 6 a) 7 c) 8 b)

Exercise 4

2 any 3 a 4 An 5 no 6 some 7 some
8 some

c It was raining when we landed.

Exercise 1

2 d) 3 b) 4 e) 5 a) 6 i) 7 j) 8 f) 9 h) 10 g)

Exercise 2

2 plumber 3 electrician 4 chef 5 housewife
6 builder

Exercise 3

2 while I was taking 3 While I was giving
4 When I finished 5 the actress was
walking 6 while he was standing

Exercise 4

2 The electricity went off while I was
  playing computer games.
3 While the police officer was driving, he
  saw the bank robbers.

d What is it?

Exercise 1

2 b) 3 b) 4 c) 5 c) 6 a) 7 a) 8 b)

Exercise 2

2 Where 3 How far 4 How 5 What kind
6 How old 7 How many 8 How often

Exercise 3

jumper 2 gloves 1 dress 4 sleeveless 4
baggy 2 plain 3 patterned 2 striped 1
tight 3 spotted 4

Exercise 4

2 scarf 3 checked shirt 4 belt 5 pocket
6 zip 7 jeans 8 socks 9 sandals

Unit 1 Performance
1a I'm going to apply.

Exercise 1

2 Latin 3 reggae 4 soul 5 techno
6 classical 7 rock 8 heavy metal
9 country, western

Exercise 2

2 double bass 3 violin 4 guitar 5 drums
6 trumpet 7 clarinet 8 flute 9 saxophone
10 keyboard

Exercise 3

2 prediction without evidence 3 decision
4 prediction with evidence 5 promise
6 plan

Exercise 4

2 you'll have 3 You'll be 4 You won't be
5 you'll be 6 I'm not going to pass

Exercise 5

2 'm going to put 3 'll be 4 'll make
5 won't get 6 won't do 7 are you going to
call 8 'll think

1b I'm going out.

Exercise 1

2 can't make it 3 hang on 4 can make it

Exercise 2

2 Simon is meeting 3 Tom and I are
playing 4 My mum and dad are having
5 What are you doing 6 We aren't going
7 Are you working 8 I'm getting

Exercise 3

1 **A:** No, I'm not. I'm playing the Prince.

   B: Who's playing Romeo?

2 **A:** Are you meeting Simon this
     weekend?

   B: Yes, I am. We're going to the
     cinema.

   A: Is he taking you out for dinner as
     well?

   B: No, he isn't. He's coming to my
     house for dinner.

3 **A:** Are you doing anything tomorrow?

   B: No, I'm not. Why?

   A: I'm meeting Kate at Pizza Palace.

   B: She's bringing her friend, Theresa.

Exercise 4

2 c) 3 a) 4 c) 5 a) 6 c) 7 b)

Exercise 5

2 I'd love 3 for asking 4 Do you 5 I can't
6 fancy going 7 sounds great 8 I'm afraid
9 What about 10 I'd love

1c They're the best films ever!

Exercise 1

2 a) 3 a) 4 b) 5 b) 6 a) 7 b)

Exercise 2

2 awesome 3 excellent 4 exciting
5 enjoyable 6 interesting 7 awful 8 boring
9 disappointing 10 dull

Exercise 3

2 worse 3 as 4 worst 5 more 6 the 7 sad
8 isn't 9 much

Exercise 4

2 The best 3 the most exciting 4 as
good 5 The scariest 6 more exciting than
7 duller than 8 as enjoyable 9 the dullest
10 better than

Exercise 5

2 The old Star Wars films are much more
  enjoyable than the new Star Wars films.
3 The best film is the first one.
4 The worst film is the fifth one.
5 The acting in the old film isn't (wasn't) as
  good as the acting in the new film.
6 The actors in the original film are (were)
  as cool as the actors in the new film.
7 They aren't (weren't) as good-looking as
  George Clooney and Brad Pitt though!

Language round-up
(page 14)

Exercise 1

1 clarinet, flute, violin
2 techno, classical, jazz
3 awesome, enjoyable
4 dull, awful

Workbook answer key

Exercise 2

2 **A:** When are you going to do your homework?

B: Er, I'll do it after this film, I promise.

3 **A:** When are you meeting/going to meet Amy?

B: I'm meeting her tomorrow at eleven o'clock.

4 **A:** Do you fancy going to the cinema tonight?

B: I can't. We're going to my grandmother's tonight.

5 **A:** Would you like to come to my party on Saturday?

B: I'm afraid I can't but thanks for asking.

6 **A:** Will you still live here in ten years' time?

B: No, I won't. It's boring here.

Exercise 3

2 better 3 good 4 worse 5 funnier 6 more enjoyable 7 most complicated 8 the worst 9 interesting 10 most beautiful 11 scariest

Exercise 4

2 going to get a summer job 3 visiting my cousin 4 is the best actor 5 as good as 6 more difficult than

Skills practice (page 15)

Exercise 1

B 3 C 2

Exercise 2

2 F 3 F 4 DS 5 T

Exercise 3

2 How's 3 going 4 Do 5 fancy 6 Do 7 want 8 Bye 9 now

Unit 2 That's life
2a I've just told you.

Exercise 1

2 empty 3 make 4 tidy 5 wash 6 do 7 take

Exercise 2

2 do the cooking 3 do the washing 4 do the shopping 5 make the bed 6 do the ironing 7 do the washing up

Exercise 3

2 b) 3 a) 4 a) 5 b) 6 a)

Exercise 4

2 **A:** Have you tidied your room yet?

B: I've started but I haven't finished yet.

3 **A:** Have you ever found money in the street?

B: No, I haven't but I've lost lots of money!

4 **A:** Has Jack done the washing up yet?

B: Yes, he has and he's already emptied the dishwasher.

Exercise 5

2 No, I haven't finished it yet.
3 Yes, I've just bought it.
4 I've never been there.
5 I've never made one/a cake.

2b He asked me out.

Exercise 1

2 with 3 be 4 out 5 out 6 on 7 get 8 out 9 up

Exercise 2

2 broke up with 3 got engaged to 4 got married to

Exercise 3

2 did, 've already done 3 've never been, wasn't 4 Have you ever been, Did you go

Exercise 4

2 **A:** When are you going to ask Melanie out?

B: I've already asked her. I asked her yesterday.

3 **A:** Have you ever been in love?

B: Yes, I have. I fell in love last night.

4 **A:** I've never had an argument with my sister.

B: Yes, you have. You had one last week.

Exercise 5

2 bit 3 matter 4 Maybe 5 Why 6 fed-up 7 should 8 worried

Exercise 6

2 What's up? 3 I'm a bit worried about 4 I don't know what to do 5 why don't you 6 Maybe you should 7 I don't think you should

2c People who you can trust.

Exercise 1

2 Jessica 3 Harold and Kathy 4 Charlene and Russell 5 Phil 6 Phil 7 Charlene 8 Charlene 9 Phil 10 Harry

Exercise 2

2 single 3 stepmother 4 fiancé 5 sister-in-law 6 fiancée

Exercise 3

2 where 3 whose 4 which 5 where 6 who

Exercise 4

2 a) 3 a) 4 c) 5 b)

Exercise 5

3 (which) 4 which 5 whose 6 (which) 7 where

Exercise 6

2 She's a woman who was in a pop group.
3 It's an art gallery where you can see the Mona Lisa.
4 It's an art gallery which lots of people visit each year.
5 He's an actor who has won the Best Actor Oscar three times.
6 He's an actor whose father was a famous poet.
7 It's a place which is a district of Los Angeles.
8 It's a place where lots of films are made.

Skills practice (page 23)

Exercise 1

B

Exercise 2

2 F 3 F 4 T 5 F

Exercise 3

c)

Exercise 4

2 Sylvia
3 He was really upset.
4 Break up with Sylvia/tell Sylvia he has finished with her.
6 after football practice

Exercise 5

2 It will be 3 are coming 4 I'm not having 5 Do you want 6 What about going 7 I'll ask 8 tell me 9 See you tomorrow

Language round-up
(page 22)

Exercise 1

2 ago 3 get 4 stepfather 5 stepbrother 6 aunt 7 cousins 8 on 9 do 10 make 11 tidy 12 fell 13 out 14 up 15 has

Exercise 2

2 c) 3 a) 4 b) 5 a) 6 b) 7 c)

Exercise 3

2 Have 3 yet 4 out 5 which 6 ago 7 who 8 whose 9 just 10 went 11 has

Exercise 4

2 up on, with to 3 already yet, saw seen 4 on in, what who 5 made done, done made 6 get make, do have

151

Unit 3 City life

3a Too big to see it all on foot.

Exercise 1
2 to 3 hard 4 too 5 enough

Exercise 2
2 a) It's too far. b) I'm not rich enough.
3 a) I'm too scared. b) It's too dangerous.
4 a) It's too rainy. b) My Italian isn't good enough. 5 a) It's too big. b) The food isn't tasty enough.

Exercise 3
2 My PC isn't fast enough for this game.
3 I ran too slowly to win the race.
4 I'm too short to play for the school basketball team.
5 I don't speak French well enough to understand this book.
6 It's too late to go out for a meal.

Exercise 4
2 high 3 big 4 fast 5 old 6 far 7 wide 8 long

Exercise 5
2 c) 3 h) 4 i) 5 a) 6 f) 7 b) 8 d) 9 g)

Exercise 6
2 ferry 3 caravan 4 minibus 5 ship 6 plane
7 coach 8 lorry 9 tram

3b You can't miss it.

Exercise 1
2 d) 3 d) 4 a) 5 g) 6 a) 7 e) 8 b) 9 f) 10 a)

Exercise 2
2 bank 3 factory 4 hospital 5 newsagent(s)
6 office 7 travel agent(s) 8 library
9 restaurant 10 supermarket

Exercise 3
2 museum 3 park 4 zoo 5 theatre 6 hotels
7 pharmacy 8 school

Exercise 4
2 suppose 3 mean 4 now

Exercise 5
2 Take the second on the left. 3 Cross the road. 4 Go past the bank. 5 Go straight on. 6 The bank is opposite the station.
7 Turn left. 8 Go right out of the station.
9 The bank is next to the station. 10 Take the first on the right.

Exercise 6
2 take 3 left 4 past 5 left 6 opposite 7 out
8 right 9 first 10 next

Exercise 7
2 way 3 straight 4 past 5 cross 6 on
7 bother 8 how 9 out 10 Take 11 to
12 welcome

3c We throw away too many things.

Exercise 1
2 b) 3 b) 4 a) 5 c) 6 a)

Exercise 2
3 ✓ 4 ✓ 5 ✗ 6 ✓ 7 ✓ 8 ✗ 9 ✗ 10 ✗ 11 ✓
12 ✗ 13 ✓ 14 ✗

Exercise 3
2 isn't enough 3 too many 4 aren't enough
5 isn't enough 6 aren't enough 7 too many
8 too much

Exercise 4
A 2 too many 3 aren't enough 4 isn't enough
B 5 aren't enough 6 too much 7 too much
8 isn't enough 9 too many
C 10 too much 11 enough 12 isn't enough
13 too many 14 are, enough

Exercise 5
2 nothing 3 nowhere 4 Everyone 5 nobody
6 anywhere 7 anyone 8 somewhere

Exercise 6
1 someone/somebody, something
2 Everything, anything, anyone, anywhere, everyone/everybody
3 No one/Nobody, nothing, nowhere

Language round-up
(page 30)

Exercise 1
2 taxis 3 far 4 underground 5 theatre 6 art galleries 7 expensive 8 restaurant 9 boat
10 traffic 11 parks

Exercise 2
2 take 3 someone 4 past 5 anywhere
6 centres 7 nothing 8 too 9 enough
10 supermarket 11 to

Exercise 3
2 ~~much~~ many 3 ~~slowly~~ slow 4 ~~Are~~ Is
5 ~~nothing~~ anything 6 ~~deep~~ depth
7 ~~informations~~ information 8 ~~anything~~ nothing 9 ~~is~~ are 9 ~~width~~ wide 10 ~~many~~ much

Exercise 4
2 far 3 turn 4 office 5 take 6 on 7 to
8 many 9 enough 10 much 11 anything

Skills practice (page 31)

Exercise 1
1 Washington Monument 2 Smithsonian
3 Pentagon City

Exercise 2
2 100 3 The Washington Monument
4 one of nineteen 5 one part
6 an underground station

Exercise 3
2 a) 3 d) 4 c)

Unit 4 Time passes

4a I haven't seen the sun for weeks.

Exercise 1
Make: an appointment, a decision, a noise, friends with someone
Do: some exercise, your best, your homework, the shopping, the housework

Exercise 2
2 made 3 done 4 doing 5 make 6 made
7 make 8 made

Exercise 3
2 for, since, February 3 since, for, 2013 4 since, for, ten 5 for, since, first

Exercise 4
2 I've (have) had this book for a (one) week.
3 I've (have) been at this school since 2008.
4 I haven't seen this film for five years.
5 Tim hasn't been late for school since last year.
6 Meg's (has) been here for thirty seconds.
7 My dad hasn't had a holiday since 2010.

Exercise 5
2 **A:** How long has your mum been a teacher?
B: She's been a teacher since 1993.
3 **A:** How long have you liked Justin Bieber?
B: I've liked him since last year.
4 **A:** How long have you had a dog?
B: We've had her for about two months.
5 **A:** How long has this building been here?
B: It's been here since 2009.

4b You've been talking for ages.

Exercise 1
1 last 2 just, tell 3 about, in, on

Exercise 2
2 up 3 forward to 4 for 5 after

Exercise 3
2 looking for 3 looking forward to
4 looking up 5 looking at

Exercise 4

2 've (have) been reading, for 3 've (have) been talking, for 4 's (has) been learning, since 5 's (has) been singing since 6 's (has) been raining for 7 've (have) been going, since

Exercise 5

1 **B:** I've been reading for two hours.
2 **A:** He's been swimming since four o'clock
  A: So, he's been swimming for two hours.
  B: I've been telling him to come out for half an hour.

Exercise 6

1 **B:** I've been cycling around Europe.
  B: I've been working since October.
2 **A:** Have you been waiting long?
  B: Yes, I have., I've been waiting for 45 minutes.
  A: I've been shopping.
  B: I've been watching that boy and girl for the last ten minutes. They've been arguing since they arrived.
  B: haven't been listening to their conversation!

4c She used to be a Goth.

Exercise 1

2 used to be 3 didn't use to like 4 didn't use to work 5 Did you use to go 6 Did she use to have 7 used to work 8 Did your brother use to go

Exercise 2

2 used to go 3 used to wear 4 didn't use to wear 5 used to play 6 used to play 7 used to make 8 used to cycle 9 used to dream

Exercise 3

1 **B:** I used to have tennis lessons but I didn't use to like them.
2 **A:** What music did you use to like when you were ten?
  B: I used to like pop music. I didn't use to listen to rock at all.
3 **A:** Where did you and your family use to go on holiday when you were younger?
  B: We used to go to Cornwall. We didn't use to go abroad.
4 **A:** Did your dad use to have long hair?
  B: No, he didn't but my mum used to have pink hair!

Exercise 4

2 Haven't 3 Did 4 Doesn't 5 Is 6 Are 7 Didn't 8 Isn't

Exercise 5

1 *Have you,* Doesn't it 2 Did he, Was she, Did you 3 Did you, Didn't you, Is it

Exercise 6

2 c) 3 a) 4 b) 5 a) 6 c), c)

Skills practice (page 39)

Exercise 1

2 F 3 T 4 T 5 F

Exercise 2

2 Peter 3 Lisa 4 Lisa

Exercise 3

2 Monday 3 Wednesday
4 thrillers or crime 5 morning 6 cinema

Exercise 4

2 1st February 2013 3 306 metres
4 72 5 Renzo Piano 6 Southwark
7 London Bridge

Language round-up (page 38)

Exercise 1

2 f) 3 c) 4 a) 5 b) 6 g) 7 e)

Exercise 2

2 after 3 been 4 for 5 forward 6 since 7 do 8 made 9 Have 10 Is 11 Why 12 used 13 Did

Exercise 3

2 didn't use to like 3 look after my dog 4 had this scarf since 5 've been going out for 6 use to be noisy 7 used to go

Exercise 4

2 Did your sister use to go out on school nights?
3 Have you been playing football (for) a long time?
4 How long have your parents had that car?
5 How did you use to get to primary school?
6 How long have you had a headache?

Unit 5 Around the world

5a They were made in Thailand.

Exercise 1

2 true 3 but 4 fiver 5 on 6 earth

Exercise 2

2 silk 3 cardboard 4 wooden 5 silver 6 fur 7 denim 8 leather 9 plastic

Exercise 3

2 suede 3 glass 4 gold 5 wool 6 cotton 7 paper

Exercise 4

2 gave 3 is sold 4 is read 5 were you asked 6 heat

Exercise 5

2 are thrown 3 was given 4 are killed 5 isn't/is not paid 6 wasn't written 7 were you stopped

Exercise 6

2 Glassmakers were sent there from Venice in 1291.
3 Lots of glass objects are still made there now.
4 The glassmaking factories are visited by thousands of tourists every year.
5 The glass is coloured with gold and other metals.
6 I was given these by my aunt.

5b I couldn't sleep.

Exercise 1

2 drop 3 took off 4 land 5 pull 6 push 7 floating 8 sink 9 lift

Exercise 2

2 I could read. 3 I could write my name.
4 I could speak. 5 I couldn't ride a bike.
6 I couldn't ski. 7 I couldn't cook.
8 I couldn't use a computer.

Exercise 3

2 wasn't able to take 3 couldn't fix
4 Could you see 5 were you able to hear
6 weren't able to help 7 Were you able to swim

Exercise 4

2 We weren't able to find a hotel.
3 We were able to go online in a cafe.
4 So, we were able to look for hotels in Athens.
5 Were you able to find one?
6 He wasn't able to pay the driver.
7 He was able to get some money out.

5c Plato, who was born in Athens, ...

Exercise 1

2 harbour 3 path 4 stream 5 valley 6 forest 7 hill 8 bush

Exercise 2

2 mountain 3 valley 4 waterfall 5 rocks 6 river 7 island 8 lake 9 coast 10 woods

Exercise 3

2 who 3 where 4 whose 5 whose 6 which 6 which 8 who 9 who

Exercise 4

2 Some friends, who we knew from school, came too.

3 We swam to the other side of the lake, where some teenagers were making a fire.

4 One of my friends, whose parents are strict, had to leave.

5 The walk home, which took a lot longer than the walk there, was very tiring.

Exercise 5

1 agree 2 opinion, know, mean 3 stand, sorry 4 love, true

Exercise 6

2 true 3 think 4 afraid/sorry 5 agree 6 In 7 too 8 what 9 but

Language round-up (page 46)

Exercise 1

2 who 3 were able to 4 which 5 where 6 wasn't 7 who 8 whose 9 which

Exercise 2

2 was 3 who 4 which 5 able 6 are 7 were (are) 8 to 9 whose 10 was 11 were

Exercise 3

2 coastline 3 lakes 4 forests 5 Ocean 6 river

Exercise 4

2 f) Kilts are worn in Scotland.

3 a) I was given this scarf by my aunt.

4 g) My shirt (It) is made of cotton.

5 b) I could smell gas.

6 c) No, they aren't. They're made in Japan.

7 e) The pyramids were built in Egypt.

Skills practice (page 47)

Exercise 1

B

Exercise 2

2 DS 3 F 4 F 5 T 6 DS

Exercise 3

2 then 3 Next 4 After 5 Before that 6 Finally 7 afterwards 8 after

Unit 6 Things to remember
6a It might snow.

Exercise 1

2 Mr and Mrs Brown 3 Mr and Mrs Bailey 4 The Patel family 5 The Taylor family 6 John and Beth 7 The Ford family 8 Jenny

Exercise 2

2 a) 3 g) 4 d) 5 f) 6 b) 7 e)

Exercise 3

2 won't 3 will 4 might 5 won't 6 will/'ll

Exercise 4

2 won't have 3 might be 4 won't wait 5 will see 6 won't sleep

Exercise 5

1 worry 2 Make sure, I will 3 Would you, would 4 Shall, no need 5 you like 6 promise, I'll remember

6b If she's here, we'll invite her.

Exercise 1

2 Come on up 3 That's him, Quick 4 How are you doing, obviously 5 Who else?

Exercise 2

2 a) 3 h) 4 f) 5 b) 6 e) 7 c) 8 d)

Exercise 3

2 if 3 unless 4 unless 5 if 6 unless

Exercise 4

3 I'll go to the party if he sends me an invitation.

4 I'll show you my photos when I see you.

5 ✓

6 Will you phone me if your train is late?

7 ✓

8 What will you do if no one comes to the party?

9 I won't go out unless there is something really exciting happening.

10 ✓

Exercise 5

2 inexperienced 3 unfit 4 unfriendly 5 unhappy 6 impossible 7 unpopular 8 independent

Exercise 6

2 untidy 3 unnecessary 4 impatient 5 unattractive 6 uninteresting 7 informal 8 unlikely

6c The two men hadn't met before.

Exercise 1

2 g) 3 a) 4 f) 5 d) 6 b) 7 e)

Exercise 2

2 lose weight 3 losing my memory 4 lost interest 5 loses his temper 6 lost touch with 7 lose sight of

Exercise 3

2 we hadn't slept all night 3 he hadn't eaten anything 4 we hadn't done our projects 5 we hadn't put it up properly 6 someone had put salt in it

Exercise 4

2 had lost 3 had never forgotten 4 had asked 5 had sent 6 had come 7 had met

Exercise 5

2 He had fallen in love with another woman.

3 he had told her (that) he wanted to get divorced

4 She had left her driving licence and some clothes in the/her car.

5 But where had she gone?

6 Had she killed herself?

7 She had booked in as Mrs Teresa Neele from South Africa.

8 No one had recognised her.

9 Why had she done it?

10 How had she got there without her car?

Skills practice (page 55)

Exercise 1

c)

Exercise 2

2 didn't know 3 Alain's 4 older 5 got on quite well 6 Julie 7 she realised she loved someone else

Exercise 3

2 cheese and juice

3 20°C

Exercise 4

2 He showed them everything.

3 They are about 200 metres from the sea.

4 She's wearing a T-shirt and shorts.

5 He's going (on a) camping (holiday).

Language round-up (page 54)

Exercise 1

2 temper 3 If 4 might 5 unless 6 I'll

Exercise 2

2 tent 3 self 4 touch 5 swim 6 play

Exercise 3

2 might not be 3 arrived, the party had 4 lost interest 5 If we don't get 6 as soon as I know

Exercise 4

2 impossible 3 written 4 unnecessary 5 been 6 unlikely

Unit 7 Reporting speech
7a He told her to throw it.

Exercise 1

2 to wear 3 not to be 4 to buy 5 not to talk 6 to cook 7 to take 8 not to go 9 not to phone

Exercise 2

2 Be quiet. 3 Don't use my computer.
4 Don't talk during the exam. 5 Phone me at 6 p.m. 6 Do your schoolwork.

Exercise 3

2 to meet 3 not to be 4 to buy 5 to give
6 to look 7 to be 8 to listen 9 not to talk

Exercise 4

2 My brother asked me to help him with his homework.
3 I told David to go away.
4 My mum told my sister to hurry up.
5 Our teacher told us not to look at the answers.
6 My mum told my brother to switch off his computer.

Exercise 5

2 Venice is a beautiful old Italian city.
3 Kangaroos are strange brown Australian animals.
4 It is a pretty small glass Chinese lantern.

7b He said he was writing a book.

Exercise 1

2 was going to need 3 would be 4 couldn't fight 5 was talking 6 had/'d seen

Exercise 2

2 he hadn't tried windsurfing 3 she would be in London soon 4 the dentist was waiting for me 5 they hadn't done anything interesting 6 he was going to learn Spanish

Exercise 3

2 had seen 3 would be happy 4 she'd got
5 would be 6 he'd failed 7 he was going
8 he would wash up 9 would be

Exercise 4

2 Middle-aged. 3 Square. 4 No, quite thin.
5 No, but he had a moustache. 6 It was blond. 7 Yes, very. And straight. 8 She had a fringe.

Exercise 5

2 short 3 spiky 4 glasses 5 square 6 slim
7 teens 8 long 9 wavy 10 parting 11 eyes
12 round 13 medium-height

7c She asked if I could come ...

Exercise 1

2 excited 3 Just 4 minute 5 can't 6 think
7 hard 8 luck

Exercise 2

2 I was going 3 if she liked 4 my mum worked 5 we had been 6 the dress cost
7 if he would be 8 I had gone

Exercise 3

2 They asked us where we worked.
3 She asked me what my name was.
4 He asked her why she had gone home so early.
5 I asked him if he knew Kate Simmons.
6 My dad asked us why we hadn't done our homework.

Exercise 4

2 how it had started
3 if there was anyone in the house
4 if we could take some photos

Exercise 5

1 I'm afraid she's out. Can I take a message?
2 Who's calling, please? It's Mandy. Hang on.

Exercise 6

1 calling, Just, minute, get
2 speaking, This, there, sorry, out, take, message

Language round-up
(page 62)

Exercise 1

Size: enormous
Age: modern, teenage
Origin: Mexican, Spanish
Hair style: parting, fringe
Opinion: horrible, weird
Shape: round, square
Hair colour: fair, blond
Build: overweight, slim

Exercise 2

2 if 3 told 4 been 5 me 6 did 7 not 8 length
9 looking 10 built 11 to 12 gave

Exercise 3

2 not to worry about my exams 3 he was driving too fast 4 she didn't like pizza
5 if I often ate fast food 6 if she had read *The Lord of the Rings* 7 her watch had stopped

Exercise 4

2 twenties 3 wavy 4 Italian 5 colourful
6 spiky 7 useful 8 beautiful 9 Chinese

Skills practice (page 63)

Exercise 1

2 Thomas Gonzales 3 Edgar Mitchell
4 Thomas Gonzales 5 Frank Kaufmann
6 Edgar Mitchell

Exercise 2

2 c) 3 c) 4 a) 5 b) 6 b) 7 c)

Unit 8 Feelings

8a How would you feel?

Exercise 1

2 d) 3 c) 4 h) 5 g) 6 a) 7 e) 8 f)

Exercise 2

2 didn't have, would/'d go 3 would you do, were 4 had, would you want 5 stopped, wouldn't know 6 would you go, could
7 Would your neighbours be, had 8 would your parents say, decided

Exercise 3

2 If this exercise wasn't difficult, I could do it.
3 If there was/were more wind, we could/would go windsurfing.
4 We would go to the concert if the tickets weren't so expensive.
5 If I understood French, my parents wouldn't want me to go to extra lessons.

Exercise 4

2 If someone made a film of your life, who would play you?
3 If someone offered you a job in Australia, would you go?
4 What would you say if your friends asked you to go camping this summer?
5 Which photo would you keep if you could only keep one?
6 If you had a blog, what would you write about?

Exercise 5

2 interested, interesting 3 frightening, frightened 4 boring, bored 5 disappointing, disappointed 6 annoying, annoyed

Exercise 6

2 amusing 3 tired 4 shocked 5 exciting

8b I wish we could stay longer.

Exercise 1

1 out 2 out, up, on 3 up, up

Exercise 2

2 got on with 3 turned on 4 ran out of
5 get up 6 look up 7 look out 8 cheer, up

Exercise 3

2 didn't 3 was 4 weren't 5 wasn't 6 was
7 could

Exercise 4

2 didn't argue 3 could 4 wasn't 5 had
6 was 7 were 8 knew

Exercise 5

2 I wish she could come to England with us.
3 I wish I spoke better Spanish.
4 I wish my friends could see me now.

5 I wish my parents were somewhere else.

6 I wish I knew somewhere interesting to take her.

7 I wish I had cooler clothes.

8 I wish this evening could last forever.

Exercise 6

2 I wish I could swim.

3 I wish I didn't have to tidy my room every Saturday.

4 I wish we didn't have a test tomorrow.

5 I wish I had a job.

6 I wish my friend and I didn't keep arguing.

8c It was so boring I fell asleep.

Exercise 1

2 What a waste of money.

3 in a minute

Exercise 2

2 news 3 talent 4 cookery 5 Reality TV
6 quiz 7 wildlife 8 comedy

Exercise 3

2 such 3 so 4 such 5 such 6 so

Exercise 4

2 so sad 3 so old 4 such a powerful 5 so popular 6 so convinced 7 so disappointing 8 such a waste

Exercise 5

2 h) 3 b) 4 e) 5 g) 6 c) 7 i) 8 a) 9 d)

Exercise 6

1 sounds, Let, about, sure

2 Shall, rather, prefer, how, really

Skills practice (page 71)

Exercise 1

2 Cathy and Nicola

3 She turned on her computer and wrote a blog.

4 She had written the names of the cheats on her blog.

5 She came top of the school in Maths.

Exercise 3

3 ✓ 4 ✓ 5 ✓

Exercise 4

2 b) 3 b) 4 b) 5 a)

Language round-up
(page 70)

Exercise 1

2 **A:** What would you do if you were on a talent show?

   B: If I was/were on a talent show, I'd sing.

3 **A:** If you lost your phone, would you cry?

   B: No, I wouldn't.

4 **A:** What do you wish you could do?

   B: I wish I could speak a foreign language.

5 **A:** Would you wear a suit if you went on a date?

   B: No, I wouldn't. I'd wear jeans.

Exercise 2

2 had, 'd (would) drive 3 spoke, 'd (would) understand 4 not to do 5 didn't have, couldn't 6 didn't have 7 didn't live 8 would come, liked

Exercise 3

2 give up 3 interesting 4 don't 5 wish 6 stopped 7 would 8 find out 9 was 10 turn on 11 such 12 bored 13 rather

Exercise 4

2 opera 3 goes 4 out 5 if 6 would 7 so 8 not 9 such 10 get

Unit 9 Moving on

9a You can't afford to buy it.

Exercise 1

2 I'd so like, That's all 3 go halves 4 Nice try

Exercise 2

2 delete 3 connected 4 download 5 burn, stick

Exercise 3

2 wi-fi 3 apps (applications) 4 tablets 5 touchscreen 6 player 7 upload

Exercise 4

2 to finish 3 borrowing, breaking 4 to go 5 trying 6 buying 7 to save 8 wasting 9 to help

Exercise 5

2 keep 3 offered 4 fancy 5 suggest 6 seems

Exercise 6

2 to write 3 playing 4 to change 5 studying 6 to live 7 to find 8 seeing

9b He had to swim on his back.

Exercise 1

2 court 3 spectators 4 umpire 5 net 6 racket 7 hitting 8 goal 9 goalkeeper 10 referee 11 pitch 12 kicking 13 bat 14 helmet 15 glove 16 pad 17 throwing

Exercise 2

2 b) 3 a) 4 a) 5 b) 6 a)

Exercise 3

2 match 3 teams 4 pass 5 throws 6 basket 7 draw 8 goals 9 goalkeepers 10 beat

Exercise 4

2 don't have to run 3 have to throw 4 mustn't throw 5 don't have to bowl 6 mustn't bowl 7 have to keep 8 have to run

Exercise 5

1 mustn't 2 didn't have to 3 doesn't have to, mustn't, had to

9c It's so different from London.

Exercise 1

2 i) 3 b) 4 f) 5 a) 6 j) 7 c) 8 g) 9 d) 10 h)

Exercise 2

2 c) 3 b) 4 c) 5 c) 6 a) 7 b)

Exercise 3

2 with, with 3 of, of 4 in, in 5 by, by 6 to, from 7 on, with

Exercise 4

2 good 3 keen 4 interested 5 scared 6 impressed 7 similar 8 famous

Exercise 5

2 Take care 3 Look 4 I hope so 5 Keep 6 Let us know 7 I won't

Exercise 6

2 trip 3 great 4 will 5 care 6 after 7 forget 8 touch 9 won't 10 know 11 soon

Language round-up
(page 78)

Exercise 1

2 pads 3 send 4 score 5 pitch 6 charge 7 throw 8 reboot

Exercise 2

2 didn't have to 3 had to do 4 to eat 5 stand playing 6 up going 7 breaking the 8 to come to

Exercise 3

2 team 3 to 4 for 5 about 6 online

Exercise 4

2 doesn't have to 3 stand 4 about 5 win
6 running 7 coach 8 to listen 9 to watching
10 mustn't

Skills practice (page 79)

Exercise 1

2 C 3 C 4 B 5 B 6 A

Exercise 2

2 Although I spend a lot of time on the
 internet, I don't send any emails.
 I spend a lot of time on the internet.
 However, I don't send any emails.
3 Although I love watching football on the
 TV, I don't like playing it.
 I love watching football on the TV.
 However, I don't like playing it.

Exercise 3

2 However 3 although 4 although
5 However 6 However

Workbook audio script

Unit 2 That's life
Skills practice (page 23)

🎧 4 **Audio script**

Liz: Hi Max. Have you heard about the party on Wednesday?

Max: No. What party?

Liz: Shelly's having a party. I can't go because my parents won't let me go out on a school night.

Max: That's what my mum said to me.

Liz: It's not fair.

Max: I think she's right. I have been very tired recently.

Liz: What about Sylvia? What does she think about it?

Max: She's not very happy but she'll enjoy the party without me.

Liz: I'm sure she will.

Max: What do you mean by that?

Liz: I mean her old boyfriend, Kevin Gates, will be there. He hasn't forgotten her. He was really upset when she broke up with him. He might try to get back together with her.

Max: You know, I don't think it would worry me very much. I haven't got time for a girlfriend at the moment. I just don't know how to tell Sylvia that I want to break up.

Liz: Well, you should tell her to her face. My last boyfriend sent me a text to tell me.

Max: Really? That's terrible.

Liz: Come on, football practice is starting. Give me the ball.

Max: Hey Liz. You're beautiful, you play football really well, you never argue. Why can't I find a girlfriend like you?

Liz: Why do you want a girl like me? Why not me?

Max: You ... but ... we're friends. We've never been on a date.

Liz: You've never asked me.

Max: So ... will you go out with me?

Liz: Not yet. First tell Sylvia that you've finished with her and then ask me.

Max: I will. I promise. I'll go to her house after football practice.

Unit 4 Time passes
Skills practice (page 39)

🎧 7 **Audio script**

Peter: Hi, Lisa. How's things?

Lisa: Hi, Peter. Not too bad. I've been studying hard for the History exam tomorrow.

Peter: History? Isn't it Geography tomorrow?

Lisa: No. That's on Monday.

Peter: Oh. I've been studying the wrong subject.

Lisa: Really? Well, you can study History this evening.

Peter: No, I can't. I'm going out.

Lisa: Are you? Where?

Peter: I go to a film club every Wednesday. We've been watching some old Film Noir films.

Lisa: Film Noir? What's that?

Peter: They're old black and white films, usually thrillers or crime films. The camera work is very interesting and artistic.

Lisa: Oh, right. I don't like black and white films. So, when are you going to study?

Peter: I guess I'll get up very early. I'm a morning person. I can get up at four o'clock and find it easy to concentrate.

Lisa: Really? I can't. I can stay awake until two in the morning, but when I get up I can't do anything apart from eat breakfast. I'm not fully awake until the second or third lesson of the day!

Peter: I used to be like that, but I didn't work until 2 a.m., I played computer games. Now, I fall asleep at ten o'clock. I fell asleep in the cinema last week. Elaine wasn't very happy with me. We argued all the way to her house. We broke up for two days, but we've made up now.

Lisa: That's good. Right. I must go.

Peter: Me, too. See you tomorrow.

Unit 6 Things to remember
Skills practice (page 55)

🎧 10 Audio script

Rob: Hi Cathy. How are you?

Cathy: Hi Rob. I'm OK. We're here. We left home at six o'clock this morning and arrived here at seven o'clock this evening. It was so boring.

Rob: Where are you staying?

Cathy: In a cottage. It's lovely. A man met us and showed us everything. When he left, Dad looked in the fridge and found some cheese and juice. He was very happy!

Rob: Are you close to the sea?

Cathy: Yes. I can see the sea from my bedroom window. It's about 200 metres away. I want to go to the beach tomorrow. It was 25 degrees today. It's still about 20 degrees now. I'm in my shorts and T-shirt and I'm still hot. The problem is that Mum wants to visit a castle. She loves old castles. I hate them, especially when the weather is hot and sunny. I want to go to the beach every day. We live so far from the sea.

Rob: Yes, but the mountains are only an hour away. It's great in the winter when we can go skiing.

Cathy: I know. I'm not complaining but when I'm near the sea, I don't want to be in a castle or go shopping or visit museums.

Rob: I know.

Cathy: Anyway, when are you leaving on your camping holiday?

Rob: Tomorrow. I hope it doesn't rain. We got the tent out today and put it up. I remembered how to do it!

Cathy: Have a great time and see you in two weeks.

Rob: OK. Bye.

Unit 8 Feelings
Skills practice (page 71)

🎧 13 Audio script

Ian: Hi, Laura. You look excited.

Laura: Hi, Ian. I am. I'm going to be on TV next week.

Ian: Really? Wow! Which programme?

Laura: *What Do You Know?* I won a school quiz and the prize was to appear on the show.

Ian: Hey! You could win a million pounds.

Laura: No, it isn't like that. I can win something for the school. Laptops or DVDs or books. Things like that.

Ian: If I was on TV, I'd want a prize for myself.

Laura: Well, I could win a hundred pounds. It would be great if I won that. I could buy fifteen or twenty books. That would be enough for a whole year.

Ian: It would be enough for my whole life! So, do you know what the questions will be about?

Laura: School subjects. Geography, History, Science. That sort of thing. And I can also answer questions on my own special subject.

Ian: What did you choose?

Laura: Jane Austen of course. What would you choose if it was you?

Ian: Adventure games for computers.

Laura: I mean something intellectual.

Ian: I don't know. Maybe twentieth-century British history. I like history.

Laura: Really? I hadn't noticed!

Ian: Well, I enjoy playing Second World War games on my computer!